DE PROPRIETATIBUS LITTERARUM

edenda curat

C. H. VAN SCHOONEVELD

Indiana University

Series Maior, 35

PERSPECTIVES OF IRONY IN MEDIEVAL FRENCH LITERATURE

by

VLADIMIR R. ROSSMAN
Columbia University

1975

MOUTON

THE HAGUE · PARIS

ISBN 90 279 3291 3

Printed in The Netherlands by Mouton & Co., The Hague

ACKNOWLEDGMENTS

I owe a debt of gratitude to Professor Lawton P. G. Peckham. Before and after his retirement from Columbia, he made many valuable comments and always proved a vivid example of scholarship and courtesy. My deep thanks go to Professor Daniel F. Penham, who helped me acquire a broader view of the subject by his knowledge of medieval and Renaissance philosophy. Through his personal interest in the progress of my work, he conveyed to me some of his great enthusiasm for literature.

Professor W. T. H. Jackson suggested intricate thematic relations among texts. Besides following my work step by step, he provided continuous moral support, for which I am most grateful. His courses, publications, and friendly advice have been for me a standard of comparison and a source of inspiration.

Professor Donald M. Frame's remarks in his Rabelais seminar led me to an investigation of the theoretical problems of irony. My thanks are also due to Professor Bert M.-P. Leefmans, whose seminar on satire and irony uncovered new areas of research. Professor Joan M. Ferrante indicated useful critical works. I owe to the late Professor Nathan Edelman my knowledge of Villon and my awareness of relations between literature and the history of ideas. I am sorry he could not see this study, with which he was familiar and which he encouraged from the beginning.

Professors Jeanne Varney-Pleasants and Laura Fleder and Richard Pachella, Rare Book Librarian, Union Theological Seminary, read and commented on the manuscript. The Columbia University Library supplied various unpublished materials on microfilm.

My parents, Irina and Adolf Rossman, discussed with me some of the thorny theoretical problems involved in this study. My deepest gratitude goes to Dorothy, my wife, who criticized the manuscript and offered encouragement when it was most needed. I affectionately dedicate this book to her.

CONTENTS

INTRODUCTION

The term *ironia*, borrowed from classical antiquity, was usually described as a trope or as a figure of thought. It is only one of many medieval tropes which we would consider ironic today — e.g., *permutatio*, *abusio*, *subiectio*, *contrarium*, *occupatio*, *commutatio*, *occultatio* — all familiar to medieval readers, but not necessarily considered by them ironic. Modern definitions of irony, which date from the end of the eighteenth century and the beginning of the nineteenth,[1] combine concepts known from antiquity to the present. While *ironia* was limited in size, modern irony may originate also in episodes or works wholly ironic. Discussions of medieval irony usually reflect the characteristics of both *ironia* and modern irony. Like *ironia*, the ironic contexts are small. Like modern irony, they can result from several devices. Since such discussions include something more than *ironia* but less than modern irony, their purpose is hard to understand and their conclusions hard, if not impossible to check.

In my study, modern irony is defined and then applied to a variety of texts from Old French literature. This method has several purposes: to offer a new interpretation of very important medieval works by means of detailed stylistic analysis; to show how much irony in medieval literature differs from *ironia*; to provide precise criteria for determining irony not only in medieval literature but in literature in general; to point to the extraordinary scope of irony; and finally to indicate new areas that students of irony might pursue.

Chapter I is devoted to Socratic irony, irony as a rhetorical device, and irony of fate or dramatic irony, in order to formulate a unique definition applicable to all texts. The question of irony has been the subject of considerable controversy, largely because it is used in a variety of contexts

1 Ronald Paulson, *The Fictions of Satire* (Baltimore: Johns Hopkins Press, 1967), 97-98; D[ouglas] C. Muecke, *The Compass of Irony* (London: Methuen, 1969), 119-158, which also contains a good bibliography.

for many different effects. As early as the eighteenth century, the *Richelet* asserted the impossibility of defining the concept:

Il n'est pas possible de donner une idée générale de l'ironie; on en trouve de tant d'espèces différentes, & elles se forment en tant de manières, que pour la faire connoître, on ne peut qu'en rapporter quelques exemples...[2]

(It is not possible to give a general idea of irony. There are so many different kinds and they are formed in so many manners that in order to describe it, one can only give a few examples...)

In fact, as already mentioned, the meaning of the term has changed in the course of time. In Greek antiquity it meant primarily dissimulation. Today most theoreticians characterize irony as a discrepancy between what an author thinks and what he writes. Such a description, however, presents the difficulty of determining what an author thinks. In examples used by rhetoricians or lexicographers, "what an author thinks" turns out to be what is commonly thought. To create irony, an author refers to an accepted reality or makes an assertion concerning it and then makes a contradictory or incongruous statement.[3]

The remaining chapters apply the criteria arrived at in Chapter I to medieval works. These works represent different genres, themes, and periods as well as ironic contexts of varying size and extent, and thus show that irony appears throughout medieval literature. While most medievalists would take for granted the use of irony in a particular medieval genre, theme or period, many would refrain from discussing a broad

[2] Pierre Richelet, *Dictionnaire de la langue française ancienne et moderne: Nouvelle édition augmentée d'un très-grand nombre d'articles* (Lyons: Frères Duplain, 1759), II, 473. Translation mine.

[3] Extremely helpful is the formulation offered by Angus Fletcher, in his *Allegory: The Theory of a Symbolic Mode* (Ithaca, N.Y.: Cornell Univ. Press, 1964), 229-230: "Irony we often equate with paradox, that is with seemingly self-contradictory utterances where tenets normally in polar contradiction to each other are collapsed together into one single ambivalent statement. In irony and paradox extremes meet, while the tension of ambivalence increases proportionately. Because irony seems to collapse the multileveled segregations of allegory (e.g., a fourfold schema would collapse), it has been called 'anti-allegorical.' This seems to me an unfortunate usage, since irony still involves an otherness of meaning, however tenuous and shifty may be our means of decoding that other (*allos*) meaning. Rather, I think we might call ironies 'collapsed allegories,' or perhaps 'condensed allegories.' They show no diminishing, only a confusion, of the semantic and syntactic processes of double or multiple-leveled polysemy. Where they do differ from an allegorical norm might instead be in the degree of emotive tension they manifest; anxiety increases in European literary works as they approach... their 'ironic phase.'"

See also Paul Zumthor, *Essai de poétique médiévale*, Coll. Poétique (Paris: Seuil, 1972), 104-106.

ironic context, whose concept was formulated after the Middle Ages. This is why my discussion will bear mainly on the unexplored area of contexts varying in size and extent. Size refers to the actual length of the context, whereas extent involves the relation of a particular passage to the whole work. While one often accompanies the other, they sometimes require distinction. As I shall show, the wide contexts, despite their belated theoretical formulation, are not unmedieval.[4] In Old French literature, they are the product of converging medieval rhetorical devices, medieval narrative patterns and medieval ideas. They give the literature of the period another dimension that relates the texts to the vision of the universe in the Middle Ages.

Chapters II through V present a progression from small to wide ironic contexts — i.e., from contexts probably associated with *ironia* to those belonging exclusively to modern irony. Irony of words, treated in Chapter II, corresponds most closely to medieval definitions, where irony results from the interaction of small elements, such as words or sentences. The passages discussed are "Je meurs de soif" by Charles d'Orléans, the Story of Alexander and Diomedes by Villon, and the "Mariage Rutebeuf". Episodic irony, discussed in Chapter III, results from the juxtaposition of two or more episodes usually not ironic in themselves. The selection includes passages from André de la Vigne's *Moralité de l'Aveugle et du boiteux*, Chrétien's *Cligés*, the *Voyage de Charlemagne*, the *Chanson de Roland* and Béroul's *Tristan*. Chapters IV (*Aucassin et Nicolette* and *Yvain*) and V (*The Romance of the Rose*) deal with irony in works wholly ironic. Their contexts consist also of juxtaposed episodes, but unlike the former level, bear on the structure of the entire work. In addition the *Rose*, by Guillaume de Lorris and Jean de Meun, reflects the viewpoints of two persons and thus offers a wider perspective than *Aucassin* and *Yvain*.

The wider the context, the more intricate its ironic structure. As we shall see, word irony sometimes adds to episodic, while both often occur in wholly ironic works. The presentation of contexts gradually leads from *ironia* to modern irony, and thus explores simpler levels before more intricate ones. Throughout this study, we realize more and more that irony is not an artificial concept, arbitrarily applied to Old French, but rather an integral part of medieval literature.

[4] Cf. D. H. Green, "Irony in Medieval Romance", in *Arthurian Romance: Seven Essays*, ed. D. D. R. Owen (Edinburgh and London: Scottish Academic Press, 1970), 50.

I

TOWARD A DEFINITION OF IRONY

The meaning of irony has undergone several modifications in literary function or terminology from Greek antiquity until today. Some contemporary definitions are sufficiently inclusive to account for the variations that occur in the history of different cultures; others tend to be exclusive. It will be useful to explore past acceptations of the term in order to distinguish a principle common to them and to them alone that would be meaningful to either a medieval or a contemporary audience.

In dictionaries as well as in theoretical treatises, from the nineteenth century on, irony usually appears under three headings: Socratic irony, irony as a rhetorical device, and irony of fate. Larousse, for example, distinguishes an

> *Ironie socratique*, Méthode de Socrate qui, feignant l'ignorance, questionnait ses disciples, et par ses questions mêmes les amenait à reconnaître leur erreur.
>
> (*Socratic Irony*, Method of Socrates, who, feigning ignorance, questioned his disciples and, through these very questions, led them to recognize their errors.)

He also mentions the rhetorical device, a "raillerie, sorte de sarcasme qui consiste à dire le contraire de ce qu'on veut faire entendre" (Raillery, kind of sarcasm which consists of saying the opposite of what one wants [the people] to understand) and irony of fate, an "Opposition, contraste pénible, réunion de circonstances qui ressemble à une moquerie insultante" (Opposition, painful contrast, meeting of circumstances which resembles an insulting mockery).[1] It is possible to define the distinguishing features

[1] Pierre Larousse, *Grand Dictionnaire universel du XIXe siècle* (Paris: Larousse et Boyer, 1866-1870), IX, 793. Other dictionaries consulted which contain the same classification are: Emile Littré, *Dictionnaire de la langue française* (Paris: Jean-Jacques Pauvert, 1956-1958), I, 1152-1153; *Dictionnaire de l'Académie française*, 8th edition (Paris: Hachette, 1932-1935), II, 79; Paul Robert, *Dictionnaire alphabétique et analogique de la langue française* (Paris: Société du Nouveau Littré, 1957-1964), IV, 83; Larousse, *Grand Dictionnaire encyclopédique* (Paris: Larousse, 1960-1968), VI, 229; Adolphe Hatzfeld and Arsène Darmesteter, *Dictionnaire général de la langue fran-*

of each variety, even though the three concepts are closely related. The Greeks associated irony with Socrates. Latin antiquity understood irony as either Socratic or rhetorical, or both, and the nineteenth and twentieth centuries added to this already complex notion the term "irony of fate". Dictionaries of rhetoric attempt a deeper analysis, using the technical vocabulary of the specialist, but sometimes confusing the issues for lack of precise definitions.[2] They too stress the three connotations listed in less specialized dictionaries. Recent treatises elaborate these concepts and often comment on semantic problems. An excellent study on the subject is that by C. G. Sedgewick, "Dramatic Irony: Studies in Its History, Its Definition and Its Use Especially in Shakespere and Sophocles".[3] Professor Sedgewick illustrates with various texts the different meanings of irony and points to their common ground. Although he sees several varieties of irony, he occasionally underlines the three main groups, as labeled in the preceding pages.

The generally accepted tripartite definition of irony proves to be inadequate when applied to the analysis of literary texts, since it depends on non-verifiable criteria such as the author's intention, the nature of the audience (sympathetic, intelligent), and value judgments (good, bad, funny).[4] Inevitably the interpretation of any text is subject to the limita-

---

çaise du commencement jusqu'à nos jours (Paris: Delagrave, 1964), II, 1335; *Oxford English Dictionary* (Oxford Univ. Press at Clarendon Press, 1933), V, 484; William Little, H. W. Fowler, J. Coulson, ed., *The Oxford Universal Dictionary on Historical Principles,* revised and ed. C. T. Onions, 3rd edition (London: Oxford Univ. Press at Clarendon Press, 1964), 1045; Noah Webster, *Webster's New Twentieth-Century Dictionary of the English Language,* revised by Jean L. McKechnie, 2nd edition (New York: Publisher's Guild, 1960), 969-970; Philip Babcock Gove, ed. *Webster's Third New International Dictionary of the English Language* (Springfield, Mass.: G. & C. Merriam, 1968), 1195; *Encyclopedia Britannica* (Chicago: William Benton, 1967), XII, 637.

2 Particularly helpful are: Henri Morier, *Dictionnaire de poétique et de rhétorique* (Paris: Presses univ. de France, 1965), 219; Josph T. Shipley, ed. *Dictionary of World Literature: Criticism, Forms, Technique,* New Revised Edition (New York: Philosophical Library, 1953), 233-234; Alex Preminger, ed. *Encyclopedia of Poetry and Poetics* (Princeton: Princeton Univ. Press, 1965), 407; M. H. Abrams, *A Glossary of Literary Terms* (1941; rpt. New York: Holt, Rinehart & Winston, 1957), 44-46.

3 Diss. Harvard 1913. See also Sedgewick, *Of Irony, Especially in Drama* (Toronto: Univ. of Toronto Press, 1948); Norman Knox, *The Word Irony and Its Context, 1500-1755* (Durham: Duke Univ. Press, 1961), 3-32; David Worcester, *The Art of Satire* (=*Norton Library,* 472) (New York: Norton, 1969), 71-144.

4 See, for example, John J. Enck, Elisabeth T. Forter, and Alvin Whitley, ed. *The Comic in Theory and Practice* (New York: Appleton, 1960), 4. The scheme provided by the editors does not always explain the differences among the terms it proposes to define. Some criteria are vague (e.g., who is to say what is an intelligent audience?) and not

tions of the reader. Nevertheless, it will be useful to look more closely at the traditional concepts — Socratic and rhetorical irony and the irony of fate — from the viewpoint of their history in European culture.

1. SOCRATIC IRONY

Etymologically, the Greek *eironeia* means dissimulation or pretense, and this connotation was preserved throughout the centuries.[5] Thus, Cicero talks about "dissimulatio"[6] in Latin antiquity, and Evrard l'Allemand about "simplicitas simulata",[7] in the Middle Ages. In the seventeenth century, Furetière insists on false appearance as characteristic of irony: "Ce mot vient du Grec *eironeia: dissimulation, feintise...*"[8] (This word comes from the Greek *eironeia*; dissimulation, feigning...). Modern definitions regularly refer to Socratic dissimulation as a technique of deceiving the adversary or enlightening the young,[9] or both. However,

relevant to all texts (e.g., the motive may not be apparent). See also Robert A. Dutch, *The Original Roget's Thesaurus of English Words and Phrases* (New York: St. Martin's Press, 1965), 274, 318, 518, 526-527, 582; John M. Aden, "Towards a Uniform Satiric Terminology", *SNL*, 1 (1964), 31; G. L. Hendrickson, "Satura tota nostra est", *Classical Philology*, 22 (1927), 46; F. Baldensperger, "Les Définitions de l'humour", *Annales de l'Est*, 14 (1900), 177-200; Raymond Bayer, "L'Humour: Conférence", *RE*, 2 (1949), 319-322; A. E. Dyson, *The Crazy Fabric: Essays in Irony* (London: Macmillan and New York: St. Martin's Press, 1965); Rudolf Jancke, *Das Wesen der Ironie: Eine Strukturanalyse ihrer Erscheinungsformen* (Leipzig: Johann Ambrosius Barth, 1929).

5 For a general account of Socratic irony, see Søren Kierkegaard, *The Concept of Irony, with Constant Reference to Socrates*, trans. and ed. Lee M. Capel, Midland, MB 111 (Bloomington and London: Indiana Univ. Press, 1965), 276-288.

6 "Urbana etiam dissimulatio est..." ("Irony too gives pleasure..."). Cicero, *De Oratore*, II, lxvii, 269, ed. H. Rackham, Loeb Classical Library (Cambridge, Mass.: Harvard Univ. Press, 1942), I, 402-403. All translations from Cicero are according to the above edition.

7 "Simplicitas simulata, mali simulatio simplex
Incautos telo praegraviore ferit" (ll. 899-900).
(Dissimulated innocence, the simple simulation of evil,
Strikes the incautious with a very heavy spear. [trans. mine])
Evrard l'Allemand, *Laborintus*, in Edmond Faral, *Les Arts poétiques du XIIe et du XIIIe siècle: Recherches et documents sur la technique littéraire du Moyen Age* (Paris: Champion, 1962), 367.

8 Antoine Furetière, *Dictionnaire universel contenant generalement tous les mots françois tant vieux que modernes & les termes de toutes les sciences et des arts* (La Haye & Rotterdam: Arnout & Reinier Leers, 1690), Vol. II. See also Gustave Servois, ed. "Lexique de la langue de La Bruyère", in *Oeuvres*, by Jean de La Bruyère, Les Grands Ecrivains de la France (Paris: Hachette, 1865-1878), III, ii, 201.

9 The relationship of master to pupil or of mature man to youth had a great influence on teaching in all ages and became a literary theme. See H. I. Marrou, *A History of*

the favorable connotations of the term originated after Socrates' time. In 400 B.C. *eironeia* had a derogatory meaning, and the *eiron*, a dissimulator, was a person to fear. Sedgewick, in his "Dramatic Irony", p. 172, explains the "meaning of irony which was dominant in Athens of the fifth and early fourth centuries — namely 'cunning deceit,' 'vulgar, mocking pretence' — the irony of the fox".[10] Evrard l'Allemand preserves this meaning when, in describing irony, he writes:

> Decipiunt multi natura vulpis iniquae, 891
> In ficta fabricant simplicitate dolos.
> Angelicum vultum praetendunt, daemonis artem
> Occultant, fraudis ebrietate fluunt. 894

(Faral, *Arts poétiques*, 367).

(Many people deceive, whose character resembles that of the hostile fox. They nourish evil thoughts with feigned simplicity. They show an angel's face but hide a demon's skill. They flow in the drunkenness of deceit.)

Aristotle describes *eironeia* "self-depreciation" as the exact opposite of boastfulness.[11] He says that both are to be condemned, although boastfulness is even less praiseworthy than self-depreciation (*Nichomachean Ethics*, IV, 7). As Sedgewick humorously notes, irony "was the evil term that had the good luck to be applied to Socrates..." (p. 173).[12]

Education in Antiquity, trans. George Lamb, Mentor (New York: New American Library, 1964), 58-61.

[10] Cf. Gilbert Highet, *The Anatomy of Satire* (Princeton: Princeton Univ. Press, 1962), 56: "This 'irony' of Socrates produced divergent effects on the Athenians. Some admired it, and became his pupils. Others detested it, and condemned him to death.

In this time the word irony with its cognates was uncomplimentary. In Aristophanes (who is the first we know to have used it — in his satire against Socrates, *The Clouds*) and later in Demosthenes it is a harsh word, connoting sly cleverness. The type of irony is the fox; the user of irony is something very like a hypocrite. Socrates himself is never recorded as saying that 'irony' defined his method of philosophizing; in the works of his pupil Plato the word is used (whether of Socrates or of others) as a joke or a reproach. It was Plato's pupil Aristotle who used irony in a good sense to describe the gentle assumption of weakness and ignorance, coupled with a polite desire to be enlightened, which was the characteristic dialectic technique of Socrates; and he passed on the concept of Socratic irony through the Romans to us."

See also Mikhaïl M. Bakhtine, *Problèmes de la poétique de Dostoïevski*, trans. Guy Verret, Slavica (1963; Lausanne: L'Age d'Homme, 1970), 155.

[11] See Martin Oswald, ed. and trans. "Glossary", *Nichomachean Ethics*, by Aristotle (= *Library of Liberal Arts*, 75) (Indianapolis and New York: Bobbs-Merrill, 1962), 305.

[12] Socrates used dissimulation to uncover the truth, yet he was considered a liar (*eiron*). Professor Sedgewick attempts to explain this paradox: "... Socrates' method of procedure *was* a pretence; it *had* an element of the 'sly' and the 'cunning' in it: it

One of the major documents describing irony is a passage from Theophrastus' *Characters*. His comments were influential enough throughout the seventeenth century to deserve La Bruyère's translation.[13] La Bruyère calls irony "dissimulation", and adds that Theophrastus "parle de celle qui ne vient pas de la prudence, et que les Grecs appeloient ironie" (speaks of that dissimulation which does not come from prudence and which the Greeks called irony). Below is Theophrastus' description of the *eiron* in La Bruyère's translation:

La dissimulation

. . . .

[1] Un homme dissimulé se comporte de cette manière: il aborde ses ennemis, leur parle, et leur fait croire par cette démarche qu'il ne les hait point; il loue ouvertement et en leur présence ceux à qui il dresse de secrètes embûches, et il s'afflige avec eux s'il leur est arrivé quelque disgrâce; il semble pardonner les discours offensants qu'on lui tient; il récite froidement les plus horribles choses que l'on lui aura dites contre sa réputation, et il emploie les paroles les plus flatteuses pour adoucier ceux qui se plaignent de lui, et qui sont aigris par les injures qu'ils en ont reçues. [2] S'il arrive que quelqu'un l'aborde avec empressement, il feint des affaires, et lui dit de revenir une autre fois. [3] Il cache soigneusement tout ce qu'il fait; et à l'entendre parler, on croiroit toujours qu'il délibère. [4] Il ne parle point indifféremment, il a ses raisons pour dire qu'il ne fait que revenir de la campagne, tantôt qu'il est arrivé à la ville fort tard, et quelquefois qu'il est languissant, ou qu'il a une mauvaise santé. [5] Il dit à celui qui lui emprunte de l'argent à intérêt, qu'il ne s'est jamais vu si dénué d'argent; pendant qu'il dit aux autres que le commerce va le mieux du monde, quoiqu'en effet il ne vende rien. [6] Souvent, après avoir écouté ce que l'on lui a dit, il veut faire croire qu'il n'y a pas eu la moindre attention; il feint de n'avoir pas aperçu les choses où il vient de jeter les yeux, ou s'il est convenu d'un fait, de ne s'en plus souvenir. [7] Il n'a pour ceux qui lui parlent d'affaires que cette seule réponse: "J'y penserai." [8] Il sait certaines choses, il en ignore d'autres, il est saisi d'admiration, d'autres fois il aura pensé comme vous sur cet événement, et cela selon ses différents intérêts. [9] Son langage le plus ordinaire est celui-ci: "Je n'en crois rien, je ne comprends pas que cela puisse être, je ne sais où j'en suis"; et ensuite: "Ce n'est pas ainsi qu'il me l'a fait entendre; voilà une chose merveilleuse et qui passe toute créance; contez cela à d'autres; dois-je vous croire? ou me persuaderai-je qu'il m'ait dit la vérité?" paroles doubles et artificieuses, dont il faut se défier comme de ce qu'il y a au monde de plus pernicieux. [10] Ces manières d'agir ne

---

did result in mockery of the Sophists... To the mind of the man on the street who could not see below the surface into Socrates' motive for adopting such questionable ways, *eiron* must have seemed a right and proper term for the philosopher; *a fortiori* to the mind of the victim, many of whom were men of influence" "Dramatic Irony...", 174).

[13] See Octave Navarre, "Théophraste et La Bruyère", *Revue des études grecques*, 27 (1914), 384-440.

partent point d'une âme simple et droite, mais d'une mauvaise volonté, ou d'un homme qui veut nuire: le venin des aspics est moins à craindre.[14]

(Dissimulation

. . . .

[1] A dissimulator behaves in the following manner: he accosts his enemies, talks to them, and thus makes them believe that he does not hate them at all. He openly praises in their presence those for whom he prepares secret ambushes, and seems afflicted if some mishap has occurred to them. He seems to forgive the insulting discourses held against him. He dispassionately recites the most horrible things said against his reputation and uses the most flattering words to sweeten those who complain about him and who are soured by the wrongs that he has done to them. [2] If it happens that someone eagerly accosts him, the dissimilator pretends to be busy and tells him to come back another time .[3] He carefully conceals everything he does. To hear him speak, one would think that he always reflects. [4] He does not talk without purpose: he has his reasons for saying that he has just returned from the country, sometimes that he arrived in town too late, other times that he is languishing or ill. [5] He tells his debtor that he has never been so penniless, while he tells others that business cannot be better, although he is actually selling nothing. [6] Often, after listening to what he is told, he wants to make believe that he paid no attention whatsoever. He pretends not to have noticed things upon which he has just gazed, or if a fact is established, he feigns not to remember it. [7] He has only one answer for those who talk to him about business: "I shall think about it." [8] He knows certain things, he does not know others, he is struck by admiration; other times he will have thought like you on a certain matter — all these according to his momentary interest. [9] His most common expressions are as follows: "I don't believe a word of it, I don't see how this can be, I don't know where I stand." And then: "It is not thus that he led me to believe. That is an unlikely thing, that goes beyond belief. Tell this to others. Must I believe you or should I make myself believe that he told me the truth?" These are deceitful words with double meanings, which we must mistrust as the most pernicious thing in the world. [10] Such behavior does not originate in a simple, straightforward soul, but in bad will or in a man who wants to make trouble: the asp's venom is less to be feared.)

According to this passage, the *eiron* is a dangerous person (10) who hides his thoughts and deeds. His personality originates in the contrast between truth and untruth. His words do not convey a precise meaning; they are "paroles doubles et artificieuses" (9). In sentence 9, for example, the *eiron* casts doubt on his interlocutor's honesty, by an accumulation of statements amounting to "I do not believe you." Two expressions come into contact, one supposedly true, the other false. A similar discrepancy appears be-

[14] La Bruyère, trans. *Les Caractères de Théophraste, traduits du grec*, in *Oeuvres*, ed. Gustave Servois, I, 34-36. The sentence numbers are mine. Comments on this passage refer to the numbers inserted in the text.

tween the dissimulator's words and his actions: "Il cache soigneusement tout ce qu'il fait" (3). He pretends to have just arrived from the country, or not to feel well (4). In this case, his words represent an untrue description of his actions and thus create a contrast between reality and lies.

This contrast sometimes acquires special qualities. Not only do the facts belie the words, but the two are directly opposed. He maintains that he does not hate his enemies, and he seems to forgive them, yet he secretly plots against them (1). The plot annihilates his friendly appearance, for a person cannot conceivably be friend and enemy to the same individual at the same time. The *eiron* says that business is good, although in fact he sells nothing (5). Since selling nothing means bad business, the fact contradicts the *eiron's* evaluation. The dissimulator pretends not to have paid attention to, and not to have seen that which he actually saw (6). The truth cancels out his assertion.

In all these examples, whether the *eiron*'s pretenses are merely different from, or directly opposed to, the truth, reality is described on two levels: one provided by the context, the other by the *eiron*. If one description is true, the other cannot be. According to the context, the *eiron* lies. The clash between the two levels characterizes some of Plato's dialogues, where Socrates plays the part of the *eiron*. Yet the discrepancies that occur between Socrates' pretense and reality differ from those in Theophrastus' text. While Theophrastus' *eiron* does not admit to reality, Socrates eventually does. Also, Socrates' dissimulation, the so-called "mock-ignorance", is directly opposite to reality, which was not always the case with Theophrastus' *eiron*.

Plato's dialogues usually involve two characters: the *eiron* and the *alazon*. The former feigns ignorance, the latter feigns omniscience. Eventually they appear as they really are. Pretended ignorance serves to describe knowledge, while affected knowledge stands for actual ignorance. Whereas irony referred only to hidden knowledge,[15] hidden knowledge

15 "It is proper to apply the name of *irony*, in the first place, to the elementary humor of understatement, not only because of its peculiar flavor, but because in its origin that is what the word implied. In Aristotle's *Ethics* we find the two nouns [*alazon* and *eiron*]... set off against each other as opposites — the one meaning a man who 'talks big,' the other a dissembler, or one who avows less than he intends. And it was the application of this latter term to the peculiar humor of Socrates that gave popularity to that word irony... Socrates would come up to some complacent citizen in the streets of Athens and ask him if he knew a certain thing. And when the citizen replied, 'Of course,' Socrates would say: 'I just wanted to ask you, because I myself don't know anything, and I wondered if it would be possible for you to enlighten me a little.' From such a beginning would ensue a conversation in which the ignorant folly of the citizen and the adroit profundity of his question became equally apparent." Max

appeared together with masked ignorance.[16] The two are therefore linked by the common situation in which they occur, as well as by their common characteristic — namely, description of a quality through its opposite. Since knowledge characterizes the *eiron*, and ignorance the *alazon*, and since each character uses the opposite quality in order to describe his own, the *eiron*'s quality and description correspond respectively to the *alazon*'s description and quality. Thus when Aristotle, Cicero, Evrard l'Allemand, and Furetière mention Socratic irony, they refer to the interplay of knowledge and ignorance on two levels of reference — the quality and its description.

2. IRONY AS A RHETORICAL DEVICE

Not entirely foreign to the Greeks, irony as a rhetorical device becomes increasingly popular in Latin antiquity and, from the Middle Ages on, in French vernacular writing.[17] All theoretical treatises define rhetorical irony in a similar manner — i.e., expression of an idea by its opposite — although they may add to it different overtones. While the definitions may vary from simple[18] to subtle and intricate, they are all based on Cicero's and Quintilian's discussions.

Cicero writes about irony under two headings: verbal witticisms and witticisms of matter. Whereas the former concern only a short context, the latter refer to the whole speech:

> Urbana etiam dissimulatio est, cum alia dicuntur ac sentias, non illo genere de quo ante dixi, cum contraria dicas, ut Lamiae Crassus, sed cum toto genere orationis severe ludas, cum aliter sentias ac loquare.
>
> (Cicero, *De Oratore*, II, lxvii, 269)

(Irony too gives pleasure, when your words may differ from your thoughts, not

---

Eastman, *The Sense of Humor* (New York: Charles Scribner's Sons, 1922), 52. I have used the following edition of Plato's works: Edith Hamilton and Huntington Cairns, ed. *The Collected Dialogues of Plato* (= *Bollingen Series*, LXXI) (Princeton: Princeton Univ. Press, 1961).

16 "... the word *irony*, having named the jokes which say less in order to mean more, came also to include those which say more in order to mean less" (Eastman, 55).

17 For a general view of rhetorical irony, see Charles Sears Baldwin, *Ancient Rhetoric and Poetic Interpreted from Representative Works* (New York: Macmillan, 1924).

18 For example, Boiste writes under *ironie* only "*Ironia*, raillerie fine; figure de rhétorique." P[ierre] C. V. Boiste, *Dictionnaire universel de la langue françoise*, 2nd edition (Paris: Desray, 1803), 230. See also *Le Dictionnaire de l'Académie françoise dédié au roy* (Paris: Jean Baptiste Coignard, 1694), I, 612; Walther von Wartburg, *Französisches Etymologisches Wörterbuch* (Basel: Helbing & Lichtenhahn, 1952), IV, 814.

in the way of which I spoke earlier, when you assert exactly the contradictory, as Crassus did to Lamia, but when the whole tenor of your speech shows you to be solemnly jesting, what you think differing continuously from what you say...[p. 403])

Yet from the viewpoint of their implications, the examples Cicero gives do not justify such a distinction. As verbal witticism, irony figures among devices such as the use of ambiguity, the unexpected, the play on words, quotation of verses or proverbs, words taken literally rather than in the sense intended, allegory, metaphor, and antithetical expressions (*De Oratore*, lxvi-lxxi, 265-289, pp. 398-418).[19]

To illustrate irony as a verbal witticism, Cicero tells a story where Crassus called Lamia, a cripple and a bad orator, first "handsome child", then "eloquent speaker":

Invertuntur autem verba, ut, Crassus apud M. Perpernam judicem pro Aculeone cum diceret, aderat contra Aculeonem Gratidiano L. Aelius Lamia, deformis, ut nostis; qui cum interpellaret odiose: 'Audiamus,' inquit, 'pulchellum puerum,' Crassus. Cum esset arrisum, 'Non potui mihi,' inquit Lamia, 'formam ipse fingere; ingenium potui.' Tum hic, 'Audiamus,' inquit, 'disertum.' Multo etiam arrisum est vehementis."

(Cicero, lxv, 262, pp. 394–396)

(And meanings were ironically inverted when Crassus was representing Aculeo before Marcus Perperna as arbitrator, and Lucius Aelius Lamia, a cripple as you know, was for Gratidianus against Aculeo, and kept on interrupting vexatiously, until Crassus said, 'Let us hear the little beauty.' When the laughter at this had subsided, Lamia retorted, 'I could not mould my own bodily shape; my talents I could.' Thereupon Crassus remarked, 'Let us hear the eloquent speaker.' At this the laughter was far more uproarious. [pp. 395–397])

Laughter arises when Crassus attributes beauty to a cripple, whose deformities imply ugliness.[20] The context attaches also moral defects to physical deformity ("Lamia... qui cum interpellaret odiose"), thus reinforcing the disparity between reality and its description by Crassus. "Disertum"[21] contrasts to "interpellaret odiose",[22] since the same orator's speech is

19 See Auguste Haury, *L'Ironie et l'humour chez Cicéron* (Leiden: E. J. Brill, 1955), 3-29.

20 "Dē-formis... *Departing*, either physically or... *morally*, *from the right shape*, *quality*, etc.; *misshapen*, *deformed*, *unsightly*, *ugly*, *odious*, *disgusting: disgraceful*, *base*..." Charlton T. Lewis and Charles Short, *A Latin Dictionary Founded on Andrews' Edition of Freund's Latin Dictionary* (London: Oxford Univ. Press, at Clarendon Press, 1879), 532. The fact that this word refers to either physical or moral defects reinforces physical and moral ugliness as expressed by "deformis" and "odiose".

21 "dĭsertus... *skilful in speaking on a subject; clear, methodical in speaking; well spoken, fluent*..." (Lewis and Short, 594).

22 "ŏdiōsē, *in a hateful manner, odiously, vexatiously*..." (Lewis and Short, 1256).

described by contradictory words. The oppositions between "interpellaret odiose" and "disertum" and between the former and "ingenium potui" supervene. The text suggests that Lamia can dominate his talents no more than he can his bodily shape. Crassus' attack appears on two levels, physical and intellectual. As the context asserts a quality which Crassus' description contradicts, the context and Crassus' assertions are incompatible.

In order to illustrate witticism of matter, Cicero relates a story in which Scaevola told Septumuleius of Angania, who had received a large quantity of gold for Gaius Gracchus' head, that since there were so many wicked citizens in Rome, Septumuleius would become rich, if he only remained there:

> ... noster Scaevola Septumuleio illi Anagnino, cui pro C. Gracchi capite erat aurum repensum, roganti ut se in Asiam praefectum duceret, 'Quid tibi vis,' inquit, 'insane? tanta malorum est multitudo civium ut tibi ego hoc confirmen, si Romae manseris, te paucis annis ad maximas pecunias esse venturum.'
> (Cicero, lxvii, 269, p. 402)

> (... our friend Scaevola observed to the notorious Septumuleius of Angania (to whom its weight in gold had been paid for the head of Gaius Gracchus), when he prayed to be taken into Asia as his lieutenant, 'Madman,' said Scaevola, 'what would you have? There is such a host of wicked citizens in Rome that I guarantee you, if you remain there, the attainment within a few years, of enormous wealth.' [p. 403])

The reader expects that wicked citizens would harm rather than make someone prosperous. But since Septumuleius receives gold for the heads of the evil, the larger their number, the richer he becomes. Good and evil — that is, opposite connotations — applied to the same people at the same time are incompatible.

A similar mechanism characterizes the following illustration of witticism of matter, where Africanus degraded one of his men, who failed to participate in the battle because he had stayed in camp on guard. When the soldier inquired about his commander's action, the latter replied that he did not like overcautious people:

> ... cum Africanus censor tribu movebat eum centurionem qui in Pauli pugna non adfuerat, cum ille se custodiae causa diceret in castris remansisse quaereretque cur ab eo notaretur, 'Non amo,' inquit, 'nimium diligentes.' (Cicero, 272, p. 404).

> (... when Africanus as censor removed from his tribe that centurion who failed to appear at the battle fought under Paulus, though the defaulter pleaded that he had stayed in camp on guard, and sought to know why he was degraded by

the censor: 'I am no lover of the over-cautious,' was the answer of Africanus. [p. 405])

The centurion may have stayed in camp either to guard it or to guard himself. Guarding the camp against the enemy is a valiant, praiseworthy action; avoiding battle is sheer cowardice. "Nimium diligentes" can apply to either, but not simultaneously. Yet the text attributes with the same words opposite qualities to one person with respect to one issue at one time.

According to these illustrations, irony as witticism of matter closely resembles irony as verbal witticism. Despite what Cicero says, verbal witticism too, like witticism of matter, can appear on several levels throughout the speech ("cum toto genere orationis"), and witticism of matter contains, like verbal witticism, clashes of opposite qualities ("cum contraria dicas").

Cicero associates witticism of matter with Socratic irony.[23] Africanus and especially Socrates excelled in assumed simplicity, whose Greek equivalent is irony:

In hoc genere Fannius in Annalibus suis Africanum hunc Aemilianum dicit fuisse egregium et Graeco eum verbo appellat εἴρωνα: sed, uti ferunt qui melius haec norunt, Socratem opinor in hac ironia dissimulantiaque longe lepore et humanitate omnibus praestitisse.

(Cicero, II, lxvi, 270, p. 402).

(Fannius in his 'Chronicles' records that Africanus (the one named Aemilianus) was outstanding in this kind of thing, and describes him by the Greek word 'dissembler,' but upon the evidence of those who know those subjects better than I do, my opinion is that Socrates far surpassed all others for accomplished wit within this strain of irony or assumed simplicity. [p. 403])

Whereas in Socratic irony ignorance would stand for knowledge and knowledge for ignorance, in Cicero's examples of irony beauty stands for ugliness, eloquence for bad speech, valiance for cowardice, the good for the bad. Each ironic situation equates antonyms, which by definition are not identical.

Quintilian preserves the essence of Ciceronian irony and presents it both as trope and as rhetorical figure. As a trope, it is associated with allegory[24] and is defined as

[23] Mary A. Grant, *The Ancient Rhetorical Theories of the Laughable* (= *Univ. of Wisconsin Studies in Language and Literature*, 21) (Madison: Univ. of Wisconsin Press, 1924), 125-129.

[24] "'Ἀλληγορία, quam inversionem interpretamur, aut aliud verbis, aliud sensu ostendit, aut etiam interim contrarium. prius fit genus plerumque continuatis translationibus..." Quintilian, *Institutio Oratoria*, VIII, vi, 44, ed. Ludwig Radermacher, revised by

In eo vero genere, quo contraria ostenduntur, εἰρωνεία est: inlusionem vocant. quae aut pronuntiatione intellegitur aut persona aut rei natura: nam si qua earum verbis dissentit, apparet diversam esse orationi voluntatem. quamquam in plurimis id tropis accidit, ut intersit, quid de quoque dicatur, quia quod dicitur alibi verum est. et laudis adsimulatione detrahere et vituperationis laudare concessum est...

(Quintilian, *Institutio*, VIII, vi, 54-55, p. 127).

(On the other hand, that class of allegory in which the meaning is contrary to that suggested by the words, involves an element of irony, or as our rhetoricians call it, *illusio*. This is made evident to the understanding either by the delivery, the character of the speaker or the nature of the subject. For if any of these three is out of keeping with the words, it at once becomes clear that the intention of the speaker is other than what he actually says. In the majority of tropes it is, however, important to bear in mind not only what is said, but about whom it is said, since what is said may in another context be literally true. It is permissible to censure with counterfeited praise and praise under a pretence of blame. [Butler, trans., p. 333])

Quintilian's distinction between the trope and the figure calls to mind Cicero's verbal witticism and witticism of matter:[25]

in duobus demum verbis est ironia, ergo etiam brevior est τρόπος. at in figura totius voluntatis fictio est, apparens magis quam confessa, ut illic verba sint veris diversa, his sensus sermoni et voci et tota interim causae conformatio, cum etiam vita universa ironiam habere videatur, qualis est visa Socratis (nam ideo dictus εἴρων, agens imperitum et admiratorem aliorum tamquam sapientium)...

(Quintilian, IX, ii, 45-46, p. 155).

(In this case the irony lies in two words, and is therefore a specially concise form of trope. But in the figurative form of irony the speaker disguises his entire

---

Vinzenz Buchheit, Academia Scientiarum Germanica Berolinensis, Bibliotheca Scriptorum Graecorum et Romanorum Teubneriana (Berlin: Teubner, 1965), II, 124. For a translation of the above passage, see H. E. Butler, trans. *The "Institutio Oratoria" of Quintilian, vol. III*, Loeb (London: William Heinemann and New York: G. P. Putnam's Sons, 1922), 327: "*Allegory*, which is translated in Latin by *inversio*, either presents one thing in words and another in meaning, or else something absolutely opposed to the meaning of the words. The first type is generally produced by a series of metaphors."

"Contrarium" calls to mind Cicero's "cum contraria dicas". Allegory and allegorism are important in the Middle Ages. See Edgar de Bruyne, *Etudes d'esthétique médiévale* (= *Rijksuniversiteit te Gent, Werken uitgegeven door de Faculteit van de wijsbegeerte en letteren*, 97-99) (Bruges: De Tempel, 1946), II, 302-370.

[25] On Cicero's influence upon Quintilian, see Jean Cousin, *Etudes sur Quintilien* (Paris: Boivin, 1935), I, 338 and 342-344. On the various meanings of irony in Quintilian, Cousin, II, 70-71. See also Ernst Robert Curtius, "Mittelalterlische Literaturtheorien", *ZRP*, 62 (1942), 424-429.

meaning, the disguise being apparent rather than confessed. For in the *trope* the conflict is purely verbal, while in the *figure* the meaning, and sometimes the whole aspect of our case, conflicts with the language and the tone of voice adopted; nay, a man's whole life may be coloured with *irony*, as was the case with Socrates, who was called an *ironist* because he assumed the rôle of an ignorant man lost in wonder at the wisdom of others. [H. E. Butler, trans., p. 401])

In addition to certain notions already present in *De Oratore* — e.g., classification (simple and complex irony) and general characteristics ("contraria", "vituperationis laudare"), Quintilian introduces the writer's or speaker's intention, which must differ from his words ("diversam esse orationi voluntatem", "totius voluntatis fictio est").[26] Most subsequent definitions, whether classical, medieval or modern, consider irony in the same light as Quintilian.[27] Some rhetoricians discard the "per contrarium" from their definitions but maintain it in their examples (e.g., Aquila Romanus and Martianus Capella). If the two elements are not opposed, any type of allegory or simple substitution would become ironical.[28] In Pompeius' words, irony is "non ita, ut diximus de allegoria, quando aliud dicimus et aliud significamus, non, sed isdem verbi potes et negare et confirmare..." (*Commentum Artis Donati*, Keil, V, 310).

Some theorists after Quintilian and most modern dictionaries and treatises base their definitions on the writer's or speaker's intention (e.g., Aquila Romanus and Martianus Capella, "significamus" vs. "sentimus"; Julius Rufinianus, "in pectore" vs. "in lingua"; Oresme, "l'en veult donner a entendre..."; Godefroy, Académie, Mortier, etc., "on veut faire entendre"). While this criterion may prove useful to writers or producers of irony, it is irrelevant in literary analysis, unless the context offers some indication of a particular intention. Socrates, who is Quintilian's prototype of the *eiron*, expresses no sly intention to play the underdog or the naïve. In fact, any apparent devious intention of Socrates could have prevented the *alazon* from answering. When Socrates considers himself ignorant, when Crassus calls a cripple "pulchellum puerum", when Scae-

[26] Quintilian's *Institutio* influenced the rhetorical theories of all ages. See A. Mollard, "La Diffusion de l'*Institution oratoire* au XIIe siècle", MA, 44, 3rd series, 5 (1934), 161-175, and 45, 3rd series, 6 (1935), 1-9; [Denis] Diderot, *Encyclopédie ou Dictionnaire raisonné des sciences et des arts* (Lausanne and Bern: Sociétés typographiques, 1781), XIX, 83; Raoul Mortier, ed., *Dictionnaire encyclopédique Quillet* (Paris: Aristide Quillet, 1935), III, 2424.

[27] For a list of grammarians, rhetoricians, and theoreticians who mention irony in the same light as Quintilian, see Appendix I.

[28] This is the case in Northrop Frye, *Anatomy of Criticism: Four Essays* (Princeton: Princeton Univ. Press, 1957), partic. 223-239 ("The Mythos of Winter").

vola urges Septumuleius to stay in Rome, or when Africanus says that he does not like the overcautious, there is no evidence of the speaker's intention, other than the incompatibility of two assertions. This incompatibility is perceived by the reader, but not necessarily intended by the speaker. Socrates may have desired only to uncover the truth, not to trick his adversary, and his pledge of ignorance may have been modesty rather than pretense. Lamia may have seemed handsome to Crassus, Scaevola may have seen in the wicked a regular source of income, and Africanus may have sincerely disliked an exaggerated concern for the camp in time of war. The text neither indicates nor denies such intentions. It merely suggests to the reader certain incongruities produced by its elements. Irony as a rhetorical device seems therefore to consist of the equation of two opposed elements.[29]

3. IRONY OF FATE OR DRAMATIC IRONY

Irony of fate implies a discrepancy between appearance and reality in events:

[29] Modern treatises on irony center on the older definitions and multiply the types of opposition or contradiction involved. Jankélévitch mentions the "Désaccord de la pensée avec l'action, et finalement désaccord de la pensée avec elle-même". Vladimir Jankélévitch, *L'Ironie*, Nouvelle Bibliothèque scientifique (Paris: Flammarion, 1964), 56; *Ibid.*, 20, 60, 72-73, 82, 84, 99; Fr[édéric] Paulhan, *La Morale de l'ironie*, Bibliothèque de philosophie contemporaine (Paris: Alcan, 1909), 142. Other theorists mention pretense — J. Y. T. Greig, *The Psychology of Laughter and Comedy* (New York: Dodd, Mean, 1923), 185-186; contrary opinions — René Schaerer, "Le Mécanisme de l'ironie dans ses rapports avec la dialectique", *RMM*, 48 (1941), 185-186; absurdity — Arthur Koestler, *Insight and Outlook: An Inquiry into the Common Foundations of Science, Art and Social Ethics* (New York: Macmillan, 1949), 98; praise by blame — Maynard Mack, "The Muse of Satire", *YR*, 41 (1951-1952), 83-84; real vs. fictitious — Claude Saulnier, *Le Sens du comique: Essai sur le caractère esthétique du rire* (Paris: Vrin, 1940), 131; internal vs. external — Kierkegaard, *Concluding Unscientific Postscript*, trans. David F. Swenson and Walter Lowrle (Princeton: Princeton Univ. Press, 1941), 287. See also Ewald Hecker, *Physiologie und Psychologie des Lachens und des Komischen: Ein Beitrag zur experimentellen Psychologie für Naturforscher, Philosophen und gebildete Laien* (Berlin: Ferd. Dümmler, 1873), 72-73.

Romantic irony is a variation of irony, where the opposing incompatible terms are the real and the unreal, objectivity and subjectivity, the individual and his work. See Fritz Ernst, *Die romantische Ironie* (Zürich: Schulters, 1915); Ingrid Strohschneider-Kohrs, *Die romantische Ironie in Theorie und Gestaltung*, in *Hermaea*, VI (Tübingen: Max Niemeyer, 1960), 223; Morton Gurevitch, "European Romantic Irony", Diss. Columbia 1957, p. 42; Irving Babbitt, *Rousseau and Romanticism* (Boston and New York: Houghton Mifflin, 1919), 242, 247, 263-265; René Wellek, *A History of Modern Criticism, 1750-1950*. vol. II: *The Romantic Age* (New Haven and London: Yale Univ. Press, 1955-*0000*), 14 and 300; William K. Wimsatt, Jr. and Cleanth Brooks, *Literary Criticism: A Short History*, Borzoi (1957; rpt. New York: Alfred A. Knopf, 1965), 378-380.

This concept and name arises from a figurative extension of the concept and name as ordinarily understood... The transference is easy very often in life. Circumstances are wrongly interpreted by Man, they *seem* otherwise than they really are. Similarly, things bear a promise upon their face that is at variance with the actual issue. A man who becomes conscious that he has been duped thus, may readily conceive that circumstance — the Scheme of things — has been mocking him, "saying one and giving to understand the contrary." And the idea comes all the more easily if that man is accustomed to believe that circumstance is the expression of some Power — God, Fate, Fortune — who, if not mocking him, is at any rate pursuing ways that are past finding out.

(Sedgewick, "Dramatic Irony", 214-215).

Although the term "ironie du sort" becomes common in the nineteenth century, the phenomenon to which it points appears in literature ever since Greek drama and ancient theoretical works. While the Ancients never applied it to their theater,[30] modern theorists on irony frequently include peripeteia in their definitions.[31] Aristotle's discussion of peripeteia — i.e., reversal — still holds true today:

'Peripety' is the shift of the action towards the opposite pole in accordance with the principles previously mentioned, and in the manner we were just speaking of, i.e., in accordance with probability or necessity — as for example in the *Oedipus* the messenger who has arrived, when it seems that he will make Oedipus happy

[30] "That very name [irony of fate] is practically a nineteenth-century creation. One wonders that the Greeks never thought of the fitness of the term. Perhaps they felt 'irony' to be too undignified a word to apply to the action of their Gods. In any case, neither they nor the medieval devotees of Fortune... ever name the workings of the 'Master of the Show' by the name 'irony.'" Sedgewick, "Dramatic Irony", 217-218. See also Robert Boies Sharpe, *Irony in Drama: An Essay on Impersonation, Shock and Catharsis* (Chapel Hill: Univ. of North Carolina Press, 1959).

[31] "The *peripeteia* is the resulting from *blinded* human effort of the very opposite of its aim." F. L. Lucas, "The Reverse of Aristotle", *Classical Review*, 37 (1923), 102-103. See also Thomas Dwight Goodell, *Athenian Tragedy: A Study in Popular Art* (New Haven: Yale Univ. Press, 1920), 158; F. McD. C. Turner, *The Element of Irony in English Literature* (Cambridge, England: Cambridge Univ. Press, 1926), 3-4; Eugene H. Falk, *Renunciation as a Tragic Focus: A Study of Five Plays*, introd. by Norman J. DeWitt (Minneapolis: Univ. of Minnesota Press, 1954), 3; Seymour M. Pitcher, "Aristotle's Good and Just Heroes", *PQ*, 24 (1945), 1-11 and 190-191. Of particular importance is Jacques Scherer's comment on peripeteia in his *La Dramaturgie classique en France* (Paris: Nizet, 1950), 86-87. See also J. W. H. Atkins, *Literary Criticism in Antiquity: A Sketch of Its Development*, Vol. I, *Greek* (Gloucester, Mass.: Peter Smith, 1961), 92. Geoffrey Brereton, in his *Principles of Tragedy: A Rational Examination of the Tragic Concept in Life and Literature* (Coral Gables: Univ. of Miami Press, 1968), 14, connects irony to peripeteia in both tragedy and comedy. See William Empson, *Seven Types of Ambiguity* (New York: New Directions, 1930), 38-47; H. D. F. Kitto, *Greek Tragedy*, 2nd edition (London: Methuen, 1950), 329; Henry Alonzo Myers, *Tragedy: A View of Life* (Ithaca, N.Y.: Cornell Univ. Press, 1965), 17-18; Alan Reynolds Thompson, *The Anatomy of Drama* (Berkeley and Los Angeles: Univ. of California Press, 1946), 142-145.

and relieve him of his fears towards his mother by revealing who he was, brings about the opposite; and in the *Lynceus* the hero being led off as though to execution, and Danaus following him as if to perform the execution, it follows logically as a result of what has happened that the latter dies and the former is saved...[32]

The appreciation of probability and necessity may vary from person to person. If a spectator knows Oedipus' story, he may expect a certain development of the action, which could seem improbable to someone hearing the subject for the first time. Also, depending on the individual sense of justice or poetic instinct, a particular consequence would appear either necessary or superfluous. If there are any "logical" consequences, there is usually a logical choice — i.e., one or several events which could logically take different courses. The messenger could have said that Oedipus' parents were both dead, or that Oedipus killed his father and married his mother but that the gods forgave him, or that he was guilty and he had to pay. In a culture which accepts the supernatural, all these variants and countless others seem possible.

Oedipus expects that the messenger will make him happy, yet the opposite happens. In *Lynceus*, the executioner dies, and the victim is saved. In both cases expectation and reality are at opposite poles (happiness and unhappiness, life and death). Although the expected event and the real one are incompatible, the context links them by attributing to the same character two opposite fates at the same time. Thus the expectation becomes an untrue description of the actual fact. The stronger the expectation, the more striking the shift of the action toward its opposite.[33]

Peripeteia can take many forms. If it appears in a play, it is sometimes associated with "dramatic irony". If it appears in a non-dramatic work, critics still refer to it as "dramatic irony" or, figuratively, as "irony of fate".[34] What makes it different from verbal irony (i.e., irony as a rhetorical device) is that in dramatic irony, the situation determined by destiny rep-

[32] Aristotle, *Poetics*, 5a22-30, in Gerald F. Else, *Aristotle's "Poetics": The Argument* (Cambridge, Mass.: Harvard Univ. Press, 1963), 342. See also Walter Lock, "The Use of περιπετέια in Aristotle's *Poetics*", *Classical Review*, 9 (1895), 251-253.

[33] For a discussion of the implications of peripeteia, see Else, 342-355; Lane Cooper, *An Aristotelian Theory of Comedy with an Adaptation of the Poetics and a Translation of the "Tractatus Coislianus"* (New York: Harcourt, Brace, 1922), 200; Allan H. Gilbert and Henry L. Snuggs, "On the Relation of Horace to Aristotle in Literary Criticism", *JEGP*, 46 (1947), 237. Particularly helpful is Bert O. States, *Irony and Drama: A Poetics* (Ithaca, N.Y.: Cornell Univ. Press, 1971), 27.

[34] "*Dramatic i.* is a plot device according to which (a) the spectators know more than the protagonist; (b) the character reacts in a way contrary to that which is appropriate or wise; (c) characters or situations are compared or contrasted for ironic effects...; (d) there is a marked contrast between what the character understands about his acts and what the play demonstrates about them" (Preminger, 407).

resents at least one of the contrasting terms, while in verbal irony destiny plays no part. Just as a non-dramatic work may contain dramatic irony, a play can contain verbal irony, independent of any particular circumstance.

Since dramatic irony appears in both comedy and tragedy, it can borrow the qualities of either. Hence the terms comic and tragic irony.[35] Yet they apply not only to dramatic works but also to poetry and fiction, where their meaning has been extended to verbal irony. If irony produces laughter and happiness, it is comic; if it produces tears and unhappiness, it is tragic.[36] But people do not laugh or weep at the same things. Satire could conceivably generate tears in those criticized, and laughter or no reaction at all in those not involved. Moreover, laughter and tears do not always correspond to comedy and tragedy respectively, for some people weep out of happiness, others laugh from pain, while still others laugh with tears in their eyes. There are certain literary conventions established by tradition, according to which a certain theme belongs to either comedy or tragedy. The more an author departs from tradition — that is, from Aristotle — the more his drama will differ from an "authentic" tragedy or comedy, and the more controversy on the "true nature" of his play will arise.

The link between the two dramatic genres appears early in literature. Plato mentions it in the conclusion of his *Symposium*, in the conversation of Socrates, Agathon, the tragic writer, and Aristophanes, the comic playwright. In the Middle Ages, there are several poems consisting of an accumulation of paradoxes, among which that between laughter and tears.[37] Generally, the discussion of irony reflects the same mixture of

[35] Marcos Victoria, "Notes sur la dévaluation comique", *RE*, 3 (1950), 320. See also Worcester, 71-144; Larousse, *Grand Dictionnaire universel du XIXe siècle*, IX, 793; Boiste, *Dictionnaire universel de la langue française*, New Edition, Revised by Charles Nodier (Brussels: J. P. Meline, 1835), 407.

[36] See for example, Nicolas Boileau-Despréaux, *L'Art poétique*, III, ll. 150-351, 363-366, 141-144, ed. Charles-H. Boudhors, Les Textes français (Paris: Belles Lettres, 1939), 106-107 and 100. See also Félix Gaiffe, *Le Rire et la scène française*, Bibliothèque de la Revue des cours et conférences (Paris: Boivin, 1931); Richmond Y. Hathorn, *Tragedy, Myth and Mystery*, Midland, MB 92 (Bloomington and London: Indiana Univ. Press, 1962); Marguerite Fernagu, "Le Rire tragique", *RE*, 3 (1950), 413; H. Heath Bawden, "The Comic as Illustrating the Summation-Irradiation Theory of Pleasure-Pain", *Psychology*, 17 (1910), 336; Salomon Reinach, *Cultes, mythes et religions* (Paris: Ernest Leroux, 1912), IV, 127. For a general treatment of the subject, see Joyce O. Hertzler, *Laughter: A Socio-Scientific Analysis* (Jericho, N.Y.: Exposition Press, 1970); this book contains a good bibliography.

[37] Curtius, "Jest and Earnest in Medieval Literature", Excursus IV, in his *European Literature and the Latin Middle Ages*, trans. Willard R. Trask (= *Harper Torchbooks*, 2015) (= Bollingen Library, 36) (New York and Evanston, 1963), 417-435. See also

comic and tragic. For example, although he identifies irony with comedy, Voltaire admits that a tragic context can also be ironic.[38] Bergson maintains that "On obtiendra un effet comique en transposant l'expression naturelle d'une idée dans un autre ton" ("A comic effect will be obtained by transposing the natural expression of an idea to a different tone") and that "il y a d'abord deux termes de comparaison extrêmes, le très grand et le très petit, le meilleur et le pire, entre lesquels la transposition peut s'effectuer dans un sens ou dans l'autre" ("first there are two extreme terms of comparison, the very big and the very small, the best and the worst, between which the transposition can take place in one direction or the other").[39] The comic opposition between two incompatible terms also appears in Lalo,[40] Freud,[41] and Monro,[42] but McMahon uses the same type of contrast to define tragedy.[43] The similarity of these definitions underlines the link between comic and tragic, the difficulty in distinguishing one from the other, and the fact that both partake of the nature of irony. As already noted, dramatic irony functions according to the same criteria, regardless of the comic or tragic character of the text.

Mikhail Bakhtin, *Rabelais and His World*, trans. Helene Iswolsky (Cambridge, Mass. and London: M. I. T. Press, 1968), 1-58; Hanns Fluck, "Der Risus paschalis: Ein Beitrag zur religiösen Volkskunde", *Archiv für Religionswissenschaft*, 31 (1934), 188; States, 59.

38 Voltaire, "Remarques sur Médée", *Commentaires sur Corneille*, in *Oeuvres*, ed. Adrien J. Q. Beuchot, vol. 35 (Paris: Lefèvre and Werdet & Lequien, 1829), I, 23-24.

39 Henri Bergson, *Le Rire: Essai sur la signification du comique*, 237th edition, Bibliothèque de philosophie contemporaine (Paris: Presses univ. de France, 1969), 94 and 96.

40 Charles Lalo, "Le Comique et le spirituel", *RE*, 3 (1950), 321. See also Lalo, *Esthétique du rire*, Bibliothèque de philosophie scientifique (Paris: Flammarion, 1949), 233-234.

41 Sigmund Freud, *Wit and Its Relation to the Unconscious*, in *The Basic Writings of Sigmund Freud*, trans. A. A. Brill (= *Giant*, 39) (New York: Modern Library, 1938), 757.

42 D.H. Monro, *Argument of Laughter* (Indiana: Univ. of Notre Dame Press, 1963), 235. Similar theories appear in E. Aubouin, "Humour et transfert", *RE*, 3 (1950), 369-370; L. Cazamian, "Pourquoi nous ne pouvons pas définir l'humour", *Revue germanique*, 2 (1906), 607 and 629; Arthur Schopenhauer, *The World as Will and Idea*, trans. R. B. Haldane and J. Kemp (London: Kegan Paul, Trench, Trübner, 1886-1907), II, 271; Ralph Waldo Emerson, "The Comic", *Letters and Social Aims*, in *Complete Works* (Boston: Houghton, Mifflin, 1883), VIII, 151; L. J. Potts, *Comedy*, Hutchinson's Univ. Library, 41 (London: Cheltenham and London, 1948), 76-78; Marie Collins Swabey, *Comic Laughter: A Philosophical Essay* (New Haven and London: Yale Univ. Press, 1961), 7-25; James Sully, *An Essay on Laughter: Its Forms, Its Causes, Its Development and Its Value* (New York and Bombay: Longmans, Green, 1902), 343-391; Henry L. Snuggs, "The Comic Humorous: A New Interpretation", *PMLA*, 52 (1947), 121; Willard Smith, *The Nature of Comedy* (Boston: Richard G. Badger, 1930), 29-65.

43 A. Philip McMahon, "Seven Questions of Aristotelian Definitions of Tragedy and Comedy", *Harvard Studies in Classical Philology*, 40 (1929), 97-189.

4. CRITERIA FOR ANALYZING IRONY

The three types of irony discussed share certain characteristics. In each, an assertion establishes a fact which another assertion contradicts. Irony therefore implies two opposite and incompatible terms qualifying the same object simultaneously. The opposition is in accordance with linguistic and cultural habits. Good is opposed to bad, long to short, knowledgeable to ignorant, high to low. The terms are incompatible if they cannot apply to the same object in the same circumstances (e.g., the same time, place, etc.). The two terms form an ironic context[44] if, despite their incompatibility, they apply to the same object in the same circumstances. The ironic reality is the common ground of the terms. Two opposed and incompatible qualities characterize Socrates: ignorance and knowledge. They constitute the ironic context, whose ironic reality is Socrates. Lamia appears ugly and handsome, untalented and eloquent. These contradictory qualities represent the ironic context, while Lamia and all the circumstances that bring together the incompatible terms are the ironic reality. Oedipus is associated with the ironic reality when the actual message contradicts the expected one.

It is possible for one person to see incompatibility and opposition, while another perceives only one of them or neither. Differences of perception occur particularly when analysis involves value judgments not expressed in the text, which change with each reader, population segment, culture, and period. Everybody will agree that "good" and "bad" are direct opposites. Therefore, applied to the same person in the same circumstances, they become ironic. In Christian societies where thieving has unfavorable connotations, a thief lacking moral compunction would probably perceive no opposition or incompatibility between "good" and "theft". However, if the context clearly establishes the formulas "stealing is bad" and "theft is a good thing", there is no ambiguity as to the ironic connotations of the latter. A thief may not like them, but he will notice them. Similarly, if the reader expects the word "excellent", and the text only gives "pretty good", the combination of the two expressions could

[44] The ironic context is a particular form of stylistic context, defined as "a linguistic *pattern suddenly broken by an element which was impredictable*, and the contrast resulting from this interference is the stylistic stimulus... The stylistic value of the contrast lies in the relationship it establishes between the two clashing elements: no effect would occur without their association in a sequence." Michael Riffaterre, "Criteria for Style Analysis", *Word*, 15 (1959), 171. See also, by the same author, "Le Contexte stylistique", in *Essais de stylistique structurale*, ed. and trans. Daniel Delas (Paris: Flammarion, 1971), 69-94.

produce an ironic context only to those readers for whom "excellent" is the only possible expectation.

Analysis becomes even more difficult when dealing with texts whose cultural and linguistic background is less familiar to the critic. Certain conventions are the same today as in antiquity or in the Middle Ages, not all of them. On one hand, since science has progressed, what seemed impossible eight hundred years ago may be possible today; hence what seemed incompatible then could seem compatible now. On the other hand, miracles and superstitions made the medieval man believe in relations which are incompatible by modern standards. Finally, in analyzing a text, we do not know if originally intonation and gestures were part of an ironic context, unless the text corroborates them.

The criteria defining the ironic context belong to all three types of irony discussed, and nothing but irony has all these criteria together. No device that I know creates alone an ironic context, because no isolated device contains two opposite and incompatible terms. Yet a few theorists have tried to classify irony according to the rhetorical figures which may express it.[45] Actually, the devices they mention may be, but are not always, ironic. Also, irony may result not only from the juxtaposition of two terms or sentences, but from that of passages of various length (with no particular rhetorical label), providing that these passages are opposed and incompatible in meaning and that the reader is forced to bring them together. However, all figures may reinforce irony, if they underline or contain one or both terms of the ironic context. In a simile, for example, the tenor (the compared object) could be one term of that context, the vehicle (the object to which the tenor is compared) the other, and the ground (the qualities common to tenor and vehicle) the ironic reality.

In addition to knowing the cultural and linguistic background of the text, stylistic convergence is also useful. If to a certain opposition and incompatibility correspond many others, the author creates an effect of insistence which is more likely to strike the reader than an isolated device.[46]

Irony, as I shall apply it in this study, consists of a context of at least

[45] Norman Knox, in his *The Word "Irony" and Its Context, 1500-1755* (Durham: Duke Univ. Press, 1961), 39-98, supplies a dictionary of rhetorical devices which can express irony. See also Peter Haidu, *Aesthetic Distance in Chrétien de Troyes: Irony and Comedy in "Cligès" and "Perceval"* (Geneva: Droz, 1968), 13-23; Philippe Ménard, *Le Rire et le sourire dans le roman courtois en France au Moyen Age (1150-1250)* (*Publications romanes et françaises*, 105) (Geneva: Droz, 1969), 447-462 and 630-683; E. de Saint-Denis, *Essais sur le rire et le sourire des Latins* (*Publications de l'Univ. de Dijon*, 32) (Paris: Belles Lettres, 1965), 125.

[46] Riffaterre, *Le Style des "Pléiades" de Gobineau: Essai d'application d'une méthode stylistique* (New York: Columbia Univ. Press, 1957), 190.

two opposed terms (ironic context) characterizing the same object (ironic reality) in relation to which they are logically incompatible. The definition obviously has limitations. My discussion has shown only that these criteria are necessary, not that they are sufficient: while irony always implies opposition and incompatibility, the reverse may not be true. To be sufficient, the necessary qualities should always be considered ironic. They emerged as the common denominator of an accumulation of popular views on irony, and they are necessary because there is no ironic occurrence without them. They will be sufficient as well, if the public always considers them ironic. In order to establish sufficiency, I have therefore tried opposition and incompatibility in as many forms and on as many people as I could. I am now convinced that opposition and incompatibility are both necessary and sufficient. Moreover, the advantage of these criteria is that irony thus defined does not depend on the reader's individual value judgments (for the text usually provides its own), but can be objectively analyzed by readers of any epoch, nationality, or cultural background.

II

IRONY OF WORDS

I shall use "irony of words" to describe ironic occurrences established by single words or small groups of words, rather than paragraphs, sections or whole works. In this way, the present chapter will treat irony on a level as close as possible to that implied by medieval definitions.

Irony of words may change the meaning of, or be changed by, neighboring words, the entire work, the culture of the period, or the reader's mentality. The three poems to be discussed will be treated not chronologically, but in order of their complexity — i.e., according to the number of elements which the reader could superimpose to create and alter irony of words. The poems in question are Charles d'Orléans' "Je meurs de soif auprès de la fontaine", François Villon's story of Alexander and Diomedes from the *Testament*, and Rutebeuf's "Mariage". Besides irony, all three have in common a certain popularity owing not only to their intrinsic value or the fame of their authors, but also to certain *topoi* which connect each poem to at least one literary tradition. Some *topoi* were already ironic, others become so only in the above works. A short discussion of the traditions of the poems will demonstrate a wide distribution of irony in time and subject matter, despite a narrow perspective of the ironic context (the word).

"Je meurs de soif" and all its variants by Charles d'Orléans and his literary circle owe to tradition the *topos* of contradictions, often connected with love's suffering. Paul Meyer noticed a resemblance between certain poems where the suffering inflicted by Amor is described by means of paradoxes. The authors of these poems enumerate the circumstances when their feelings differ from those of a man in his right mind. The cause and effect of the lover's activities constantly contradict each other. Throughout the Middle Ages such poems are found not only in France, but also in Spain and Italy.[1] Several fifteenth-century French poems begin

[1] Paul Meyer, "Des rapports de la poésie des trouvères avec celle des troubadours", *Romania*, 19 (1890), 7 and 11. This *topos* is more fully established by Italo Siciliano, in

"Je meurs de soif auprès de la fontaine". Many critics attribute this recurrence to the famous "Concours de Blois", where Charles d'Orléans would have composed the ballad, and his courtiers, Villon among them, would have kept the first line and changed the rest.[2] Lucien Foulet attributes such popularity to Charles's patronage of the arts.[3] Widespread in the Middle Ages, "Je meurs de soif" appeared in many different contexts. Likewise its ironic implications belonged to many works in which irony of words played various roles.

The story of Alexander and Diomedes first appeared in Cicero's *Republic*, then in many adaptations in both Latin and French. Modern critics have sought to establish Villon's direct source. Champion asserted that this story is found in the writings of preachers such as Jean Gerson, and was well-known.[4] In his edition of Villon[5] and in his *Villon et Rabelais: Notes et commentaires*,[6] Louis Thuasne mentioned Villon's debt to John of Salisbury through Jean de Vignay. To facilitate comparison, this critic supplied the texts of several authors such as Cicero, Saint Augustine, Caecilius Balbus, John of Salisbury, Jacques de Cessoles (Latin), Denis Foullechat, Jean Ferron and Jean de Vignay (French). Whether Villon was particularly familiar with one version or another, the story itself was important enough to inspire that many adaptations and translations. Its ironic overtones lasted from generation to generation before Villon included it in his *Testament*.

The "Mariage Rutebeuf" contains a combination of different *topoi*,

---

his *François Villon et les thèmes poétiques du moyen âge* (1933; rpt. Paris: Nizet, 1967), 106-107 and R. A. Dwyer, "'Je meurs de soif auprès de la fontaine'", *FS*, 23 (1969), 225-228.

[2] Pierre Champion, *Vie de Charles d'Orléans (1394-1465)* (Paris: H. Champion, 1911), 651-652.

[3] L. Foulet, "Villon et Charles d'Orléans", in *Medieval Studies in Memory of Gertrude Schoepperle Loomis* (Paris: Champion and New York: Columbia Univ. Press, 1927), 356-357. Also helpful are [Mary] Ethel Seaton, "Charles d'Orléans and Versifiers of His Court", in her *Studies in Villon, Vaillant and Charles d'Orléans* (Oxford: B. H. Blackwell, 1957), 45-48; Grace Frank, "Villon at the Court of Charles d'Orléans", *MLN*, 47 (1932), 498 and 501. Cf. Philippe Ménard, "*Je meurs de soif auprès de la fontaine:* D'un mythe antique à une image lyrique", *Romania*, 87 (1966), 394-400.

[4] Pierre Champion, *François Villon: Sa Vie et son temps*, 2nd edition (= *Bibliothèque du XVe siècle*, vols. 20-21) (Paris: Champion, 1967), I, 47, n. 1.

[5] Louis Thuasne, ed. *Oeuvres*, by François Villon, 3 vols. (rpt. Geneva: Slatkine, 1967), III, 613-623.

[6] Thuasne, "Appendice I", *Villon et Rabelais: Notes et commentaires* (1911; rpt. Geneva: Slatkine, 1969), 419-430. See also Gaston Paris and Marcel Schwob, "Villoniana", *Romania*, 30 (1901), 385; David Kuhn, *La Poétique de François Villon* (Paris: Armand Colin, 1967), 179-180, n. 12 and 182, n. 19.

such as "the unhappy marriage",[7] or the wife's ugliness and old age.[8] To the best of my knowledge, Ulrich Leo makes the most important contribution to the analysis of *topoi* in this poem. First he compares Rutebeuf to Adam de la Halle and Colin Muset. Then he places the "Mariage" against the whole tradition of the courtly lyric. The "Mariage" is a parody of the troubadour love and its paradoxical ideology.[9]

The multiplicity of *topoi* and themes present in the "Mariage" deserves further discussion. In fact, the ironic context of the poem depends largely upon the combination of such literary conventions and will receive closer scrutiny in the third and most complex section of this chapter.

1. "JE MEURS DE SOIF" (CHARLES D'ORLÉANS, BALLADE CXXIII[c])

This ballad has long been interpreted as an accumulation of paradoxes with little or no connection among them. While many critics successfully proved the stereotyped nature of these paradoxes, few attempted to study their function in the poem. Charles may indeed merely have played a rhetorical game, with no overall conception of the structure of his poem. Nevertheless, whether intentionally or not, he produced twenty-eight lines rich in associations. His text, much like a symbolic one, offers few clues as to its intended meaning. So the reader is free to interpret it in any way that he chooses, although cultural and literary conventions as well as personal taste will determine his choice. As I shall show, many interpretations are ironic. Each line contains two contrasting statements

[7] Cf. Alfred Jeanroy, *Les Origines de la poésie lyrique en France au moyen âge: Etudes de littérature française et comparée suivies de textes inédits*, 3rd edition (Paris: Champion, 1925), 85-91.

[8] Jean Frappier, *La Poésie lyrique française aux XIIe et XIIIe siècles: Les Auteurs et les genres*, Les Cours de Sorbonne: Littérature française (Paris: Centre de documentation universitaire), 225. For a general outlook on Rutebeuf's satirical and love poetry see Léon Clédat, *Rutebeuf*, Les Grands Ecrivains français (Paris: Hachette, 1891) and *La Poésie lyrique et satirique en France au moyen âge*, Coll. des classiques populaires (Paris: Société française d'imprimerie et de librairie), 195-219; A. Kressner, "Rustebuef als Satiren-Dichter", *Franco-Gallia*, 11 (1894), 17-23; Anne-Lise Cohen, "Exploration of Sounds in Rutebeuf's Poetry", *FR*, 40 (1967), 658-667; P. Leendertz, Jr., "De Strophen van Rutebeuf", *Neophil.*, 4 (1918-1919), 202-211; Heinrich Peter Tjaden, *Untersuchungen über die Poetik Rutebeufs* (Marburg and Leer: W. J. Loendertz, 1885); Arié Serper, *La Manière satirique de Rutebeuf: Le Ton et le style* (Naples: Liguori, 1972).

[9] Ulrich Leo, "Rutebeuf: Persönlicher Ausdruck und Wirklichkeit", in *Romanistische Aufsätze aus drei Jahrzehnten*, ed. Fritz Schalk (Köln and Graz: Böhlau, 1966), 136-137.

which, taken literally, cannot both apply to one person in exactly the same circumstances (e.g., "Homme parfait, privé de corps et d'ame", l. 21).[10] However, Charles d'Orléans attributes all these contrasts to one man — to "je" or another pronoun in the first person singular — in the same circumstances. Incapable of finding a coherent literal meaning, the reader must seek a figurative one.

My analysis of the text will include the tradition of the paradoxes and their relation to each other. To avoid confusion with its variants (Charles d'Orléans, I, pp. 156-157, 191-193, 194-195, 196-203; II, 638), I shall quote the poem in full:

BALLADE CXXIII[c]

Je meurs de soif auprès de la fontaine;
Tant plus mengue, et tant plus je me affame;
Pouvre d'argent ou ma bourse en est plaine,
Marié suis et si n'ay point de fame;
Qui me honnore, grandement me diffame;
Quant je vois droit, lors est que me devoye;
Pour loz et pris, j'é tiltre de diffame;
Grief desplaisir m'est excessive joie.

Quant l'en me toult, richement on me estraine;
Dix mile onces ne me sont que une drame;
Sec et brahaing, je porte fleur et graine;
En reposant, sur mer tire a la rame;
Actainé suis en tous lieux ou n'a ame;
Acompaigné, je n'ay qui me convoye;
Tout entiere est la chose que je entâme;
Grief desplaisir m'est excessive joie.

En aspirant, je retiens mon alaine;
Quant eur me vient, maleureux je me clame;
Fort et puissant, flexible comme laine;
Transsi d'amours sans avoir nulle dame;
Homme parfait, privé de corps et d'ame;
Paisible suis, et ung chascun guerroye;
Mes ennemis plus que tous autres ame;
Grief desplaisir m'est excessive joie.

Mauvaise odeur m'est plus fleurant que basme;
Pasmé de dueil, angoisseux me resjoye;
En eaue plungié, je brule tout en flame;
Grief desplaisir m'est excessive joie.

[10] All quotations of Charles d'Orléans are from his *Poésies*, ed. Pierre Champion (= *CFMA*, nos. 34 and 56) (1923-1924; rpt. Paris: H. Champion, 1956), I, 192-193. Line numbers are inserted in the text.

(I die of thirst near the fountain. The more I eat, the hungrier I am. [I have] little money when my pocket is full. I am married and I have no wife. Whoever honors me greatly disgraces me. When I go straight, then I go astray. Praise gives me reason for dishonor. Grievous distress is excessive joy to me.

Rich gifts are bestowed upon me when they are taken away. Ten thousand ounces are but a drachma to me. Dry and fruitless, I bear flower and seed. While resting, I row at sea. I am irritated wherever there is nobody [to get angry at]. Accompanied, I have no one to invite me. The thing that I begin is completed. Grievous distress is excessive joy to me.

I hold my breath when I exhale. When happiness comes, I claim myself unhappy. [I am] strong and powerful, pliable like wool. [I am] penetrated by love though I have no lady. [I am] a whole man, deprived of body and soul. I am peaceful, and I make war on everyone. I love my enemies more than [I do] all other people. Grievous distress is excessive joy to me.

Bad odor smells better than balm to me. Having fainted from sorrow, I painfully rejoice. Plunged into water, I burn all aflame. Grievous distress is excessive joy to me.)

"Je meurs de soif" contains a whole spectrum of ironic perspectives, literal or with possible figurative connotations (e.g., l. 6). "Quant je vois droit, lors est que me devoye" (l. 6) may allude not only to the physical reality of a person who goes astray although he sees the right direction, but also, figuratively, to a person who does not find his way clearly in life. It may refer even to the speaker's paradoxical thinking throughout the poem.

The implications of line 6 go beyond physical reality.[11] Unless the speaker deliberately avoids the right way, "je vois droit" implies going in the right direction. Yet "devoye" conveys deviation. Taken literally, this line is a paradox without any particular significance. Figuratively, however, it may refer to other types of perception, such as understanding or love.[12] If the reader interprets both hemistichs on the same level, whether literal or figurative, going in the right and in the wrong directions simultaneously describes actions incompatible, opposed, and, therefore, ironic.

Equally ironic and far-reaching is line 27 ("En eau plungié, je brule tout en flame."). Water extinguishes fire. Yet plunged in water, the speaker is burning. Such an unlikely phenomenon taken literally, makes the reader question the power of fire and water. The whole line can acquire figurative

[11] Poirion, *Le Lexique de Charles d'Orléans dans les Ballades* (= *Publications romanes et françaises*, 91) (Geneva: Droz, 1967).

[12] Andreas Capellanus, *The Art of Courtly Love*, trans. John Jay Parry (New York: Ungar, 1959); Herbert Kolb, *Der Begriff der Minne und das Entstehen der höfischen Lyrik* (= *Hermaea, Germanistische Forschungen, neue Folge*, 4) (Tübingen: Max Niemeyer, 1958).

meanings, as warriors can be fiery in battle, and lovers may burn from passion. The literal interpretations imply respectively that water, supposed to extinguish fire, does not really do so, and that burning flames do not actually burn. Both interpretations annihilate basic qualities of an element by attributing to it characteristics opposite to its own, and thus both create irony.[13]

The figurative interpretation is particularly accessible to the medieval reader because of its frequency in literature. In fact, our poem contains ideas that ironically suggest passion in both battle and love, as the speaker opposes peace to war and friendship to enmity and alludes to marital and courtly love. On one hand, a military vocabulary emerges from lines 22 and 23: "Paisible suis et ung chascun guerroye; / Mes ennemis plus que tous autres ame..." Peaceful and warlike (l. 22), attributed to the same person simultaneously, are incompatible. Since enmity implies hate (l. 23), loving one's enemy suggests simultaneous love and hate toward the same person, and like the peaceful warrior of the preceding line, is ironic. On the other hand, lines 4 and 20 (Marié suis et si n'ay point de fame; / ... Transsi d'amours sans avoir nulle dame...") assert the poet's possession and lack of a woman in marriage and love. Irony originates in the contrast and incongruity of simultaneous lack and possession of women by the same person.

"Qui me honnore, grandement me diffame" (l. 5) may elucidate the immediately preceding paradox of marital love: "n'ay point de fame" could connote his abstinence or his wife's unfaithfulness. However, honor and defamation also belong to a more general concept dear to the medieval noble, which includes attitudes in love, war and everyday life.[14] "Pour loz et pris, j'é tiltre de diffame" (l. 7) insists on the same concept. Since honor and dishonor are opposed and, coming from the same person at the same time, incompatible, honor appears in an ironic context.

Honor calls to mind *largesse*, 'generosity', an important quality of the medieval knight, which in turn reflects abundance. The speaker complains of dying of thirst near the fountain, getting hungrier the more he eats, and having no money while he has plenty. He also claims that to take from him is to bestow rich gifts upon him (ll. 1-3 and 9). Lines 1-3 refer to abundance and scarcity of food, drink and money, while line 9 involves *largesse*. The whole passage is ironic, for it insists on the incongruous contrast

[13] Poirion, *Lexique*, 81 ("Feu"); Tobler-Lommatzsch, III, cols. 1785 ("*feu*") and 1904 ("*flame*").

[14] See Victoria Crane Lebovics, "The Moral Universe of Charles d'Orléans," Diss., Yale, 1962.

between abundance and scarcity, as well as between getting something and having it taken away.

Love, war, honor, abundance, *largesse*, and all the other themes of the poem are associated with joy and sorrow. This association is perceptible in the structure of the ballad owing to the refrain (ll. 8, 16, 24, 28). "Grief desplaisir m'est excessive joie" is ironic, because it equates pleasure and displeasure, incompatible and opposite terms. The refrain stresses the ironic context and provides a common denominator for the four *laisses*. Three of the four lines in the *envoi* (ll. 25, 26, 28) also point to the paradox of pleasure and displeasure. Consequently, the refrain, reinforced by lines such as "Quant eur me vient, malheureux je me clame" (l. 18), "Pasmé de dueil, angoisseux me resjoye" (l. 26), and "Mauvaise odeur m'est plus fleurant que basme" (l. 25), represents the ironic conclusion not only to each *laisse*, but also to the whole poem.

Irony of words in "Je meurs de soif" results, as we have seen, from the juxtaposition of hemistichs in each line and the accumulation of ironic paradoxes thus produced (see Kolb, "Dialektik der Minne", *Begriff*, 100-110). Incoherence draws attention to the lover's abnormal state. Unlike the lover who is personally involved, the reader can see irony in the paradoxes. The smallness of the context does not imply insignificant themes or limited interpretations. The ironic themes vary from specific aspects of everyday life to general characteristics of the medieval knight, and from concrete activities to abstract concepts. Abstract concepts result mainly from incoherent meanings on the literal level and from the reader's awareness of figurative associations in other medieval works. Themes comprise from one to six lines and may be independent of each other or closely linked. Although limited by its size, irony in this ballad displays a wide thematic perspective, for its inconsistencies and imprecision give way to imagination and association.

2. THE STORY OF ALEXANDER AND DIOMEDES (VILLON, *Testament*, XVII-XXI)

Irony in this episode originates in a sharp contrast between Alexander the Great and the pirate Diomedes. By comparing them, Villon equates good to evil, a surprising relation which, however, is justified in the moral of the story and in the *Testament* as a whole. After outlining the plot followed by Villon's text, I shall examine the portraits of the protagonists and show how their relationship is ironic.

About to sentence the pirate to death, Alexander asks why he is a thief. The prisoner answers that although a pirate in a small boat, he is no thief; had he a powerful army, he would become Alexander's equal. Impressed, Alexander decides to improve Diomedes' life. This incident illustrates reversal of fortune and is one of the many passages where "pauvre Villon" attributes his misery to fate. In "Problème", for example, Fortune, to whom François complained about his life, reprimands him. Since men much more important than he died because of her, Villon should be grateful for everything. Alexander is among those who, despite their grandeur, die at the hands of fortune.[15]

All references to the story of Alexander and Diomedes are made to the text below:

XVII Ou temps qu'Alixandre regna,
Ung homs nommé Diomedès
Devant luy on lui amena,
Engrilloné poulces et des
Comme ung larron, car il fut des
Escumeurs que voions courir;
Si fut mis devant ce cadès,
Pour estre jugié a mourir.

XVIII L'empereur si l'araisonna:
"Pourquoi es tu larron de mer?"
L'autre responce luy donna:
"Pourquoi larron me faiz nommer?
Pour ce qu'on me voit escumer.
en une petiote fuste?
Se comme toy me peusse armer,
Comme toy empereur je feusse.

XIX "Mais que veux-tu? De ma fortune,
Contre qui ne puis bonnement,
Qui si faulcement me fortune,
Me vient tout ce gouvernement.
Excuse moy aucunement
Et saiche qu'en grant povreté,
Ce mot se dit communement,
Ne gist pas grande loyauté."

XX Quant l'empereur ot remiré
De Diomedès tout le dit:
"Ta fortune je te mueray

[15] François Villon, "Poésies diverses", XII, in *Oeuvres*, ed. Auguste Longnon, 4th edition revised by Lucien Foulet (= *CFMA*, 2) (Paris: H. Champion, 1961), 94.

Mauvaise en bonne," si luy dit.
Si fist il. Onc puis ne mesdit
A personne, mais fut vray homme;
Valere pour vray le baudit,
Qui fut nommé le Grant a Romme.

XXI Se Dieu m'eust donné rencontrer
Ung autre piteux Alixandre
Qui m'eust fait en bon eur entrer,
Et lors qui m'eust veu condescendre
A mal, estre ars et mis en cendre
Jugié me feusse de ma voix.
Necessité fait gens mesprendre
Et faim saillir le loup du bois.

(Villon, *Testament*, in *Oeuvres*, pp. 16-17).

(When Alexander reigned, a man called Diomedes was brought to him. The latter was chained like a thief, for he was among the pirates whom we see running rampant. He was placed before this commander, who was to condemn him to death.

The emperor addressed him thus: "Why are you a pirate?" The other answered: "Why do you call me a pirate? Because they see me steal in a small boat? If I could arm myself like you, I would be an emperor like you.

But what do you expect? This behavior originates in my fortune, against which I can do nothing, [and] which makes me so miserable. Do not condemn me entirely. Be aware that, as the saying goes, no great loyalty lies in poverty."

When the emperor heard Diomedes' words, he spoke to him thus: "I will change your bad fortune in to a good one". So he did. After that, he never slandered anyone. Instead, he became a truthful man. Valerius [Maximus], who in Rome was called "the Great", considered him to be truthful.

If God had made it possible for me to meet another merciful Alexander, who would have given me happiness, and then who would have seen me indulge in evil deeds, I would have condemned myself with my own voice to be burned to ashes. [But] necessity leads people astray, and hunger makes the wolf come out of the woods.)

Alexander the Great, Charlemagne, and Arthur were the three monarchs who most influenced the concept of the ideal king in medieval French literature.[16] Alexander's portrait was readily accessible in many versions

16 See Dora M. Bell, *L'Idéal éthique de la royauté en France au moyen âge d'après quelques moralistes de ce temps* (Geneva: Droz, 1962).

of the *Roman d'Alexandre*, Charlemagne was the hero of the *geste du roi*, and Arthur appeared in romances of the *matière de Bretagne*. In addition, these heroes became a standard of comparison in many medieval works. An army was excellent if it was as good as theirs. Authors often associated Charlemagne with prowess in battle and Arthur with courtly love. Alexander is famous also for his generosity. In fact, *largesse* was the quality for which medieval writers proposed Alexander as an example to their protectors. His *largesse* had various connotations, such as rich gifts to his vassals, protection of the weak, and justice for the innocent and the oppressed.

In Villon's poem, Alexander, having to judge Diomedes, appears in a position of power. The opposition between the protagonists appears on several levels: military (military leader vs. enemy prisoner), legal (judge vs. accused), political (big power vs. small power), social (great king vs. low character), and humanitarian (benefactor vs. malefactor). The vocabulary describing Alexander reflects at least two of these levels. Villon calls him a "cadès" (l. 135), which means judge or captain,[17] and thus places the story in a legal and military frame. Diomedes matches both levels, as his appearance suggests the thief as well as the prisoner (ll. 132-133). This multilevel contrast will contribute to irony in the story.

In analyzing irony, it is worth noting that Diomedes is not a thief, but "like a thief". Diomedes will make the same distinction himself. When Alexander asks him why he is a pirate (l. 138), he answers "Pourquoi larron me faiz nommer" (l. 140), thus discriminating between his title and his real nature. Diomedes says that he is accused of theft because he practices piracy (l. 141) in a small boat (l. 142). In his opinion, the shift from "larron" to "empereur" would require one from a small boat to an army like Alexander's. Strictly speaking, "me peusse armer" (l. 143) is the opposite term of "en petiote fuste" alone; these terms are extremes of military power. However, since "escumer" and "en une petiote fuste" are grammatically linked, "me peusse armer" could also represent the opposite pole of "escumer" and "en une petiote fuste" together. This ambiguity suggests that as emperor, Diomedes would either give up piracy by gaining strength, or merely gain strength. The latter possibility implies that an emperor behaves like a pirate, but he is no longer called (cf. "nom-

[17] Thuasne, ed., II, 111-112. On the double meaning of "cadès", see also Pierre Demarolle, *L'Esprit de Villon: Etude de style*, Coll. "Style et esprit français" (Paris: Nizet, 1968), 36, n. 34; cf. André Burger, *Lexique de la langue de Villon* (Geneva: 1957), 41 ("cadés").

mer") thief.[18] The context allows both interpretations, the first of which referring to a change in behavior, is not ironic, while the second, based on a change in terminology, is.

Diomedes suggests the first interpretation by saying that little loyalty lies in poverty (ll. 150-152). Although these lines are ambiguous as to the loyalty of poor people, the parallel between Villon and the pirate, following the story of Alexander and Diomedes, solves that ambiguity (ll. 167-168). "Necessité" calls to mind Diomedes' humble state ("petiote fuste", "grant povreté"). Reinforced by the proverb of the hungry wolf coming out of the forest (Thuasne, ed., II, 119-120), "Necessité fait gens mesprendre" indicates that bad actions result from poverty.

The first interpretation does not rule out the second, for although virtue never comes from poverty, neither does it necessarily originate in wealth or power. In their professions, both Alexander and Diomedes seize enemy powers by force. Yet the former's deeds are considered noble, the latter's ignominious. By implying that an emperor is a powerful pirate no longer called thief, Diomedes puts an emperor and an outcast on the same level. The ambiguity of ll. 157-158 points again to the similarity between these characters. "Fu vray homme" can describe both Alexander and Diomedes: the former will no longer make unjust accusations, the latter will no longer be a pirate. "Il" (l. 157) refers to Alexander, who promises to improve his prisoner's life. Although the subject of "mesdit" and "fu" is not expressed, we can assume it to be Alexander, who wrongly called Diomedes a pirate. The contrast between "mesdit" and "fut vray homme" describes that between his unjust and just attitudes. Thus Alexander and Diomedes stand in judgment of each other, and each is both judge and accused.

Equating the two positions is nonetheless unexpected for, as already mentioned, the two men are very far apart according to both the context and literary tradition. The superposition of military, legal, social and political oppositions of the same person insists on the extreme contrast between protagonists and renders their equality impossible. Such equality implies that the emperor is like the prisoner, the judge like the

[18] Cf. "Les Animaux malades de la peste", partic. ll. 63-64:
"Selon que vous serez puissant ou misérable,
Les jugements de cour vous rendront blanc ou noir."

(Depending on whether you are powerful or wretched,
the sentences at court will make you white or black.)

La Fontaine, *Oeuvres*, ed. Henri Régnier, Les Grands Ecrivains de la France (Paris: Hachette, 1884), II, 88-100.

accused, the honest person like the dishonest one, and the benefactor like the malefactor. The extremes are incompatible and opposed, and therefore ironic.

Incongruity forces the reader to interpret as untrue either or both terms of the ironic context. The text itself does not specify if a pirate is as good as a king, or a king as bad as a pirate. Wagner insists that both Alexander and Diomedes have sinned, and that both repent.[19] Villon distinguished Diomedes from Fortune, who is solely responsible for the pirate's behavior and occupation (l. 148). The change of fortune corresponds to Diomedes' opposition between the weak and the strong ("petiote fuste" vs. "comme toy me peusse armer"), between bad and good lives or unjust and just actions, but bears no reflection on the individual's intrinsic value. However, in the rest of his work, the author seems to assert that it is the pirate who is as good as Alexander. Villon compares himself to a Diomedes in search of a "piteux Alixandre" (l. 162). He forgot his natural duty (*Test.*, l. 183) only because of material difficulties (*Test.*, l. 184). In addition, the author, always the underdog, often maintains that he is as good as others. In the lines immediately preceding the story of Alexander and Diomedes, Villon admits that he has sinned, but he also knows that God wants the sinner's repentance, not his death:

XIV Je suis pecheur, je le sçay bien;
Pourtant ne veult pas Dieu ma mort,
Mais convertisse et vive en bien...

(I know well that I am a sinner. However, God does not want my death, but rather that I repent and live a righteous life.)

The story of Alexander and Diomedes is an illustration of the relationship between God and Villon the sinner.[20] The change of fortune "mauvaise en bonne" (l. 156) in the pagan story corresponds to the sinner's repentance — i.e., to his transition from sin and damnation to mercy. Since to people of fifteenth-century France God is good, and since in the *exemplum* Alexander represents God, the story implies that Diomedes could be as good as Alexander, rather than Alexander as bad as Diomedes. Campaux makes a case for the opposite interpretation, by relating the story of Alexander and Diomedes to fifteenth-century life. Villon would

[19] R. L. Wagner, "Villon et Jean de Bueil (d'un exemple à un mythe)", in *Medieval Miscellany Presented to Eugène Vinaver by Pupils, Colleagues and Friends*, ed. F. Whitehead, A. H. Diverres, and F. E. Sutcliffe, Manchester Univ. Press (New York: Barnes & Noble, 1965), 297.

[20] See D. B. Wyndham Lewis, *François Villon: A Documented Survey*, Preface by Hilaire Belloc (New York: Literary Guild of America, 1928), 263-264.

have compared himself to the noble robbers of his time. They would have differed only in that Villon was poor and unprotected, while his nobler counterparts could hide in their castles.[21] In any case, as repentance brings Villon closer to God, so reversal of fortune brings Diomedes closer in status to Alexander.[22]

Irony of words in the story of Alexander and Diomedes originated, as we have seen, in the contrast between "larron" and "empereur" and in the description of the activities of each. In addition, there were several converging factors, such as literary tradition, context, linguistic ambiguities, which conditioned the perception of irony. The very same lines would seem non-ironic to readers who would attribute bad actions to bad people and good actions to good people exclusively. They would seem ironic to readers aware of the discrepancy of the powerful who, though bad in reality, are considered good, and of the weak who, though actually good, are considered bad. The ironic context does not clearly state who is good and who is bad. However, this information appears in lines preceding the story, which parallel not only Diomedes and Villon, but also Alexander and God, thus giving the king definitely favorable qualities.

3. THE "MARIAGE RUTEBEUF"

The "Mariage" contains irony of words and, to some extent, episodic irony: the former, in that small groups are ironic; the latter, in that several such groups have a common denominator, which enables the reader to perceive irony also in a wider perspective. These perspectives explain the discussion of the poem at the end of this chapter, as a conclusion to irony of words and an introduction to episodic irony.

Irony in the "Mariage" results from a contrast between the poet's occasional pretense of prosperity and his actual misery.[23] He married an old woman, ugly and poor. Before the marriage, he had but little wealth; even that he lost because of her, so that now he is as poor as she. His friends avoid him. Nothing can surpass his suffering.[24] Her defects —

[21] Antoine Campaux, *François Villon, sa vie et ses oeuvres* (Paris: A. Durand, 1859), 136.
[22] Pierre Messiaen, "François Villon, le Bon Larron (1431-?)", *Etudes*, 76. 238 (1939), 822-832.
[23] See Charles H. Post, "The Paradox of Humor and Satire in the Poems of Rutebeuf", *FR*, 25 (1951-1952), 368.
[24] See Harry Lucas, *Les Poésies personnelles de Rutebeuf: Etude linguistique et littéraire suivie d'une édition critique du texte avec commentaire et glossaire* (Strasbourg: Faculté des lettres de l'Univ. de Strasbourg, 1938), 59; Kressner, "Rustebuef, ein Dichterleben im Mittelalter", *Franco-Gallia*, 10 (1893), 168-169.

ugliness, old age, and poverty — sometimes appear in an ironic context:

28 Tel fame ai prise
Que nus fors moi n'aime ne prise,
Et s'estoit povre et entreprise
31 Quant je la pris.
A ci mariage de pris,
C'or sui povres et entrepris
34 Ausi comme ele![25]

(I took a wife that no one except me loves or esteems. She was poor and miserable when I took her. Here is a rich [and praiseworthy] marriage. Now I am poor and miserable like her!)

"Mariage de pris" (l. 32), where *pris* means both prize and price (Faral & Bastin, ed., n. for l. 32) makes a statement contrary to fact: Rutebeuf's marriage is neither of high quality nor rich. The statement and reality, opposed and incompatible, are ironic. Similarly, in a poem where the narrator constantly complains of his misfortune, Rutebeuf's apparent joy ("Je suis toz plains d'envoiserie", l. 42) contradicts reality and is therefore ironic. In each case, the terms of the ironic context are misery and prosperity. The reader associates the former with the true state of affairs due to Rutebeuf's marriage, and the latter with pretense.

Although based on the same opposition, the other examples of irony require closer analysis of its context. We shall therefore examine each term successively, beginning with reality — that is, the narrator's misery — followed by statements contrary to fact and the effects they produce. Such analysis will show irony functioning on several levels simultaneously. Superposition of these levels and accumulation or ironic clusters will bring out the ironic character of the poem.

Rutebeuf's misery originates in his foolishness. Quoting the proverb that a madman who does not act like one loses his power,[26] the poet connects his own foolishness to his marriage:

L'en dit que fols qui ne foloie
22 Pert sa seson:
Sui je mariez sanz reson?
Or n'ai ne borde ne meson.

(It is said that a madman who does not act like one loses his skill. Did I marry foolishly? Now I have neither lodge nor house.)

[25] Rutebeuf, *Oeuvres complètes*, ed. Edmond Faral and Julia Bastin, Fondation Singer-Polignac (Paris: A. & J. Picard, 1959-1960), I, 548. All subsequent quotations from this poem are on pp. 547-551 of this edition and line numbers are inserted in the text.

[26] Faral and Bastin, ed., p. 548, n. for ll. 21-22. See also H. Lucas, p. 103, ll. 21-22.

"Sanz reson" (l. 23), the main characteristic of a "fols" (l. 21), modifies "mariez" (l. 23) and is the cause of Rutebeuf's poverty (l. 24). God's disfavor is apparent in the passage where the author attributes his unhappiness to God's revenge:

Se Dieu ai fet corouz ne ire,
De moi se puet jouer et rire,
64 Que biau s'en vange.

(If I brought sorrow or wrath to God, He can ridicule and laugh at me, for He fully avenges himself.)

The Middle Ages had an ambivalent attitude toward poverty. Voluntary poverty was idealized as a Christlike state. Involuntary poverty was considered the result of misfortune or foolishness.[27] Rutebeuf's fate is worse than the worst possible fate, and his standards of comparison become more and more dramatic. First, a man sent to Egypt as punishment for his crimes suffers less than the narrator:

Envoyer un homme en Egypte,
Ceste dolor est plus petite
19 Que n'est la moie.

(The woe of sending a man to Egypt is smaller than my own.)

Then, a martyr would suffer less, for sooner or later his pain would end, whereas Rutebeuf's continues all his life:

Diex n'a nul martir en sa route
127 Qui tant ait fet;
S'il ont esté por Dieu desfet,
Rosti, lapidé ou detret,
130 Je n'en dout mie
Que lor paine fu tost fenie;
Més ce durra toute ma vie
133 Sanz avoir aise.

(God has no martyr who has done so much on his way. If they were condemned to death, roasted, stoned or torn to pieces for the sake of God, no doubt that their pain ended quickly. But mine will last all my life with no comfort.)

Even the destruction of Troy does not equal that of the poet:

74 Nis la destruction de Troie
Ne fu si grant comme est la moie.

(Not even the destruction of Troy was so great as is mine.)

[27] Nancy Freeman Regalado, *Poetic Patterns in Rutebeuf: A Study in Noncourtly Poetic Modes of the Thirteenth Century* (= *Yale Romanic Studies, 2nd series*, 21) (New Haven: Yale Univ. Press, 1970), 289-290.

The medieval reader must have accepted the destruction of Troy as a standard of comparison for suffering and pain (Faral & Bastin, ed., p. 549, n. for l. 74). The culmination is total destruction — that is, death. If somebody ever prayed for the dead, let him pray for Rutebeuf:

> S'onques nus hom por mort pria,
> 79 Si prit por moi!

(If ever any man prayed for the dead, let him pray for me.)

The hyperbolic descriptions of misfortune convey the husband's impossible situation on as many levels as there are standards of comparison.

Rutebeuf's misery appears not only in his self-description, but also in the attitudes of his friends and enemies. The former are saddened, the latter forgive him or even rejoice:

> 59 Or faz feste a mes anemis
> Duel et corouz a mes amis.

(Now I give reason for feast to my enemies, and for woe and sorrow to my friends.)

All those who truly love Rutebeuf share his suffering:

> Fis je toute la rien dolante
> 7 Qui de cuer m'aime.

(I saddened all those who truly love me.)

Even Rutebeuf's bitterest enemies, on whom he may have inflicted great pain, would forgive him if they only considered his suffering:

> Diex ne fist cuer tant deputaire,
> Tant li aie fet de contraire
> 13 Ne de martire,
> S'il en mon martire se mire,
> Qui ne doie de bon cuer dire:
> 16 "Je te claim cuite."

(God made no being so perverted who would not sincerely say: "I forgive you," if he looked into my suffering, no matter how much torment or suffering I might have inflicted upon him.)

Rutebeuf's unhappiness serves as his enemy's revenge. The shift from "cuer deputaire" (l. 11) to "bon cuer" (l. 15) corresponds to that from revenge of the enemy because of "contraire" (l. 12) (e.g., affliction, torment) and "martire" (l. 13), to forgiveness (l. 16). "Je te claim cuite" (l. 16), meaning "I forgive you" as well as "I exempt you from your debt",[28] reflects the poet's misfortune in general and his pecuniary difficulties in particular. Revenge reappears further in the poem, again connected to the enemies' satisfaction as well as to the two meanings of the ironic "mariage de pris" (l. 32), already mentioned. Regalado notes that Rutebeuf's ugly, poor, and old wife is altogether undesirable. A seductive old woman seemed ridiculous in the Middle Ages, where love belonged to the young and beautiful.[29]

The religious and climatic circumstances of the narrator's marriage also determine his misfortune. He married

3 Uit jors après la nascion
Jhesu qui soufri passion...

(Eight days after the birth of Jesus, who suffered the passion...)

Besides showing the day when the ceremony took place, these lines qualify the poet's misery in biblical terms, for Christ's passion calls to mind Rutebeuf's suffering. Close association of religion to life continues throughout the poem and, as shown before, underlines a cause and effect relation, since the poet attributes his misery to God's disfavor.

The marriage takes place in winter, when trees are bare and birds silent: "... arbres n'a foille, oisel ne chante..." (l. 5). The scenery contrasts to the *locus amoenus* (pleasance), the ideal landscape where scenes conducive to love take place in lyric poetry and courtly romances. Curtius describes the pleasance and traces its origin to Latin antiquity:

... from the Empire to the sixteenth century, it [*locus amoenus*] forms the principal motif of all nature description. It is... a beautiful, shaded natural site. Its minimum ingredients comprise a tree (or several trees), a meadow, and a spring or brook. Birdsong and flowers may be added. The most elaborate examples also add a breeze....

. . . .

In the Middle Ages the *locus amoenus* is listed as a poetical requisite by lexicographers and writers on style. We encounter a great number of such pleasances in the Latin poetry which flourished from 1070 onwards. Model examples are also to be found in the arts of poetry which began to appear in increasing number from 1170.[30]

Many elements of the *locus amoenus* are absent from line 5. Since the "Mariage" does not concern courtly love, the reader would hardly ex-

[28] Godefroy, X, 463 ("QUITTE") and II, 145 ("CLAMER... *clamer quitte quelqu' un...*").

[29] Regalado, *Poetic Patterns*, 297. See also Luciana Cocito, "Osservazioni e note sulla lirica di Rutebuef", *Giornale storico di filologia*, 11 (1958), 352; Pablo Kleins, "Politische Satire und 'poésie personnelle' bei Rutebeuf", *ZFSL*, 74 (1964), 256.

[30] Curtius, *European Literature and the Latin Middle Ages*, 195-197.

pect a courtly landscape. However, those elements of the pleasance which are in the text are negated. In Regalado's words: "Winter is presented as an 'anti-spring'; the basic elements of the conventional tableau — leaves and birds — are present, but Rutebeuf describes them in the negative..." (Regalado, *Poetic Patterns*, 293). In the *topos* of "anti-spring", Frappier sees a parody of courtly lyric. As if Rutebeuf wanted to mock the spring *topos*, he starts his complaint with a winter *topos* (Frappier, *Poésie lyrique*, 225). Leo ("Rutebeuf", 136) goes even further to say that this *topos* is an attack against not only the troubadours, but also courtly ideology. For our purposes it is worth noting that in the thirteenth century, while marriage was praised by some and scorned by others, courtly love almost always had laudatory connotations. Negating courtly love corresponds to the poem's annihilation of the good qualities in marriage — that is, to the restatement of the poet's misery.

As we have seen, Rutebeuf relates his misfortune directly, sometimes considering it greater than the greatest calamities, and indirectly, by mentioning the reactions of friends and enemies and by describing unfavorable religious and climatic circumstances. These different ways of complaining convey by their number and variety that Rutebeuf's suffering is beyond description. Irony in the poem originates in negating the existence of misfortune so solidly established and using the same elements which showed his unhappiness to show his well-being. The following examples of irony will also involve religion.

In the midst of his complaint, Rutebeuf says ironically that God loves him from afar:

> Je cuit que Diex li debonaires
> M'aime de loing:
> Bien l'ai prové a cest besoing.

(I think that God, who is good-natured, loves me from afar: in this matter, I experienced it well.)

Taken literally, this statement is true: according to religious belief, God is far above mortals. Moreover, since Jesus sacrificed himself for love of man, "aime" seems an appropriate word to describe Heaven's attitude toward mortals. Yet line 56 associates God's love not with these normal biblical implications, but with Rutebeuf's marriage, although the poet asserts time and again that his marriage represents God's disfavor, punishment, and revenge.

The same contrast between love and hate reappears on an erotic level. Since in medieval literature "debonaires" (l. 54) can apply only to mortals,[31] "Diex li debonaires" is an allegorization where the human meaning elucidates the divine. "M'aime de loing" too makes sense on divine and human levels. The religious belief that God loves the human race is attached to the doctrine of salvation. This doctrine thus appears in human terms, where the *amor de lonh* has been associated with passionate *fin' amor* ever since Jaufré Rudel.[32] Both levels point to God's abundant love, which the poem constantly contradicts. Its sad beginning, about God's passion and "anti-spring", annihilates all favorable connotations that the divine and courtly levels may convey. Besides adding a human dimension to God's feelings toward Rutebeuf, "debonaire" has certain connotations which reinforce God's love but contradict the poem. Godefroy defines "debonaire" as tolerant, "dont la bonté va jusqu'à un excès de tolérance" (Godefroy, IX, 277); according to Tobler-Lommatzsch (II, col. 1237), this word denotes friendliness. Since such qualifications are opposite to God's wrath and enmity, "M'aime de loing" could mean that divine love is so far away that it hardly touches the poet. In any case, Rutebeuf describes his misfortune as a sign of both divine favor and disfavor, incompatible opposites which produce irony.

Another example of irony which involves religion occurs in the passage where the poet's state astonishes everybody, so that people cannot help crossing themselves as if he were a priest:

L'en cuide que je soie prestres,
Quar je faz plus sainier de testes
(Ce n'est pas guile)
Que se je chantaisse Evangile.
L'en se saine parmi la vile
De mes merveilles;
On les doit bien conter aus veilles:
Il n'i a nules lor pareilles,
Ce n'est pas doute.

(One thinks that I am a priest. Quite seriously, I make more people cross themselves than if I sang the Gospel. In town people cross themselves at my unbelievable deeds. Such deeds ought to be recounted in the evening: they have no like, no doubt about it.)

[31] See the examples in Godefroy, IX, 277 ("DEBONAIRE") and Tobler-Lommatzsch, II, col. 1237 ("debonaire").

[32] Leo Spitzer, *L'Amour lointain de Jaufré Rudel et le sens de la poésie des troubadours* (= *Univ. of North Carolina Studies in the Romance Languages and Literature*, 5) (Chapel Hill: Univ. of North Carolina, 1944); Grace Frank, "The Distant Love of Jaufré Rudel", *MLN*, 57 (1942), 528-534; Diego Zorzi, "L'Amor de lonh' de Jaufré Rudel", *Aevum*, 29 (1955), 124-144; Irénée Cluzel, "Jaufré Rudel et l'*amour de lonh:* Essai d'une nouvelle classification des pièces du troubadour", *Romania*, 78 (1957), 87-97.

In this passage, Rutebeuf describes his marriage and its consequences as a series of extraordinary deeds which command fame, bewilderment, and respect. He describes his deeds in both religious and lay terms. The sign of the cross, although originally used in church, can also express astonishment.[33] Similarly, "merveilles" may be understood as a miracle or as an amazing deed.[34] In the poem, this deed is the narrator's foolishness. The context exploits both the lay and the religious meanings, as some people take Rutebeuf the fool for a priest. Given its strong favorable connotations in thirteenth-century France, religion (the expression of utmost human wisdom) and foolishness are incompatible. Also incompatible are the position of a priest, favored by God, and that of Rutebeuf, who experiences God's disfavor, as well as a priest's celibacy and the poet's marriage. By equating himself with a priest, Rutebeuf applies wisdom and foolishness, divine favor and disfavor, celibacy and marriage to the same person simultaneously. The accumulation of incompatible extremes creates irony, which the context does not specifically direct against the poet's foolishness or against religion. On one hand, the character of religion forbids light and disrespectful treatment. On the other hand, Rutebeuf's satire of various religious orders in his other works makes such treatment likely.[35]

Irony in the "Mariage" consists, as we have seen, sometimes of a simple contradiction, other times of the superposition of several contradictions, each belonging to a different sphere. In fact, it is the convergence of ironic contexts that distinguishes the "Mariage" from "Je meurs de soif" and the story of Alexander and Diomedes, where the poems seldom indicated two supervening ironic contexts. Whether simple or complex, the various ironic contexts in the "Mariage" are closely linked. Their common characteristics include not only irony, but also the ironic themes themselves: prosperity and misery due to marriage, divine favor and disfavor, and allegorical description of God in human terms.

In the poems of Charles d'Orléans, Villon, and Rutebeuf, the ironic context often consists of two small elements or at least of one small element against the rest of the poem. The reader can always supply several meanings to one element, no matter how small. While "Je meurs de soif" does little to encourage a particular interpretation of the ironic contexts, the story of Alexander and Diomedes, although ambiguous, limits ambiguity

33 Faral and Bastin, ed., p. 551, n. for l. 117.

34 See Godefroy, V, 263 and X, 143 ("MERVEILLE"); Tobler-Lommatzsch, V, col. 1536.

35 Cf. Omer Jodogne, "L'Anticléricalisme de Rutebeuf", *LR*, 23 (1969), 220.

to a few possibilities confirmed by the *Testament*. In addition to clues provided by the non-ironic context, the "Mariage" helps the reader perceive and interpret irony by an accumulation of ironic passages which point to the same idea (the ironic reality): Rutebeuf's unhappy marriage.

Ironic passages in the "Mariage" are episodes of the poem, and their accumulation creates episodic irony. We should note, however, that unlike most episodic irony to be discussed in the next chapter, irony in the "Mariage" consists of passages independently ironic, rather than episodes which produce irony in connection with each other.

III

EPISODIC IRONY

Irony may result from various combinations of episodes. This chapter will illustrate such combinations in five well-known works: André de la Vigne's *Moralité de l'Aveugle et du boiteux*, Chrétien de Troyes' *Cligés*, the *Voyage de Charlemagne à Jérusalem et à Constantinople* (also known as the *Pèlerinage de Charlemagne*), the *Chanson de Roland*, and Béroul's *Tristan et Iseut*. As in the preceding chapter, the order of presentation reflects the progressive complexity of ironic contexts. I deliberately omitted many aspects of these works not directly related to episodic irony. Nevertheless, irony of words is mentioned if it emphasizes episodic irony.

In the *Aveugle*, irony comes out of several statements contrary to fact. The same is true for *Cligés*, where repetition of a rhetorical device becomes ironic when used in opposed contexts. Irony in the *gab* scene of the *Voyage* is perceptible on two levels, which cancel each other out. The ambiguity of Ganelon's treason corresponds to two patterns of thought and requires closer scrutiny than the passages in the preceding works. Finally, Iseut's ordeal combines ambiguity (as in the *Roland*) and multilevel irony (as in the "Mariage Rutebeuf" and the *Voyage*). In addition, the irony of the ordeal corresponds to the ironic structure of the romance.

The five works included in this chapter represent different genres (theater, romance, and epic), and combine several traditions. The variety of genres and traditions reflects the popularity of irony in many literary forms throughout the Middle Ages and supports the view that irony as we understand it today was widely exploited as early as the twelfth century.

Jacob-Lacroix points out the popularity of the *Aveugle* by showing both its originality and its imitative character.[1] Moralities were theatrical

[1] P. L. Jacob [Lacroix], ed. *Recueil de farces, soties et moralités du quinzième siècle*, Bibliothèque gauloise (Paris: Adolphe Delahays, 1859), 215. See also Louis Petit de Julleville, *Répertoire du théâtre comique en France au moyen âge*, Histoire du théâtre en France (Paris: Léopold Cerf, 1886), 39; Gustave Cohen, "Le Thème de l'aveugle et du paralytique dans la littérature française", in *Mélanges offerts à M. Emile Picot par ses amis et ses élèves* (Paris: Damarcène Morgand, 1913), II, 393-404.

productions used to illustrate miracles. Most such plays were quite serious, but others, such as the *Aveugle*, combined religion and humor, thus providing recreation as well as preaching.[2] The *Aveugle*, performed in Seurre in 1496, enjoyed much success in a town famous for its theatrical productions.[3] André's play stands out because of its traditional content and genre, favorable circumstances of its performance, and exceptional qualities of style.

Cligés and *Tristan et Iseut* are often treated together in literary criticism. Their common features suggest a strong influence of one work on the other, probably of *Tristan* on *Cligés*.[4] Nevertheless, while *Tristan* is the product of Celtic sources,[5] *Cligés* consists of the blend of Celtic and Byzantine sources.[6]

[2] Petit de Julleville, *La Comédie et les moeurs en France au moyen âge*, 4th edition, Histoire du théâtre en France (Paris: Léopold Cerf), 349. Cf. Comte de Douhet, *Dictionnaire des mystères ou collection générale des mystères, moralités, rites figures et cérémonies singulières ayant un caractère public et un but religieux et moral, et joués sous le patronage des personnes ecclésiastiques ou par l'entremise des confréries religieuses, suivie d'une notice sur le théâtre libre, complétant l'ensemble des représentations théâtrales depuis les premiers siècles de l'ère chrétienne jusqu'aux temps modernes* (Paris: J.-P. Migne, 1854), cols. 505-507 and 1292; Grace Frank, *The Medieval French Drama* (1954; rpt. London: Oxford-Clarendon, 1967), 168 and 198.

[3] Ernest Serrigny, "La Représentation d'un mystère de Saint-Martin à Seurre, en 1496", *Mémoires de l'Académie des sciences, arts et belles-lettres de Dijon*, 3e série, 10 (1887), 277.

[4] A. G. Van Hamel, "*Cligès* et *Tristan*", *Romania*, 33 (1904), 473. See also Alexandre Micha, "*Tristan* et *Cligès*", *Neophil*, 36 (1952), 1-10 and "Le Mari jaloux dans la littérature romantique des XIIe et XIIIe siècles", *SMed*, 17 (1951), 303-320; Renée L. Curtis, "Le Philtre mal préparé: Le Thème de la réciprocité dans l'amour de Tristan et Iseut", *Mélanges de langue et de littérature du moyen âge et de la Renaissance* offerts à Jean Frappier... *par ses collègues, ses élèves et ses amis* (= *Publications romanes et françaises*, 112) (Geneva: Droz, 1970), I, 195-206.

[5] To determine the origin of *Tristan*, the following works are helpful: Gaston Paris, *Tristan et Iseut* (Paris: Emile Bouillon, 1894); Joseph Loth, "Un Parallèle au roman de *Tristan* en irlandais, au Xe siècle", *CRAIBL* (1924), 122-123; Jean Marx, "La Naissance de l'amour de Tristan et Iseut dans les formes les plus anciennes de la légende", *RPh*, 9 (1955-1956), 167-173; Helaine Newstead, "The Origin and Growth of the Tristan Legend", in *Arthurian Literature in the Middle Ages: A Collaborative History*, ed. Roger Sherman Loomis (1959; rpt. Oxford: Clarendon Press, 1961), 122-133; Gertrude Schoepperle, *Tristan and Isolt: A Study of the Sources of the Romance*, 2nd edition, ed. R. S. Loomis, 2 vols. (New York: Burt Franklin, 1960); Frederick Whitehead, "The Early Tristan Poems", *Arthurian Literature*, 134-144; Edward B. Savage, *The Rose and the Wine: A Study of the Evolution of the Tristan and Isolt Tale in Drama* (Cairo: American Univ. Cairo Press, 1961); Bruno Panvini, *La Leggenda di Tristano e Isotta*, (= *Biblioteca dell'Archivum Romanicum*, 32) (Florence: Leo S. Olschki, 1951); Sigmund Eisner, *The Tristan Legend: A Study in Sources* (Evanston, Ill.: Northwestern Univ. Press, 1969).

[6] For a stylistic discussion of sources in *Cligés*, see my "*Cligés:* Tradition in Expression", M. A. Essay Columbia 1969. The following titles are also useful: Myles Dillon,

The *Roland* and the *Voyage* have also long been associated in criticism, as opposite poles of the *chanson de geste*.[7] The former represents the literary tradition of the warrior — seriousness, pride, valiance, *compagnonnage*[8] — the latter is lighter in tone and its heroes lack usual epic grandeur.[9] The critic D. D. R. Owen showed how in the *Roland* and the *Voyage* identical themes receive serious and mock treatments respectively. He concluded that the *Voyage* parodies the *Roland*.

The indebtedness of the *Roland* to various literary conventions comes out clearly in Pidal's well-known study of the French epic tradition.[10] The main theme of the *Voyage* appears in numerous documents linked to religious practices (e.g., pilgrimages), Charlemagne's life, and different sources. Bruno Panvini gives the most complete account of traditions in the *Voyage*. According to him, the *Voyage* has six sources: the story of St. Denis' relics, a legend according to which Charlemagne conquered Constantinople, a legend concerning the *gabs* of Charlemagne and the Twelve Peers at the court of a pagan king, contemporary reality, pilgrims' stories on Jerusalem, and Celtic legends.[11] Ganelon's treason and the *gabs* have attracted numerous remarks which often indicate irony.

The preceding comments help us place these five works in relation to each other as well as in the frame of literary history. Such comments show that irony was not an isolated effect, but was related to many traditions and appealed to a wide audience over a long period of time.

"Les Sources irlandaises des romans arthuriens", *LR*, 9 (1955), 143-159; J. Fourquet, "Le Rapport entre l'oeuvre et la source chez Chrétien de Troyes et le problème des sources bretonnes", *RPh*, 9 (1955-1956), 298-312; Werner Ziltener, *Chrétien und die Aeneis: Eine Untersuchung des Einflusses auf Chrétien von Troyes* (Graz-Köln: Böhlau, 1957); Anthime Fourrier, *Le Courant réaliste dans le roman courtois en France au moyen âge* (Paris: Nizet, 1960); Micha, "*Enéas* et *Cligès*", in *Mélanges de philologie romane et de littérature médiévale offerts à Ernest Hoepffner... par ses élèves et ses amis* (= *Publications de la Faculté des lettres de l'Univ. de Strasbourg*, 113) (Paris: Belles Lettres, 1949), 237-243; D. W. Robertson, "Chrétien's *Cligés* and the Ovidian Spirit", *CL*, 7 (1955), 39-42.

[7] D. D. Roy Owen, "'Voyage de Charlemagne' and 'Chanson de Roland'", *SFr*, 33 (1967), 468-472; Ernst Johannes Groth, "Vergleich zwischen der Rhetorik im altfranzösischen Rolandslied und in Karls Pilgerfahrt", *Archiv*, 69 (1883), 391-418.

[8] The bibliography of the *Roland* is gigantic. For a general view on this epic, see P[ierre] Le Gentil, *La Chanson de Roland* (= *Connaissance des lettres*, 43) (Paris: Hatier, 1955).

[9] Jules Horrent, "*Le Pèlerinage de Charlemagne*": *Essai d'explication littéraire avec des notes de critique textuelle* (= *Bibliothèque de la Faculté de philosophie et lettres de l'Univ. de Liège*, fasc. 158) (Paris: Belles Lettres, 1961).

[10] Ramon Menendes Pidal, *La Chanson de Roland et la tradition épique des Francs*, 2nd edition, revised by René Louis, trans. Irénée-Marcel Cluzel (Paris: Picard, 1960).

[11] Bruno Panvini, "Ancora sul *Pèlerinage Charlemagne*", *SGym*, 13 (1960), 59. Other

1. THE *MORALITÉ DE L'AVEUGLE ET DU BOITEUX*

Irony in André's play consists mainly of negating an expected pattern of Christian behavior. The protagonists, a blind man and a cripple, left on the road, decide to help each other: the former will carry the latter, who in turn will see for both of them. The cripple informs his companion that St. Martin, whose body can cure any sickness, just died. When the blind man suggests that they meet the saint's procession, his interlocutor objects that if he were healthy, he would no longer be able to earn a living. Afraid for their future, both invalids attempt to run away. However, they meet the procession unexpectedly and are cured of their disabilities. While the blind man expressed gratefulness to the saint, the cripple will feign injuries and carry on as before.

The morality was performed immediately after the *Mystère de Saint Martin.*[12] Conditioned by the Bible, church teachings, and earlier religious plays, the audience must have expected the invalids to rush to St. Martin's body in order to benefit from his miracles. The morality encourages such expectations by creating the proper context — namely, invalids and miracles. At the beginning of the play, both protagonists complain about their misery:

L'AVEUGLE
L'aumosne au povre diseteux
Qui jamais nul jour ne vit goucte!
LE BOITEUX
Faictes quelque bien au boiteux,
Qui bouger ne peut pour la goucte!
L'AVEUGLE
Hélas! je mourray cy sans doubte,
Pour la faulte d'un serviteur.
LE BOITEUX
Cheminer ne puis; somme toute,

---

commentators on the sources in the *Voyage* include Gaston Paris, *Histoire poétique de Charlemagne* (Paris: A. Franck, 1865), 344; Fernand Cabrol and Henri Leclercq, *Dictionnaire d'archéologie chrétienne et de liturgie* (Paris: Letouzey & Amé, 1914), III, col. 753; Laura Hibbard Loomis, "Observations on the *Pèlerinage de Charlemagne*", *MP*, 25 (1927-1928), 331-349; Ronald N. Walpole, "The *Pèlerinage de Charlemagne:* Poem, Legend, and Problem", *RPh*, 8 (1955), 173-186; Charles A. Knudson, "Serments littéraires et gabs: Notes sur un thème littéraire", *Société Rencevals: IVe Congrès International (1967), Studia Romanica*, 14 (1969), 254-260; Guido Favati, "Il 'Voyage de Charlemagne en orient'", *SMV*, 11 (1963), 112-113, 145-146; Tom Peete Cross, "The Gabs", *MP*, 25 (1927-1928), 349-354.

[12] Edouard L. de Kerdaniel, *Un Auteur dramatique du quinzième siècle: André de la Vigne* (Paris: Champion, 1923), 38-92. On the morality itself, *Ibid.*, 99-108.

8 Mon Dieu, soyez-moi protecteur!...
. . . .
13 Hélas! je suis en grant soucy
Meshuy de gaigner ma vie![13]

(*Blind Man*: Alms for the poor needy, who never saw daylight.
Cripple: Do some good for the cripple, who cannot budge at all.
Blind Man: Alas, I shall doubtless die here for lack of a servant [to lead me].
Cripple: I cannot make my way. In a word, my God, protect me!... Alas, today I am very worried about earning a living.)

Their misfortune acquires religious implications owing to lines such as "Mon Dieu, soyez-moi protecteur" (l. 8) and to the description of St. Martin's miraculous healing powers:

108 Ung sainct est mort nouvellement,
Qui faict des euvres merveilleuses.
Malladies les plus perilleuses
Que l'on sçauroit penser ne dire,
112 Il guerist, s'elles sont joyeuses...
. . . .
L'on dit que, s'il passoit par cy,
116 Que guery seroye tout de tire,
Semblablement et vous aussi.

(A saint who makes miracles has just died. He cures the most dangerous sicknesses possible, of those who submit to him willingly.... The word goes that if he passed by, I should be completely cured, and so would you.)

After describing the saint's powers, the cripple shows opposition to being cured (l. 113). He reinforces it by several other remarks which convey that health would make life more difficult:

... s'il estoit ainsi
Que n'eussions ne mal ne douleur,
120 De vivre aurions plus grant soucy,
Que nous n'avons!...
. . . .
Quant seray gary, je mourray
De faim, car ung chascun dira:
132 "Allez, ouvrez!" Jamais n'yray
En lieu où celuy Sainct sera...."

(If we had neither sickness nor pain, it would be more difficult to live than it is

[13] André de la Vigne, *Moralité de l'Aveugle et du boiteux*, in *Théâtre français avant la Renaissance (1450-1550): Mystères, moralités, et farces*, ed. Edouard Fournier, 2nd edition (Paris: Laplace, Sanchez, 1872), 157. All quotations are from pp. 155-161 of this edition. Line numbers are mine.

now!... If I am cured, I will die of hunger, for everyone will say: "Come on, work!" I will never go near that saint.)

Economically speaking, there may be no inconsistency in the cripple's attitude. As a beggar, he does his best: the more he looks like an invalid, the more pity he gets, and the more abundant the alms. Health would be a money-losing proposition. He cannot conceive of a normal life, since he expresses distaste for work (ll. 132-133). His attitude comes nevertheless as a surprise in a tradition where the sick usually look forward to enjoying health, and the miserable run to their Savior, hoping to rid themselves of misfortune. The audience assumes that the protagonists will rush to St. Martin's procession, yet they hurry away from it. Their expected and actual attitudes, incongruous and opposed, create irony.

The ironic context consists of simultaneously accepting and refusing the transition from sickness to health. Sickness and health belong to the ironic reality (the element that the contrasting attitudes have in common), but also create their own ironic context in the cripple's behavior. He shows dissatisfaction in several passages containing irony of words. Although healthy, he vows to deceive people into pitying him, by giving the appearance of an invalid:

Puisque de tout je suis reffait,
Maulgré mes dens et mon visaige,
Tant feray, que seray deffaict,
Encore ung coup, de mon corsaige,
Car je vous dis bien que encor sçay-je
La grant pratique et aussi l'art,
Par ongnement et par herbaige,
Combien que soye miste et gaillart,
Que huy on dira que ma jambe art
Du cruel mal de sainct Anthoyne.
Reluysant seray plus que lart:
A ce faire je suis ydoyne.
Homme n'aura, qui ne me donne
Par pitié et compassion.
Je feray bien de la personne
Plaine de desolacion:
En l'honneur de la Passion,
Diray-je, voyez ce pauvre homme,
Lequel, par grant extorcion,
Est tourmenté, vous voyez comme!
Puis, diray que je viens de Romme,
Que j'ay tenu prison en Acre,
Ou que d'ici m'en voys, en somme,
En voyage à sainct Fiacre.

(Since I am back on my feet, I will do my best to harm my body again despite my teeth and my face. I tell you that I can still make people say that my leg burns with St. Anthony's sickness [ulcerous erysipelas], however able and vigorous I may actually be. I am an expert in making myself shinier than grease. Due to pity and compassion, no one will refuse me alms. I will say: "See this poor man who is greatly tormented and tortured in honor of the Passion." I will then say that I come from Rome, that I was imprisoned in Acre, or that I am about to make a pilgrimage to St. Fiacre.)

Since sickness (ll. 244-246, 252-255) and health (ll. 236 and 243) are opposed, the cripple's pretense is incompatible with his actual state and thus creates irony of words.

This ironic context is also evident on a religious level. Health is attributed to a divine miracle, so slander of one means slander of the other. Such blasphemous behavior appears even more violent, when the protagonists belittle St. Martin:

LE BOITEUX
L'on m'a dit qu'il est en l'église!
Aller ne nous fault celle part.
L'AVEUGLE
Se là nous trouvons sans feintise,
Le deable en nous auroit bien part!
....
Regarde veoir que ce puist estre!
LE BOITEUX
Maleurté de près nous poursuyt:
C'est ce Sainct, par ma foy, mon maistre!

(*Cripple*: I was told that he is in the church! We should go that way.
Blind Man: If we are there, the devil will truly have us in his power!... Look, see what it can be!
Cripple: Unhappiness follows us closely: on my faith, it is that saint, the healer!)

To associate the saint with the devil (l. 165) and misfortune (l. 184) means to equate opposites, absolute good and absolute bad, logically impossible and, consequently, ironic. The blind man finally repents and humbly thanks God and the saint for healing him (ll. 212-235). Unlike his companion, the cripple, however, persists in his erring till the end of the play. He even damns the saint at one point (ll. 204 and 211) and calls him "filz de putain" (l. 211):

Le deable le puisse emporter!
Et qui luy scet ne gré ne grace?
Je me fusse bien deporté
D'estre venu en ceste place!
Las! je ne sçai plus que je face:

> Mourir me conviendra de faim.
> De dueil j'en machure ma face...
> Mauldit soit le filz de putain!

(May the devil take him! Whoever is grateful to him? I would have managed quite well here. Alas! I no longer know what to do: I will have to die of hunger. I writhe my face in sorrow... May the son of a bitch be damned.)

His attitude calls to mind that of the thieves in Bodel's *Jeu de Saint Nicolas*. After they steal the king's wealth, St. Nicholas forces them to return it. The saint's action is just because it remedies theft and it saves the life of a Christian. The Christian had to prove the power of his faith to the pagans by praying that the treasure, though left in the open, not be removed. If the treasure disappeared, the Christian would die, and his religion would seem worthless.

Nicholas introduces himself as the saint who brings misguided people (like the thieves) back on the right path (ll. 1287-1298).[14] Although the thieves know that Nicholas is just and merciful, one thief, Pincedé, calls him "evil spirit":

> Segneur, or est pis que devant:
> Anemis nous va enchantant
> Qui nous cuide faire honnir.
> Avoirs puet aler et venir; 1337
> Mais s'on nous escille et deffait,
> Nous ne serons jamais refait.
> Honnis soit ore tés marchiés! (Bodel, p. 164).

(Gentlemen, this time it is worse than before: the evil spirit, who wants to shame us, is about to bewitch us. Riches can come and go. But if we are cut to pieces and destroyed, we will never recover. Then, the hell with such a deal.)

The thief has the same irreverent attitude as André de la Vigne's cripple.

In the *Aveugle*, the blind man's repentance contrasts to his companion's sin, and this contrast corresponds to the opposition between right and wrong. The contrast finds additional support in the nature of the infirmities. While lameness has no particular religious significance, blindness — traditionally associated with lack of faith — and sight represent sin and repentance respectively. To sum up, the protagonists, at the end of the play, have opposed attitudes toward Saint Martin. The blind man fits

[14] Jehan Bodel, *Le Jeu de Saint Nicolas*, ed. Albert Henry, 2nd edition (= *Univ. libre de Bruxelles, Travaux de la Faculté de philosophie et lettres*, XXI) (Brussels: Presses universitaires de Bruxelles, 1965), 160.

into the Christian pattern of sin and salvation, whereas the cripple does not. In the set of values that the conflict between the protagonists' views brings out, irony in the play is directed against sinners.

2. *CLIGÉS*

Irony is the subject of several critical works on *Cligés*. The most outstanding is Peter Haidu's *Aesthetic Distance in Chrétien de Troyes: Irony and Comedy in "Cligès" and "Perceval"*, 25-112. The author studies irony connected to *allegoria* (pp. 27-42), *significatio* (pp. 42-58), ironization proper (pp. 58-63), parallelism (pp. 63-81), reality and illusion (pp. 82-106). Scattered remarks about *Cligés* appear also in Philippe Ménard's *Le Rire et le sourire dans le roman courtois en France au Moyen Age* (*1150-1250*). However, the example of episodic irony that I shall give here appears in neither study, although both critics refer to some components of this ironic context as funny, comic, or even ironic. That the same elements are subject to different interpretations whose common ground is irony brings out the richness of *Cligés* and, as Haidu noticed, points to its basically ironic composition. The long monologues in *Cligés* contain many small-scale examples of irony. In addition, the work is ironic in internal structure as well as in relationship to various characters. The juxtaposition of characters is in turn ironic (Haidu, 9).

The main aspect of episodic irony to be discussed in this section involves *anadiplosis* (i.e., repetition of a key word, especially the last one, at the beginning of the next sentence or clause) in contrasting passages. Both types of passages involve love: the first stimulates it, while the second destroys it. The first appears in the love-monologues, the second in the description of Alis' and Fénice's wedding night, in itself ironic. Together, they create an ironic context. The reader, who associates this repetition with awakening love throughout the romance, must perceive irony in the abrupt change from love to its destruction. I shall describe first the love-monologues, then the wedding night and the effect that these episodes produce when connected.

There are four monologues in *Cligés*: two pronounced by Soredamor, one by Fénice, and one by Alexander. Owing to their length, they interrupt the action of the romance. The interruptions create suspense and also emphasize the importance of the monologue, which acts as a disjoining element. The reader will constantly think of the narrative in terms of the love-monologues, which show the psychological basis of subsequent action.[15] Each monologue contains a *plainte d'amour*, in which a character suffers from love and does not know if love is reciprocal. The following invariably brings that love to a happy conclusion: love is shared, and the characters involved marry each other. The disjunctions reinforce stylistically the relation between the stimulus and its effect. So, the monologues in *Cligés* stand out because of their length throughout the romance and their meaning, simultaneously narrative, stylistic, and psychological. They accustom the reader to certain patterns, among which is the association of interrogative repetition with awakening love. [16]

Soredamor's first monologue takes place on the boat during Arthur's trip to Brittany. She finds it hard to accept being in love with Alexander. She accuses her eyes of treason, devises plans to resist her feelings, loves and hates simultaneously. Often she questions that which she previously asserted:

> ...Oel, vos m'avez traïe... 469
> ....
> Or me grieve ce que je voi. 472
> Grieve? Nel fet, ençois me siet,
> Et se ge voi rien qui me griet,
> Don n'ai ge mes ialz an baillie?...
> ....
> Chose qui me feïst dolante 500
> Ne deüst mes cuers pas voloir.
> Sa volentez me fet doloir.
> Doloir? Par foi, donc sui je fole
> Quant par lui voel ce qui m'afole. 504
> Volantez don me vaigne enuis
> Doi je bien oster, se je puis.
> Se je puis? Fole, qu'ai je dit?
> Donc porroie je molt petit, 508
> Se de moi puissance n'avoie![17]

(... Eyes, you betrayed me... Now what I see hurts. It hurts? In fact, it suits me well. But if I see something that hurts me, does it follow that I have no power over my eyes?... My heart should not want something painful to me. Its desire

[15] Jean Frappier, in his *Chrétien de Troyes*, New and Revised Edition (= *Connaissance des lettres*, 50) (Paris: Hatier-Boivin, 1957), 117-121, explains the psychological value of monologues in *Cligés* by comparing them to monologues in earlier works.

[16] See Frappier, *Le Roman breton. Chrétien de Troyes: "Cligès"*, Les Cours de Sorbonne: Littérature française (Paris: Centre de documentation universitaire, 1951), 69; Valeria Bertolucci, "Commento retorico all'*Erec* e al *Cligès*", *SMV*, 8 (1960), 9-51.

[17] This and all following quotations are from Chrétien de Troyes, *Cligés*, ed. Alexandre Micha, *Les Romans de Chrétien de Troyes*, II (= *CFMA*, 84) (Paris: H. Champion, 1957). Line numbers are inserted in the text.

makes me grieve. Grieve? On my faith, I must be mad for wanting something that makes me lose my mind. I have to rid myself of a desire resulting in pain — that is, if I can. If I can? Mad that I am, what have I said? I should be able to do very little if I had no power over myself.)

Here and in the following monologues, Chrétien uses anadiplosi[illegible] interrogation simultaneously, a technique which Frappier calls "re[illegible] par interrogation" (*Chrétien de Troyes*, 118). In this passage, Soredam[illegible] by repeating certain words, emphasizes Ovidian love: it is painful ("grieve[illegible] and "griet", ll. 472-473; "doloir", ll. 502-503) and omnipotent ("se je puis [oster]", ll. 506-507). The questions may express the maiden's surprise at her own feelings and her desire to conceal them. Also during the trip to Brittany, Soredamor pronounces her second monologue. According to Frappier, this analytical and deliberative monologue has three parts. The first (ll. 897-945) seems to prolong the vacillations of her preceding monologue: misery of love, various attempts to resist it, and open avowal. In the second part (ll. 946-991), the girl in love frees herself of her worries by understanding the laws governing her. She proves to herself that her goal is to love in accordance with Amor's commands. The third part (ll. 992-1046) shows how she will inform Alexander of her feelings. She will wait for him to take the first step, but she will also make some hints (Frappier, *Chrétien de Troyes*, 119-120). This monologue is also rich in *reprises par interrogation*, as will become apparent from the following passage:

... "Fole, qu'ai je a feire, 889
Se cist vaslez est deboneire...
....
Sa biauté avec lui s'en aut.
Si fera ele maugré mien,
Ja ne l'an voel je tolir rien. 896
Tolir? Non voir! Ce ne vuel mon....
....
Cui chaut, quant il ne le savra 984
Se je meïsmes ne li di?
Que feroie, se je ne li pri?
Qui de la chose a desirrier
Bien la doit requerre et proier. 988
Comant? Proierai le je donques?...
....
Bien s'an savra aparcevoir,
S'il onques d'amors s'antremist,
Ou s'il par parole en aprist. 1012
Aprist? Or ai ge dit oiseuse.

(Mad that I am, why am I so involved just because this young man is so well-born?... Let his beauty go along with him. So it will, despite me, for I would never want to take away from it. Take away? Certainly not. I certainly do not [illegible]nt that.... Who cares if he does not know my feelings unless I myself tell him? [illegible] should I do, if I do not beg him? Whoever desires something must request [illegible]g for it. What? Should I then beg him?... He will notice it, if he has ever [illegible]nvolved with love or if he learned about it from words. Learned? Now I [illegible] spoken foolishly.)

As far as anadiplosis is concerned, the second monologue continues the tendency of the first, with more emphasis on Soredamor's attitude towards Alexander than on her own feelings. Anadiplosis (ll. 896-897, 988-989, 1012-1013) still shows hesitation, fear or contradiction, this time as they relate to a more advanced stage of love.

Fénice's monologue resembles Soredamor's, with possibly more stress on interior doubt:

Asez i poi sanblanz veoir
D'amor, se je neant en sai.
Oïl, tant que mal i panssai; 4408
Mar l'ai apris et retenu,
Car trop m'en est mesavenu.
Mesavenu? Voire, par foi,
Morte sui, quant celui ne voi 4412
Qui de mon cuer m'a desrobee,
Tant m'a losengiee et gabee....
. . . .
Par foi, donc m'a cil maubaillie
Qui mon cuer a en sa baillie, 4420
Ne m'aimme pas, ce sai je bien,
Qui me desrobe et tost le mien.
Jel sai? Por coi ploroit il dons?
Por coi? Ne fu mie an pardons, 4424
Asez i ot reison de quoi....
. . . .
Dex, que ne sont li cors si prés
Que je par aucune meniere
Ramenasse mon cuer arriere! 4472
Ramenasse? Fole mauveise,
Si l'osteroie de son eise,
Einsi le porroie tuer.

(I can see much evidence of love, even though I know nothing of it. Yes, so much so that I thought badly of it. I learned and retained it in an evil hour, for it was really unsuitable to me. Unsuitable? On my faith, I feel truly dead whenever I do not see the man who praised me so much and gave me so much joy that he stole my heart.... On my faith, he who has my heart in his power has then mistreated me. He who steals and takes away what is mine does not love me, as I well know. Or do I? Then why was he weeping? Why? It was not in vain, he had much reason to.... God, why are our bodies not so close that I might somehow bring my heart back? Bring it back? Wicked fool that I am, if I took it from its rightful place, I could kill it.)

As in Soredamor's complaint, the anadiploses in Fénice's (ll. 4410-4411, 4421, and 4423, 4423-4424, 4472-4473) contribute to the description of a girl in love, unsure of the outcome of her feelings.

The last lines of the monologue (ll. 4470-4475) display an ironic conflict between anatomy and love. The conflict stems from the meaning of "cuer" as an organ and as the seat of love (ll. 4412-4414). By stealing Fénice's heart (l. 4413), Cligès left her an imperfect human being (ll. 4419-4422) but, at the same time, a better one: he inspired love, an essential ingredient of courtly conventions. Fénice wants her heart back (l. 4472), but fears death by removing it from its rightful owner, Cligès (ll. 4474-4475). It is thus both natural and unnatural, both good and bad, for Cligès to hold Fénice's heart. She is eager and reluctant to take it back. Her eagerness is moreover questionable because of l. 4470. The bodies may be close for the return of the heart — i.e., cessation of love — or for sexual satisfaction. Owing to these various incompatible opposites, the passage is ironic.

Of particular interest is Alexander's monologue. It not only constitutes an element of episodic irony, but, like Soredamor's, also displays irony of words. In love with Soredamor, Alexander goes through the same turmoil as she and Fénice, and in a long complaint, he talks about the arrow that pierced his heart. Occasionally he stops to repeat his words by means of a *reprise* (ll. 618-619, 641-645, 656-657, 658-659, 690-691):

"Por fol, fet il, me puis tenir.
Por fol? Voirement sui ge fos,
Quant ce que je pans dire n'os,
Car tost me torneroit a pis....
....
A chascun mal n'a pas mecine.
Li miens est si anracinez,
Qu'il ne puet estre mecinez.
Ne puet? Je cuit que j'ai manti....
....
Donc n'est mervoille, se je m'esmai,
Car molt ai mal, et si ne sai
Quex max ce est qui me justise,
Ne sai don la dolors m'est prise.
Nel sai? Si faz. Jel cuit savoir:
Cest mal me fet Amors avoir.
Comant? Set donc Amors mal faire?

Don n'est il dolz et debonaire?
Je cuidoie que il eüst
En Amor rien qui boen ne fust,
Mes je l'ai molt felon trové....
. . . .
...il m'a navré si fort,
Que jusqu'au cuer m'a son dart trait,
Mes ne l'a pas a lui retrait....
. . . .
Comant le t'a il tret? Par l'uel.
Par l'uel? Si ne le t'a crevé?
A l'uel ne m'a il rien grevé,
Mais au cuer me grieve formant."

("I can consider myself mad, he said. Mad? I am truly mad, since I dare not say what I think, for fear that everything would turn for the worse.... There is not a drug for every sickness. Mine is so deeply rooted that it cannot be cured. Can't it? I think I lied.... Then no wonder that I worry, for I am very sick and do not know what sickness overpowers me, nor where my pain comes from. Don't I? Yes, of course. I think I do: Amor makes me have this sickness. How come? Can Amor harm? Isn't he sweet and friendly? I thought that there was nothing bad in Amor, but I found him to be very wicked.... He hurt me so deeply by sending his dart into my heart without drawing it back.... How did he send it to you? Through my eye. Through your eye? And didn't he split it? He did not hurt my eye at all, but he grievously hurt my heart.")

Whereas in the preceding monologues irony was only hinted at, Alexander's, as already mentioned, is rich in irony of words. For example, in line 645, "Ne puet?" introduces a contradiction of what Alexander has previously said. He lied ("J'ai manti") in asserting that his sickness had no cure. Since nobody can be cured of an incurable sickness, the opposite attributes of Alexander's sickness are incompatible and ironic.

Aware of the paradox in the conception of love, Haidu argues for the psychological soundness of the monologue. The doctor, called to cure the illness, is also its cause. Alexander's illness is not only love, but his inability to express it (Haidu, 29). Lines 656-657 display the same mechanism as ll. 642 and 645. Alexander questions his ignorance and finds it untrue. Despite his "Ne sai don la dolor m'est prise" (l. 656), he knows that Love is the cause of his sickness. Simultaneous knowledge and ignorance of the same thing by the same person is ironic (cf. Socratic irony). Irony continues in the discrepancy between Alexander's preconceived idea of Love ("dolz et debonaire", l. 660) and reality ("je l'ai molt felon trové", l. 663). The superposition of ignorance and knowledge corresponds to that of his idea and reality. Knowledge that Love is the author of all evil is the *prise de conscience*: Love is a felon.

Chrétien introduces no monologues in his description of Fénice's and Alis' wedding night. The narrative context provides anadiplosis which, contrasted to the preceding and following *reprises*, creates irony. At his barons' insistence, Alis, uncle of Cligès, decided to marry Fénice, daughter of the Emperor of Germany. For political reasons, the German emperor agreed to this union, although he had already promised Fénice to the Duke of Saxony. Alis and Cligès, leading a strong army, joined the emperor in Cologne. There Fénice and Cligès fell in love. Cligès showed his bravery by brilliantly jousting against the duke's nephew, who had come to claim Fénice for his uncle. Fénice is tormented by Love. Questioned by Thessala, her nurse, she confesses her affection for the nephew of her intended. Never will she belong to two men. Thessala, who is also a magician, prepares a drink for Alis' wedding dinner. Owing to this philter, Alis will have merely the illusion of possessing his wife, who will in fact remain faithful to Cligès.

Irony in the episode of the wedding night is complex and requires more detailed analysis. For easier reference to the text, I shall quote it in full:

Or est l'empereres [Alis] gabez.
Molt ot evesques et abez
Au lit seignier et beneïr.
Quant ore fu d'aler gesir,
L'empereres, si com il dut,
La nuit avoec sa fame jut.
Si com il dut? Ai ge manti,
Qu'il ne la beisa ne santi;
Mes an un lit jurent ansanble.
La pucele de peor tranble,
Qui molt se dote e molt s'esmaie
Que la poisons ne soit veraie.
Mes ele l'a si anchanté
Que ja mes n'avra volanté
De li ne d'autre, s'il ne dort,
Et lors en avra tel deport
Con l'an puet an songent avoir,
Et si tendra le songe a voir.
Ne por quant cele le resoingne:
Premieremant de lui s'esloigne,
Ne cil apruichier ne la puet,
Qu'araumant dormir li estuet.
Il dort et songe, et veillier cuide,
S'est en grant poinne et an estuide
De la pucele losangier.
Et ele li feisoit dongier,
Et se desfant come pucele,

Et cil la prie, et si l'apele
Molt dolcement sa dolce amie;
Tenir la cuide, n'an tient mie,
Mes de neant est a grant eise,
Car neant tient, et neant beise,
Neant tient, a neant parole,
Neant voit, et neant acole,
A neant tance, a neant luite.
Molt fu la poisons bien confite
Que si le travaille et demainne.
De neant est an si grant painne,
Car por voir cuide, et si s'an prise,
Qu'il ait la forteresce prise,
Et devient lassez et recroit,
Einsi le cuide, einsi le croit.

(Now Emperor Alis is happy. Beside his bed there were many bishops and abbots to bless his marriage with Fénice. When the time came to lie down, the emperor lay with his wife, as he should. As he should? I told a lie, for he neither kissed nor felt her. But they lay in the same bed together. The maiden, very afraid and worried, trembles with fear that the philter will not work. But it has bewitched him so that he will never want her or another, except in his sleep. Then he will have as much joy as one can have in a dream, and he will hold the dream to be true. Nevertheless, she fears him. First she goes farther from him, although he cannot get closer to her, because of his sound sleep. He sleeps and dreams and thinks he is awake. He takes pains and looks forward to caressing the maiden. She resists him and defends herself like a virgin. He begs her and very softly calls her his sweet friend. He thinks he holds her, but he holds nothing. He is very comfortable for no reason, for he holds no one, kisses no one, holds no one, talks to no one, sees no one, embraces no one, discusses with no one and fights with no one. The potion was very well prepared so as to torment and overpower him. He takes such pains to no avail, for he truly thinks and praises himself to have taken the fortress. He gets tired and worn out, he believes it to be so.)

This passage has struck critics as comic and ironic. Ménard sees a comic element in the theme of the cheated husband, especially when this husband is evil. The husband's inability to consummate the marriage appears in several *chansons de geste* at the end of the twelfth century, which were written after *Cligés*. Chrétien must have been the first French author to poke fun at the cheated husband. The author is not worried that Canon Law may condemn Fénice's attitude but seems to enjoy Alis' comic illusion. The behavior of the husband, engaged in imaginary combat, contrasts with the attitude of his wife, who, as close to the edge of the bed as possible, is afraid that the philter will not work (Ménard, 270-271). More precise in his analysis, Haidu discovers a pattern of reality and illusion throughout the romance, into which Alis' character repeatedly fits. The story opposes Alis' illusion to the reality of Alexander and Cligès. The strongest such opposition is between Alis and Cligès, in relation to Fénice. While Alis possesses only a dream, Cligès possesses Fénice forever (Haidu, p. 84).

I would add that in this passage Chrétien makes use of irony of words. In line 3293 the narrator questions the truth of "si com il dut" (l. 3291). Since nothing happens between Alis and Fénice, expected sexual activity and actual inactivity are incompatible and opposed. Their incongruity is even more striking owing to "Ai ge manti" (l. 3293) and to the detailed description of reality. The possibility of Alis' touching Fénice is systematically destroyed. Owing to the potion, Alis will never desire a woman except in dreaming (ll. 3299-3301). His attempts are unreal, constantly associated as they are with sleep (ll. 3301 and 3308), dreams (ll. 3303-3304) or both (l. 3309), and with verbs denoting belief ("cuide", ll. 3316, 3325, and 3328; "croit", l. 3328). His sexual illusion (ll. 3312-3316) also appears on a military level (ll. 3325-3326) and is reinforced by the accumulation of "neant" (ll. 3316-3321 and 3324) referring to various stages of lovemaking. "Tenir la cuide, n'an tient mie" (l. 3316) typifies the opposition between illusion and reality that occurs throughout the passage. The ironic context of this episode results therefore from an accumulation of irony of words, whose terms are often reinforced by repetition.

As I said at the beginning of my discussion of *Cligés*, the wedding night, besides being ironic in itself, creates episodic irony when placed against the love-monologues. Soredamor, Fénice, and Alexander all used anadiplosis to question their feelings, to express surprise and to contradict themselves. The reader is thus conditioned to associate anadiplosis with love happily fulfilled in marriage. The wedding night creates surprise. For the first time anadiplosis appears outside of a monologue, and love does not result in happiness nor is it consummated. Such a development seems incongruous to the reader, who is accustomed to love-monologues. Whereas the hero's turmoil in the monologues preceded happy conclusions, Alis' ends in unhappiness and death (ll. 6604-6609). Separation counterbalances marriage. Fénice draws away from her husband during their wedding night ("s'esloigne", l. 3306). Then, once again owing to witchcraft, she escaped from the palace to live with Cligès in an underground palace. Love and lack of it, happy and unhappy conclusions, union and separation are opposite and incompatible terms. The episodic irony that they produce and irony of words in the description of the wedding night repeat the contrast between powerful love and its permanent absence.

3. THE *VOYAGE DE CHARLEMAGNE*

My discussion of the *Voyage* centers on the scene of the *gabs*, which some critics see as the central episode of the work.[18] These are mock-vows, in which Charlemagne's knights promise to accomplish deeds of prowess. Throughout the text and for the first time in epic literature, the *gab*, of Scandinavian origin, is associated with boasting. The *gabs* in the *Voyage*, more than in other epics, are manifest exaggerations which defy the laws of nature and human limitations. *Gaber*, *gab*, *gabois*, *gaberie* in courtly romances appear more frequently than *joer* or *s'envoisier*. *Gab*, which originally designated the action of opening the mouth, soon took on the meaning of "joke" and "raillery". The semantic doublets "rire et gaber" are particularly common (Ménard, 22-23 and 424). In the *Voyage*, several episodes contradict playfulness, an essential quality of the *gab*.

After his coronation, Charlemagne asks his wife whether she has ever seen such a valiant king as himself. When she answers that Hugues le Fort, Emperor of Greece and Constantinople, might be that man, Charles furiously leaves for Constantinople to meet him. Having arrived in Constantinople after a journey from France to Jerusalem, Charles and his knights meet Hugues, who receives them well. After dinner, Hugues shows the Frenchmen to their quarters and offers them wine. The room has a secret recess from which, at Hugues' request, a spy listens to everything said therein. Following their custom, the guests begin to boast jokingly. Charles pretends that with one blow he could cut through Hugues' strongest knight in double armor and through his horse so that the blade would be deeply buried in the ground. Roland would blow Hugues' horn so forcefully that the whole city would crumble, and if Hugues were in the direction of the blast, he would lose his beard and clothing. Oliver would like to spend the night with Hugues' daughter, in order to "know" her a hundred times. Archbishop Turpin suggests that the King of Constantinople let three of his best horses run on the plain. Turpin would overtake the three horses on a run, jump over two and seat himself on the third and juggle four apples without a miss as the horse were given free rein. Guillaume d'Orange promises to lift in one hand a sphere which thirty men could not move, to make it roll through the palace and demolish forty fathoms of its walls. Similarly, Ogier would shake the supporting column of the palace (the palace turns on a pivot). Naimon would put on Hugues'

[18] For example, Hans-Jörg Neuschäfer, "*Le Voyage de Charlemagne en Orient* als Parodie der Chanson de geste: Untersuchungen zur Epenparodie im Mittelalter", *RJ*, 10 (1959), 90.

hauberk and shake so forcefully that he would break it to pieces. If Hugues buried all his knights' swords with the blades facing upwards, Bérenger would safely throw himself on those swords from the tallest tower. Bernard boasts to make the big river flood the city for as long as he desires. Ernaud de Gironde urges Hugues to fill up a huge caldron with molten lead. Ernaud would sit in the molten lead until it had solidified, and then shake himself so hard that all the lead would break off. Aimon in disguise would come up behind Hugues at the dinner table and knock his head down onto the table while pulling the hair of his beard and whiskers. Bertram would bring two shields together to frighten the wild beasts. Garin vows to throw a spear from a league away to a pillar on the summit of a tower, where his friends would have put two deniers one above the other; he would hit one denier without moving the other and catch the spear before it fell to the ground.

These vows are ironic when placed in either of two contexts. The first involves the spy's and Hugues' reaction to the *gabs*. Every time a knight jokingly threatens Hugues or his possessions, the spy laments his master's foolishness at sheltering such enemies. In turn, Hugues makes his guests choose between accomplishing their vows and death. The second context, the quarrel of Charlemagne and his wife, provides serious motivation for presumably frivolous *gabs*. I shall comment on irony in each context and then on the interrelation of all episodes involved.

The first context leaves no ambiguity as to the levity of the *gabs*. The French are intoxicated, for Hugues sent them wine:

Franceis furent as cambres, si unt veüd les liz:
Casquun des duze pers i ad ja le son pris.
Li reis Hugun li Forz lur fait porter le vin.[19]

(The French were in their quarters and saw the beds. Each of the Twelve Peers has already taken his. King Hugues le Fort has wine brought to them.)

They go to bed at leisure (l. 445) and boast (l. 446). Ordered by Hugues to fulfill the *gabs*, Charles qualifies them as games practiced at bedtime by all Frenchmen:

"Sire, dist Carlemaines, er sair nus herbergastes,
Del vin e del claret asez nus en donastes:
Sist tel custume en France, a Paris e a Cartres,
Quant Franceis sunt culchiez, que se giuent e gabent..."

[19] Paul Aebischer, ed. *Le Voyage de Charlemagne à Jérusalem et à Constantinople*, TLF, 115 (Geneva: Droz, 1965), 57. All quotations of the *Voyage* are from Aebischer's emended text, rather than his diplomatic one, which appears on facing pages in his edition. Line numbers are inserted in the text.

("Sire, said Charlemagne, last night you sheltered us, you gave us a lot of wine and mead. In France, in Paris and in Chartres it is customary for the French to fool around and boast at bedtime.)

These games are solely for enjoyment and seem to have no serious basis in fact. By vowing to perform such impossible deeds, the jovial knights make fun of themselves.[20] However, neither the spy nor Hugues appreciates the joke.

Here are a few of the spy's reactions, most of which concern the violence of the vows, Hugues' foolishness in harboring such guests, or the boasters' punishment in the near future:

465 "Par Deu, ço dist l'eschut, fort estes e membret!
Fols fud li reis Hugun quant vus prestat ostel.
Si anuit meis vus oi de folie parler,
Al matin, par sun l'albe, vus ferai cungeër!"
. . . .
482 "Par Deu, ço dist li eschut, ci ad mal gabement:
Que fouls fist li reis Hugue, qu'il herbergat tel gent!"
. . . .
490 "Par Deu, ço dist li eschut, vus recrerez anceis!
Grant huntage avez dit: mais quel sacet li reis,
En trestute sa vie mès ne vus amereit!"
. . . .
515 "Par Deu, ço dist li eschut, ja ne vus en crerai:
Trestut sait fel li reis, s'asaier ne vus fait!
Ainz que seiez calcet, le matin le dirrai!"
. . . .
"Par Deu, ço dist li eschut, cist hom est enragez!
Unques Deus ne vus duinst cel gab a cumencer,
530 Que fols fist li reis Hugue qui vus ad herberget!"
. . . .
600 "Par Deu! ço dist li eschut, mal gabement ad ci:
Quant le savrat li reis, grains en iert e maris."

("By God, said the spy, you are strong and muscular! King Hugues was out of his mind to shelter you. If I still hear you speak foolishly tonight, I will have you thrown out tomorrow at dawn!"

. . . .

"By God, said the spy, here is an evil boast: how mad was King Hugues to shelter such people!"

. . . .

[20] Horrent, "*Le Pèlerinage de Charlemagne*", 74. The author restates these ideas in his "La Chanson du Pèlerinage de Charlemagne et la réalité historique contemporaine", *Mélanges... Frappier*, I, 412. See also H. Morf, "Etude sur la date, le caractère et l'origine du Pèlerinage de Charlemagne", *Romania*, 13 (1884), 204.

"By God, said the spy, you will eat your words! You have greatly insulted Hugues. But if the king knew it, never in his life would he be your friend!"

. . . .

"By God, said the spy, I will never believe you. May the king be damned if he does not test you! I will talk to him in the morning before you will be shod."

. . . .

"By God, said the spy, this man is wild! May God never allow you to begin [performing] such a boast. How mad was King Hugues to shelter you!"

. . . .

"By God! said the spy, here is an evil boast. When the king finds out about it, he will be distressed and saddened.")

These reactions, conspicuous by their similar position (at the end of a *laisse*), form, and content, are summed up by the spy, when he tells Hugues what he heard:

627 Tuz les gas li cuntat, quancque il en oïd.

(He recounted all the boasts to him, everything that he had heard.)

By applying Bergson's theory, Horrent finds the spy's reactions comic in themselves. The spy's error would contain comedy of situation. Taking the French seriously, he acts more or less violently according to the greater or smaller aggressiveness of the boasts. Comedy would result not from exact repetition of the same gesture, but from mechanic repetition of an attitude subtly modified according to circumstances (Horrent, *Pèlerinage*, 79).

Hugues takes the *gabs* even more seriously, and his anger replaces the spy's amazement, displeasure or fright. Charles and his men will pay with their lives for their foolish boasts, unless they can fulfill them:

Quant l'entent li reis Hugue, grains en fud e mariz:

"Par ma fei, dist li reis, Carles a feit folie,
630 Quant il gaba de moi par si grant legerie.
Herberjai les er sair en mes cambres perines:
Si ne sunt aampli li gab cum il distrent,
Trancherai lur les testes od m'aspee furbie!"

(When King Hugues hears him, he is distressed and saddened: "On my faith, says the king, Charles behaved foolishly when he boasted on my account so lightly. Last night I sheltered them in my stone chambers. If the French do not fulfill their boasts, I will cut off their heads with my polished sword!")

The general assumption in the narrative is, as mentioned, that the French are joking. The guests reinforce that assumption, whereas the hosts contradict it. The *gabs* are conventionally frivolous, but offensive in reality.

Such incompatibility may have several explanations: Hugues could have only pretended to take the *gabs* seriously; or he could have misunderstood their flippant nature; or the Frenchmen's joviality could have meant hatred and enmity. Since he is never ambiguous, Hugues' seriousness is hardly to be questioned. The other explanations seem possible, but they represent the reader's adjustment of incompatibility to compatibility: there would be no reason to surmise misunderstanding or pretense, if nothing undermined congruity in the character's behavior. The incompatible terms (levity and seriousness) are also opposite and consequently produce irony.

Questioning the Frenchmen's honesty is related to the second ironic pattern in the *Voyage*. As he exculpates himself from Hugues' accusations (ll. 652-658), Charles says that at bedtime the French play, boast, and say both wise and foolish things ("E si dient ambure, e saver e folage", l. 656).[21] Line 656 leaves open the possibility of pretense among the guests. The beginning of the *Voyage* offers, as we shall see, further reasons for pretense, for Charlemagne comes to Constantinople as Hugues' rival.

When Charlemagne asked his wife whether she had ever seen a knight as valiant as himself, she answered foolishly that there was such a man — namely, Hugues le Fort. Despite his wife's tearful pleas, Charlemagne promised to find Hugues, see for himself if the queen had told him the truth and, if not, behead her.[22]

During the conversation with his wife, Charlemagne was angry:

17 Quant l'entent Charlemaine, mult en est curecez,
Pur Franceis ki l'oïrent mult en est embrunchiez...
. . . .
30 Quant ço vit la reïne ke Charles est si iriez,
Forment s'en repentit, vuelt li chaïr as pez....
. . . .
"Par ma fei, dist li reis, mult m'aveis irascud,
M'amisted e mun gred en avez tut perduz.
55 Uncor quid qu'en perdrez la teste sur le buc:
Nel deüsez penser, dame, de ma vertuz!
Ja n'en prendrai mais fin tresque l'avrai veüz!"[23]

[21] Cf. Gaston Paris, "La Chanson du Pèlerinage de Charlemagne", *Romania*, 9 (1880), 13.

[22] Jules Coulet, *Etudes sur l'ancien poème français du "Voyage de Charlemagne en Orient"* (Montpellier: Coulet, 1907), 324.

[23] See Horrent, "Contribution à l'établissement du texte perdu du 'Pèlerinage de Charlemagne'", in *Studi in onore di Italo Siciliano* (= *Biblioteca dell'Archivum Romanicum*, 86) (Florence: Leo S. Olschki, 1966), I, 560. The author of this article sees a connection between Charlemagne's anger and the style of his discourse.

(When Charlemagne hears her, he becomes very angry. He seems in a very bad mood to the French who heard him... When the queen saw that Charles was so angry, she strongly repented and wanted to fall at his feet.... "On my faith, said the king, you angered me very much, you lost all my friendship and kindness. Moreover, I think that you will lose your head on the block. Milady, you should not doubt my strength! I will not rest until I have seen Hugues!)

The reason for his trip to Constantinople is to compare his valor to Hugues's. In the Middle Ages, confrontation can take place only in combat. In view of his feelings toward his wife, as well as the rivalry between him and Hugues, Charlemagne appears as Hugues's enemy. The French king's boast to cut Hugues's strongest knight and his horse in two reinforces the importance of combat suggested at the beginning of the *Voyage*:

Li reis Hugun li Forz nen at nul bacheler,
De tute sa mainee, qui tant seit fort membré,
Ait vestu dous haubers e dous heaumes formet,
Si seit sur un destrer curant e sujurnet;
Li reis me prest s'espee al poin d'or adubet:
Si ferrai sur les heaumes u il erent plus chers,
Trancherai les haubercs e les heaumes gemmez,
Le feutre avec la sele del destrer sujurnez;
Le branc ferrai en terre...

(Let the king lend me his golden-pointed sword. Let any young man, however muscular, from King Hugues's household, put on two hauberks and two beautiful helmets and mount a fast and rested battle-horse. I will hit the helmets where they are thicker. I will cut the hauberks and the gemmed helmets, the padding with the saddle of the rested horse. I will hit the ground with my sword.)

Alfred Adler explains the queen's guilt and Charlemagne's rivalry in folkloristic and historical terms. Folkloristically, the claim that Hugues is better than Charles activates the pattern of a king who seeks someone more significant than himself. Historically, this claim may point to the issue whether Louis VII ranked higher or lower than Manuel of Constantinople. Louis, who had to do homage to Manuel in Constantinople, occupied, according to the Greek historian Kinnamos, a seat lower than his rival's.[24] Adler's testimony gives more weight to Charles' hatred for Hugues, already attested by literary evidence. If we bear in mind the French king's rivalry, the *gabs* no longer seem trifles, but serious threats. Hugues may have sensed Charlemagne's enmity. The ironic context is the same as before, but the ironic reality is somewhat different. In the previous context it was in the hosts' expected and actual views that frivolity and

[24] Alfred Adler, "The *Pèlerinage de Charlemagne* in New Light on Saint-Denis", *Speculum*, 22 (1947), 551-552.

seriousness supervened. Here Charles's rivalry and friendship, corresponding to different episodes, make the *gabs* both flippant and threatening. Charles's behavior is ironic and his pretense juxtaposes illusion and reality. The same is true for Oliver. He jokingly commits himself to "knowing" Hugues's daughter a hundred times:

> 486 Prenget li reis sa fille, qui tant ad bloi le peil,
> En sa cambre nus metet en un lit en requeit:
> Si jo n'ai testimonie anut de li cent feiz,
> Demain perde la teste, par covent li otrai!

(Let the king take his daughter, who has such blond hair. Let him put us in bed together in privacy. I agree to lose my head tomorrow if I do not have testimony from her a hundred times tonight.)

However, Oliver's *gab* has a serious foundation. At the banquet in honor of Charlemagne and his knights, Oliver sees the girl and falls in love with her:

> Carlemaine s'asist, e sis ruiste barnez,
> Li reis Hugun li Forz e sa muiller delez,
> Sa fille od le crin bloi qu'ad le vis bel e cler,
> E out la char tant blanche cumme flur en ested.
> Oliver l'esgardat, si la prist a amer:
> "Pluüst al rei de glorie de saincte majestet
> Que la tenise en France, u a Dun la citet:
> Kar jo'n fereie pus tutes mes voluntez!"

(All sat down: Charlemagne and his courageous barons, King Hugues with his wife and his blond daughter, who had a beautiful white complexion and flesh white like the flower in the summer. Oliver looked at her and fell in love with her: "May it please the King of Glorious and Holy Majesty that I take her to France or to Dun: for then I will do with her as I please.)

The actual fulfillment of vows, negating their unreality, shows that the spy was right in fearing for his master and that Charles was stronger than Hugues.

Irony originating in the juxtaposition of the beginning of the *Voyage* and the *gab* scene makes the playful nature of the boasts seem false. Irony produced by the hosts' reactions to the boasts suggests that levity is true, and suspicion unjustified. Paradoxically, in the *Voyage*, the playfulness of vows seems both true and false. Its attributes, incompatible and opposite, are ironic. The ironic patterns strengthen irony in the work, yet reality in one context annihilates reality in the other: what seemed true before is now false. Perhaps the following quotation from Robert C. Bates, concerning the variety of the *Voyage*, will prove useful in a discussion of ironic intricacy:

How can a work of art be so variable and so varied? The final answer lies in the fact that it may be compared to one of those elaborate, entertaining imitation trees filled with mechanical birds which still existed in Constantinople in the twelfth century, which were a wonder and a toy at once; it is a baroque plaything, and as in every work of baroque art one knows, disparate parts are blended into a vigorous synthesis; it has movement and humor. Like all baroque, its chief concerns are not primarily scale and proportion except insofar as they create effects — effects which, though they seem to contradict fact, give a sense of unity of the mass and a feeling that the whole is true.[25]

Whether or not we agree with Bates, his article brings out the contradiction — i.e., reinforcement and destruction — between the two ironic patterns of the *Voyage*. The negation of irony will become more evident in Ganelon's treason, which, placed in various contexts, will sometimes seem normal, other times incongruous.

4. GANELON

Ganelon is one of the most controversial characters in the *Chanson de Roland*. His behavior has given birth to many interpretations that acknowledge ambiguity and attempt to solve it. The ambiguous elements follow an ironic pattern of friendship vs. enmity. Bédier considers Ganelon a traitor but praises the courage with which he carried out Charles's mission. Ganelon never forgets his hatred for Roland. In communicating Charles's conditions to the enemy, Ganelon also prepares Roland's death. However, Ganelon behaves like a royal messenger when, defying death, he asks Marsile to surrender.[26] Burger sees the tragic hero, noble but erring. Ganelon does not consider himself a traitor. His treason is not the act of a base person, but the tragic error of a man blinded by pride, jealousy, and hatred.[27] Pellegrini rehabilitates him by reducing his treason to a regular feudal quarrel and comparing him to Roland. In daring terms, Ganelon

[25] Robert C. Bates, "*Le Pèlerinage de Charlemagne:* A Baroque Epic", in *Studies by Members of the French Department of Yale University: Decennial Volume*, ed. Albert Feuillerat (= *Yale Romanic Studies*, 18) (New Haven: Yale Univ. Press, 1941), 22.

[26] Joseph Bédier, *Les Légendes épiques: Recherches sur la formation des chansons de geste*, 3rd edition (Paris: Champion, 1929), II, 415-417. Cf. Edmond Faral, "*La Chanson de Roland*"*: Etude et analyse*, Chefs-d'oeuvre de la littérature expliqués (Paris: Mellotée, 1932), 209-210; Paul R. Lonigan, "Ganelon before Marsile ('Chanson de Roland,' laisses XXXII-LII)", *SF*, 14.41 (1970), 277 and 280; Eugène Vinaver, *The Rise of Romance* (New York and Oxford: Oxford Univ. Press, 1971), 13.

[27] André Burger, "Le Rire de Roland", *CCM*, 3 (1960), 9. Le Gentil expressed a similar viewpoint in his *Chanson de Roland*, 134-135.

defies Marsile three times, ready to pay for his courage with his life.[28] Gaston Paris goes as far as to dismiss as unaccountable the scene where Ganelon defies Marsile and to suggest its deletion from the text.[29] This critic thus brings the perception of incompatibility to its culmination and prepares the way for an interpretation of Ganelon's behavior from an ironic perspective.

The irony of treason hardly originates in isolated fragments. It rather consists of a composite, whose episodes accumulate throughout the epic. Charlemagne has conquered all Spain except Sarragossa, which King Marsile holds. When Roland suggests Ganelon, his stepfather, as a possible messenger to the Saracen court, Ganelon is furious. Overwhelmed by the danger of such a mission, he threatens to harm Roland,[30] Oliver and the Twelve Peers (ll. 322-326). Charlemagne's glove falls as the emperor gives it to Ganelon, and the French wonder about the evil in this omen (ll. 331-335). On their way to Sarragossa, Ganelon and Blancandrin, the Saracen messenger, praise Charlemagne but plan Roland's death (ll. 366-413). Later, Ganelon first risks his own life in defying Marsile (ll. 428-440), then consents to devise a plan for murdering Roland and his companions (ll. 603-616). Although his plan succeeds (e.g., ll. 2375-2396), Charles amply avenges his nephew's death by both slaughtering the Saracens (ll. 2458-2475) and causing Ganelon to die miserably (ll. 3960-3974). While using pertinent information from all related episodes, I shall concentrate on the scenes of the trial and of treason.

In planning Roland's death, has Ganelon actually betrayed Charlemagne, or has he merely avenged himself against another knight who offended him? This dilemma disturbs not only critics, but also the char-

28 Silvio Pellegrini, *Studi rolandiani e trobadorici* (= *Biblioteca di filologia romanza*, 8) (Bari: Adriatica, 1964), 134-135. See also Martin de Riquer, *Los Cantares de gesta franceses* (*su problemas, su relacion con España*), Biblioteca romanica hispanica (Madrid: Gredos, 1952), 98.

29 Gaston Paris, "Le *Carmen de Prodicione Guenonis* et la légende de Roncevaux", *Romania*, 11 (1882), 491.

30 "Se Deus ço dunet que je de la repaire,
Jo t'en muvra un si grant contraire
Ki durerat a trestut tun edage."

(If God wills it that I return from there, I will bring you so much harm that it will last your whole life long [trans. mine].)

Bédier, ed. and trans. "*La Chanson de Roland*", *publiée d'après le manuscrit d'Oxford*, 237 edition (Paris: H. Piazza, 1937), 26. All quotations from the *Roland* are according to this edition, and line numbers are inserted in the text. I have also consulted T. Atkinson Jenkins' "*La Chanson de Roland*": *Oxford Version*, Revised edition, Heath's Modern Language Series (Boston: D. C. Heath, 1924), for its excellent introduction, textual notes, glossary and index.

acters of the epic. Ganelon's trial brings out two claims, the plaintiff's and the defendant's, the former asserting that Ganelon is a traitor, the latter that he has been loyal to Charlemagne but not to Roland:

"Seignors barons," dist Carlemagnes li reis,
"De Guenelun car me jugez le dreit!
Il fut en l'ost tresqu'en Espaigne od mei,
Si me tolit .XX. milie de mes Franceis
E mun nevold, quo ja mais ne verreiz.
E Oliver, li proz e li curteis;
Les .XII. pers ad traït por aveir."
Dist Guenolon: "Fei sei se jol ceil!
Rollant me forfist en or e en aveir
Pur que jo quis sa mort e sun destreit;
Mais traïsun nule n'en i otrei."
. . . .
"Pur amor Deu, car m'entendez, barons!
Seignors, jo fui en l'ost avoec l'empereür,
Serveie le par feid e par amur.
Rollant sis niés me coillit en haür,
Si me jugat a mort e a dulur.
Message fui al rei Marsiliun;
Par mun saveir vinc jo a guarisun.
Je desfiai Rollant le poigneor
E Oliver e tuiz lur cumpaignun
Carles l'oïd e si nobilie baron.
Venget m'en sui, mais n'i ad traïsun."

("Barons, says King Charlemagne, judge my case against Ganelon! He was with me till Spain, and took away from me 20,000 of my Frenchmen as well as my nephew, whom you will never see again, and Oliver, the valiant and courteous. He betrayed the Twelve Peers in exchange for riches." Ganelon says: "May I be damned if I hide it! Roland wronged me in my gold and my riches. This is why I sought his death and destruction. But I admit to no treason."

. . . .

"For the love of God, barons, listen to me! Gentlemen, I was in the army with the emperor, I served him with faith and love. Roland, his nephew, nourished a grudge against me and doomed me to death and pain. I was a messenger to King Marsile. Through my wisdom I managed to save myself. I challenged Roland the warrior, and Oliver, and all their companions. Charles and his noble barons heard my challenge. I avenged myself, but I did not betray.")

The suspense of the trial is great, as the barons decide to acquit Ganelon (ll. 3793-3804) and as Thierry, the only one to challenge their verdict, comes forward to champion Charles's cause (ll. 3815-3830) against Pinabel, a relative of the defendant's (ll. 3838-3849). The barons are on Ganelon's side because they may not want Charlemagne to be all-powerful.

Feudal interests are thus related to feudal law. However, when Thierry slays Pinabel, Charles's claim is satisfied. According to medieval law, Ganelon must die:

> Ço veit Tierris que el vis est ferut:
> Li sancs tuz clers en chiet el pred herbut.
> Fiert Pinabel sur l'elme d'acer brun,
> Jusqu'al nasel li ad fait e fendut,
> Del chef li ad le cervel espandut,
> Brandit sun colp, si l'ad mort abatut.
> A icest colp est li esturs vencut.
> Escrient Franc: "Deus i ad fait vertut!
> Asez est dreis que Guenes seit pendut
> E si parent, ki plaidet unt pur lui." AOI.

(Thierry sees that he has been struck in the face. His red blood spills on the grassy meadow. He strikes Pinabel's helmet of burnished steel, breaks and splits it till the nosepiece, scatters Pinabel's brains out of his cranium, turns the sword in the wound, and kills him. Owing to this blow, the battle is won. The French shout: "God made a miracle! It is only right that Ganelon hang together with his relatives who pleaded for him.")

Since the outcome of the duel represents God's judgment (l. 3931), Ganelon's guilt is real and universally recognized.[31] In addition, the epic frequently describes Ganelon as a traitor, in either the narrative context or direct discourse.[32] When Charles summoned his barons for the council, long before the trial, even before the choice of a messenger, the author warned that Ganelon would become guilty: "Guenes i vint, ki la traïsun fist" (l. 178) (Ganelon, who committed treason, came along). The French too mention betrayal. For example, Oliver tells Roland:

> Devers Espaigne vei venir tel bruur,
> Tanz blancs osbercs, tans elmes flambius!
> Icist ferunt nos Franceis grant irur.
> Guenes le sout, li fel, li traïtur,
> Ki nus jugat devant l'empereür.

(From Spain I see so much uproar, so many white hauberks, so many shiny helmets! Those will cause great distress to our Frenchmen. Ganelon, the wicked, the traitor, who condemned us before the emperor, knew about it.)

[31] Ruggero M. Ruggieri, *Il Processo di Gano nella "Chanson de Roland"* (= *Publicazioni della Scuola di filologia moderna della R. Università di Roma*, III) (Florence: G. C. Sansoni, 1936), 9-11.

[32] Adalbert Dessau, "L'Idée de la trahison au moyen âge et son rôle dans la motivation de quelques chansons de geste", *CCM*, 3 (1960), 23-26.

Convinced that the Saracens have attacked the rear guard, Naimon reveals Ganelon's treason and urges Charlemagne to come to Roland's help:

> ... Baron i fait la peine!
> Bataille i ad, par le men escientre,
> Cil l'at traït ki vos en roevet feindre.
> Adubez vos, si criez vostre enseigne,
> Si sucurez vostre maisnee gente...

(A valiant man must be fighting. There is a battle, I am sure. The very person who now urges you to hesitate betrayed the valiant man. Arm yourself, shout your war cry and help your noble household.)

When he challenges Pinabel, Thierry is also convinced of Ganelon's guilt:

> Que que Rollant a Guenelon forsfesist,
> Vostre servise l'en doüst bien guarir.
> Guenes est fels d'iço qu'il le traït;
> Vers vos s'en est parjurez e malmis.

(However much Roland may have wronged Ganelon, your service should have saved Roland. Ganelon is wicked because he betrayed. He perjured himself to you and compromised himself.)

Thierry asserts that Roland should have been exempt from any obligations interfering with his vassalage to Charles, just as Ganelon's vassalage — i.e., obligation to respect Charles — should have superseded the quarrel with Roland. Thierry's victory over Pinabel proves that vassalage has priority over everything else. Ganelon is thus guilty for not having respected the proper set of values.

Even the Saracens call Ganelon a traitor. Marsile demands that he swear Roland's death: "La traïsun me jurrez de Rollant" (l. 605). Also, Aëlroth, Marsile's nephew, shouts to the French:

> 1191 Feluns Franceis, hoi justerez as noz.
> Traït vos ad ki a guarder vos out.

(Wicked French, today you will joust against our men. The one supposed to protect you has betrayed you.)

The accumulation of such remarks leads the reader to condemn Ganelon's crime rather than sympathize with his plight. Set against his unequivocal guilt, Ganelon's claim to innocence is untenable. The positions of defendant and plaintiff are incompatible. Since they demand opposite verdicts for the same deeds, they create an ironic context.

The irony of the trial is related to that of Ganelon's treason at the beginning of the epic. After delivering his message, Ganelon praised

Charlemagne as he gradually shifted the emphasis from the emperor to Roland.[33] Praising Charlemagne while betraying Roland produced irony:

Ço dist Marsilies: "Guenes, par veir sacez,
En talant ai que mult vos voeill amer.
De Carlemagne vos voeill oïr parler....
....
Quant ert il mais recreanz d'osteier?"
Guenes respunt: "Carles n'est mie tels.
N'est hom kil veit e conuistre le set
Que ço ne diet que l'emperere est ber.
Tant nel vos sai ne preiser ne loer
Que plus n'i ad d'onur e de bontet.
Sa grant valor, kil purreit acunter?
De tel barnage l'ad Deus enluminet
Meilz voelt murir que guerpir sun barnet."
XLI
Dist li paiens: "Mult me puis merveiller
De Carlemagne, ki est canuz e vielz!
....
Quant ert il mais recreanz d'osteier?
— Ço n'iert," dist Guenes, "tant cum vivet sis niés:
N'at tel vassal suz la cape del ciel.
Mult par est proz sis cumpainz, Olivier;
Les .XII. pers, que Carles ad tant chers,
Funt les enguardes a .XX. milie chevalers.
Soürs est Carles, que nuls home ne crent." AOI.

(Marsile says: "Ganelon, I truly have it in my heart to be your friend. I want to hear you speak of Charlemagne.... When will he tire of making war?" Ganelon answers: "Charles is not as you describe him. Any man who sees and knows him would say that the emperor is valiant. I am unable to praise him as much as he deserves, for there is not more honor and goodness in any other man. Who could describe his great valor? God bestowed upon him so much heroism that he would rather die than fail his barons."

XLI

The pagan says: "I am much amazed at Charlemagne, who is gray-haired and old!... When will he tire of making war? — This will never happen, says Ganelon, as long as his nephew will be alive: there is no such hero under the cape of the sky. Oliver, his companion, is also valiant. The Twelve Peers, whom Charles holds so dear, are on guard duty with 20,000 soldiers. Charles, fearing no one, is safe.")

In order to understand the irony of this passage, it is worth noting that while he is Charlemagne's vassal and right arm (ll. 545-549), Roland be-

[33] William S. Woods, "The Symbolic Structure of *La Chanson de Roland*", *PMLA*, 65 (1950), 1251.

comes Ganelon's bitter enemy. Revenge is in order in a feud between two knights. However, by killing Roland, Ganelon also hurts Charlemagne sentimentally and militarily. Declaring war not only on Roland but also on Oliver and the Twelve Peers, reinforces that offense especially since, in Ganelon's words, Charles and his barons are equally praiseworthy (ll. 530-536). "Meilz voelt murir que guerpir sun barnet" (l. 536) is a general statement which presumably applies to Ganelon as well and which implies reciprocal faithfulness.

In defying Roland, Ganelon asserted before the French army:

> ... "Ço ad tut fait Rollant!
> Ne l'amerai a trestut mun vivant,[34]
> Ne Oliver, por ço qu'il est si cumpainz,
> Li duze per, por ço qu'il l'aiment tant,
> Desfi les ci, sire, vostre veiant."

("Roland did all this! As long as I live, I will befriend neither him, nor Oliver, for being his companion, nor the Twelve Peers, for loving him so much. Sire, here before you, I challenge them all.")

If a knight's friends (*compagnons*, vassals) must share his fate, to betray Roland means to betray Charlemagne, just as to be faithful to one means to be faithful to the other. Since Roland, Oliver, and the Twelve Peers are among the best warriors, Ganelon failed the king and his barons. At the traitor's advice Marsile would offer Charles gifts, then attack his rear guard, and kill Roland and his men. Charlemagne would thus lose his pride and never again wage war on the Saracens:

> "L'empereür tant li dunez aveir
> N'i ait Franceis ki tot ne s'en merveilt.
> Par .XX. hostages que li enveiereiz
> En dulce France s'en repairerat li reis;
> Sa rereguarde lerrat derere sei.
> Iert i sis niés, li quens Rollant, ço crei,
> E Oliver, li proz e li curteis.
> Mort sunt li cunte, se est ki mei en creit.
> Carles verrat sun grant orguill cadeir;
> N'avra talent que ja mes vus guerreit." AOI.

34 On the legal and political meaning of *amer*, see George Fenwick Jones, "Friendship in the *Chanson de Roland*", *MLQ*, 24 (1963), 89; T. Atkinson Jenkins, "Why did Ganelon hate Roland?", *PMLA*, 36 (1921), 119-133; Ruggieri, "A proposito dell'ira di Gano", *CN*, 4-5 (1944-1945), 163-165; Robert A. Hall, "Ganelon and Roland", *MLQ*, 6 (1945), 263-269; William S. Woods, "The Choice of Ganelon as Messenger to the Pagans", *SP*, 48 (1951), 706-716.

("Give the emperor so much wealth that the French would all be amazed. The king will return to sweet France, for twenty hostages that you will send. He will leave his rear guard behind. I believe that his nephew, Count Roland, and the valiant and courteous Oliver will be in it. The counts are dead, if someone trusts me. Charles will see his great pride fall. He will never desire to make war on you.")

In this passage, the speaker associates Charles's fate with his barons' even more clearly, for the former would lose his power by the latter's death. Although he had claimed loyalty to Charlemagne, Ganelon betrayed him by plotting against his power and against those who had helped him build and maintain it. Ganelon's behavior is ironic, because it includes opposite and incompatible attitudes.

Irony in the treason scene and that in the trial are closely linked. Both scenes display incongruous superpositions of friendship and enmity toward Charlemagne and his army. The ironic contexts often contain more than one episode. For example, Charles's accusation and Ganelon's defense acquire additional weight in the context of the whole epic. Also, the treason, besides originating in earlier episodes, contains in germ the conflict between loyalty and treason that will constitute the dilemma of the trial. The reader learns that nobody can attack Roland and still be considered faithful to Charlemagne.

Conditioned by Roland's bravado in the earlier scenes, the medieval audience might accept Ganelon's argument at the trial. Nevertheless, because of the feudal law that an attack on a vassal is an attack on his lord, Ganelon in fact cannot take refuge in the legal fiction that his was a personal feud not aimed against Charlemagne. Legally Ganelon has no case, although in equity he may have one. Morally he is totally wrong, for his actions were motivated by hatred of Roland and disregard for Charlemagne. Ganelon's behavior becomes ironic when set against the reader's expectations in law and in the morality of the poem. Irony in Ganelon's treason thus bears on the whole work. Together with irony in Iseut's ordeal, next to be discussed, we come closer to patterns which exceed the bounds of episodic irony.

5. ISEUT'S ORDEAL (BÉROUL'S VERSION)

Irony in Iseut's ordeal is perceptible only by placing that episode in the context of what precedes. Before she swears that nobody entered between her thighs except Mark and the leper who carried her on his back, the reader already knows that Tristan and Iseut had a love affair and that the leper was none other than Tristan. However, Mark, Arthur, and their courts do not possess this information.[35] Their ignorance brings out the ironic ambiguity of the ordeal. Iseut's innocence is at stake, and her oath exculpates her in the eyes of her witnesses (with the exception of Tristan and Dinas) and incriminates her in the eyes of the reader.[36] The ironic superposition of guilt and innocence, present in Ganelon's trial, appears here in the context of marriage vs. extra-marital love, rather than in military terms, as it did in the *Chanson de Roland.*

An important detail that prepares us for irony by strengthening the ambiguity of the oath is Tristan's disguise as a leper. His performance is so perfect that nobody questions his disease or suspects his true identity:

> Il lor dit que il a toz boit,
> Si grant arson a en son cors
> A poine l'en puet geter fors.
> Tuit cil qui l'oient si parler
> De pitié prenent a plorer;
> Ne tant ne quant pas nu mescroient
> Qu'il ne soit ladres cil quil voient.[37]

[35] For general discussions of Iseut's ordeal, see Hans Helmut Christmann, "Sur un passage du *Tristan* de Béroul", *Romania*, 80 (1959), 85-87 and "Nochmals zu Berols *Tristan*, v. 4332-4335", *ZFSL*, 76 (1966), 243-245; G. Raynaud de Lage, "Du style de Béroul", *Romania*, 85 (1964), 521. For a comparison among similar episodes in different languages, see Wolfgang Golther, *Tristan und Isolde in den Dichtungen des Mittelalters und der neuen Zeit* (Leipzig: S. Hirzel, 1907), 59-63; Friedrich Ranke, "Isolder Gottesurteil", in *Medieval Studies in Memory of Gertrude Schoepperle Loomis* (Paris: H. Champion and New York: Columbia Univ. Press, 1927), 87-94; Joan M. Ferrante, "TRISTAN: A Comparative Study of Five Medieval Works", Diss., Columbia, 1963.

[36] On the legal connotations of Iseut's oath, the following works are useful: Pierre Jonin, *Les Personnages féminins dans les romans français de Tristan au XIIe siècle: Etude des influences contemporaines* (= *Publications des Annales de la Faculté des lettres Aix-en-Provence, Nouvelle série*, 22) (Aix-en-Provence: Ophrys, 1958), 104; Frappier, "Structure et sens du *Tristan:* version commune, version courtoise", *CCM*, 6 (1963), 450; Stephen G. Nichols, Jr., "Ethical Criticism and Medieval Literature: *Le Roman de Tristan*", in *Medieval Secular Literature: Four Essays*, ed. William Matthews (= *Contributions of the UCLA Center for Medieval and Renaissance Studies*, 1) (Berkeley and Los Angeles: Univ. of California Press, 1965), 82-83; Gertrude Schoepperle, *Tristan and Isolt*, I, 226; Rosemary Norah Combridge, *Das Recht im 'Tristan' Gottfrieds von Strassburg* (= *Philologische Studien und Quellen*, 15) (Berlin: Erich Schmidt, 1964), 83-120. Also helpful are Helaine Newstead, "The Equivocal Oath in the Tristan Legend", in *Mélanges offerts à Rita Lejeune* (Gembloux: Duculot, 1969), II, 1081; Eugene Watson Burlingame, "The Act of Truth (Saccakiriya): A Hindu Spell and Its Employment as a Psychic Motif in Hindu Fiction", *JRAS* (1917), 461-463 ("Mock Proofs of Chastity").

[37] Béroul, *Le Roman de Tristan*, ed. Ernest Muret, 4th edition, revised by L. M. Defourques (= *CFMA*, 12) (Paris: Champion, 1962), 112. All quotations are from this edition and line numbers are hereafter inserted in the text.

(He tells them that he drank everything. He has so much burning in his body that he can hardly cast it out. All those who hear him speak begin to cry of pity. Those who see him do not doubt that he is a leper.)

Leprosy was associated with many sins in the Middle Ages. In S. Brody's words,

> ... Christian biblical commentators, like their Jewish counterparts, propagate the moral associations of leprosy. They variously connect scriptural leprosy with heresy, cupidity, pride and absence or weakness of faith, carnal sin, the sins of the Decalogue, the cardinal sins, and with sin itself.[38]

The disease often meant punishment for sexual depravity, all the more so that "leprosy was commonly assumed to be a venereal disease" (Brody, 127). Paradoxically, the leper also enjoyed divine favor: "The association of the disease with Jesus is seen in numerous sermons. The preachers told stories of how Jesus would appear before the faithful in the form of a leper" (Brody, 102). Thus from a moral viewpoint, the leper was a living contradiction:

> ... the leper was by turns the object of vilification and sympathy. A physician could assure the leper himself that his disease was a sign that God had chosen to grant his soul salvation, but he might simultaneously include in his diagnosis that his patient was morally corrupt. The Church might similarly decree that leprosy was a gift of God, but its bishops and priests would nonetheless use the disease as a metaphor for spiritual degeneration. The leper was seen as diabolical and sainted, as punished by God and as given special grace by him. (Brody, 55-56).

Tristan's attire before a jury that must determine Iseut's guilt or innocence is significant. Traditionally, the ordeal has divine connotations, and its outcome, like that of the duel between Thierry and Pinabel, shows that the protagonists are either right or wrong in their claims. The leper, with his double standing as saint and sinner, reflects the ambiguity of divine innocence and guilt (cf. Ferrante, 123).

There are two groups of episodes that lead to an understanding of irony in the ordeal. The first insures the reader's omniscience. While telling the truth, Iseut must present her guilt so as to make Mark and his company believe in her innocence. Since Béroul describes her manipulations in detail, the reader becomes fully aware of Tristan's disguise and of the two levels of understanding. The second group prevents those present at

[38] Saul Nathaniel Brody, "The Disease of the Soul: A Study in the Moral Associations of Leprosy in Medieval Literature", Diss., Columbia, 1968, p. 131. The literature on leprosy is immense. Brody, whose doctoral dissertation constitutes my sole authority on the subject, provides a substantial bibliography.

the ordeal from finding out the truth. They will perceive only one meaning of the oath.

Iseut is completely in command of the machinery of the ordeal. It is she who offers to take the oath in front of the two kings and their vassals, in order to belie the assertions made by the treacherous courtiers:

> Se il vuelent avoir ma jure 3244
> Ou s'il volent loi de juïse,
> Ja n'en voudront si roide guise
> (Metent le terme) que ne face.
> A terme avrai en mié la place 3248
> Li roi Artus et sa mesnie.
> Se devant lui sui alegie,
> Qui me voudroit après sordire,
> Cil me voudroient escondire, 3252
> Qui avront veü ma deraisne,
> Vers un Cornot ou vers un Saisne.[39]

(If they want to have my oath or if they want a trial, they could never find a way too hard for me to follow. Let them set the date. On that date, I will have King Arthur and his household on the very spot that they will choose. If I am exculpated before him, the witnesses having seen my defense would want to exculpate me against a Cornish or a Saxon, whoever would want to speak ill of me afterwards.)

It is also Iseut who, before returning to Mark's palace from the forest of Morois, asked Tristan to stay in the vicinity of the palace until her safety was assured. Iseut's messenger would inform Tristan of events at his uncle's court:

> Por Deu vos pri, beaus douz amis,
> Que ne partez de cest païs 2812
> Tant qos saciez conment li rois
> Sera vers moi, iriez ou voirs.
> Gel prié, qui sui ta chiere drue,
> Qant li rois m'avra retenue, 2816
> Que chiés Orri le forestier
> T'alles la nuit la herbergier.
> Por moi sejorner ne t'ennuit!...
> ....
> Sovent verrez mon mesagier: 2834
> Manderai toi de ci mon estre
> Par mon vaslet et a ton mestre... (2832)

[39] See Carlo François, "*Tristan et Iseut*, poème d'amour et manuel de la ruse", *Mercure de France*, 338 (1960), 611-625; François Rigolot, "Valeur figurative dans le *Tristan* de Béroul", *CCM*, 10 (1967), 452.

(In God's name, I beg you, sweet noble friend, not to leave this country until you find out how the king will be to me, angry or faithful to his promise. I, your dear friend, beg you to spend the night at the place of Orris the forester. Do not be distressed by the delay on my account...

....

You will often see my messenger. Through him and your tutor Governal, I will inform you of my condition.)

When Mark consents to Iseut's ordeal (ll. 3283-3287), she sends for Tristan. In her message, she discloses the time and place of the trial, requests him to dress as a leper, and prescribes his behavior step by step:

> Yseut ne s'ert mie atargie:
> Par Perinis manda Tristan
> Tote la paine et tot l'ahan
> Qu'el a por lui ouan eüe.
> Or l'en soit la bonté rendue!
> Metre la puet, s'il veut, en pes:
> "Di li qu'il set bien un marchés,
> Au chief des planches, au Mal Pas:
> G'i sollé ja un poi mes dras.
> Sor la mote, el chief de la planche,
> Un poi deça la Lande Blanche,
> Soit, revestuz de dras de ladre;
> Un henap port o soi de madre
> (Une botele ait dedesoz),
> O coroie atachié par noz;
> A l'autre main tienge un puiot,
> Si aprenge de tel tripot.
> Au terme ert sor la mote assis:
> Ja set assez bociez son vis;
> Port le henap devant son front,
> A ceus qui iluec passeront
> Demant l'amosne sinplement.
> Il li dorront or et argent:
> Gart moi l'argent, tant que le voie
> Priveement, en chanbre coie."

(Iseut waited no longer. Through Perinis she informed Tristan of all the pain and suffering that she had on his account. Her goodness should now be reciprocated! Tristan can, if he wants, bring her peace. "Tell him that he knows well the place at the head of the board by the swamp, at Mal Pas, where I soiled my clothing a little. Dressed as a leper, he should be on the hillock, at the head of the board, a little within Lande Blanche. He should carry a wooden goblet with a bottle underneath, attached by knots to a strap. He should hold a crutch in his other hand and learn this trick. That day he should be seated on the hillock. His face should be much disfigured. He should carry the goblet in front of his forehead and confidently ask for alms those who will pass by. They will give him gold and silver. He should keep the silver until I will see him privately, in a quiet chamber.)

As mentioned before, only Tristan, Iseut, and a few faithful servants know the leper's true identity. Perinis, the queen's messenger (l. 3289), is obviously one of them. Dinas, Mark's seneschal and Tristan's faithful friend, is another (ll. 3853-3858). But the remaining observers, including Mark and the accusers, are far from suspecting the truth. In fact, they think that Tristan is far away: when Iseut returned to the palace, Mark, at the advice of the three felons who had accused her of unfaithfulness, ordered Tristan to leave Cornwall for a year. Their pretext was that if Tristan remained at Cornwall and if people saw him together with Iseut, rumors that Mark consented to adultery would ensue. To the contrary, they said, in his nephew's absence, Mark could ascertain Iseut's innocence:[40]

"Sire," font il, "a nos entent:
Consel te doron bonement.
La roïne a esté blasmee
E foï hors de ta contree.
Se a ta cort resont ensenble.
Ja dira l'en, si con nos senble,
Que en consent lor felonie:
Poi i avra qui ce ne die.
Lai de ta cort partir Tristran;
Et, quant vendra jusqu'a un an,
Que tu seras aseürez
Qu'Yseut te tienge loiautez,
Mande Tristran qu'il vienge a toi.
Ce te loons par bone foi."
Li rois respont: "Que que nus die,
De vos conselz n'istrai je mie."

("Sire," they say, "listen to us: we will give you honest advice. The queen was blasphemed and fled from your country. If Tristan and the queen are together again at your court, people will say, as it seems to us, that you consent to their wickedness. Few will not say that. Let Tristan leave your court; and within a year, when you will be sure that Iseut is loyal to you, call Tristan back. We sincerely advise you to do as we tell you." The king answers: "Whatever anyone may say, I will not ignore your advice.")

It is significant that Mark does not recognize the leper's true identity.

At Lande Blanche, where the ordeal takes place, Arthur requests Iseut to swear that she and Tristan never committed adultery:

Entendez moi, Yseut la bele,
Oiez de qoi on vos apele:

[40] Cf. John H. Fisher, "Tristan and Courtly Adultery", *CL*, 9 (1957), 150-164.

Que Tristran n'ot vers vos amor
De puteé ne de folor,
Fors cele que devoit porter
Envers son oncle et vers sa per.

(Listen to me, beautiful Iseut, hear what you are called upon to swear: that besides the love he had to feel for his uncle and his mate, Tristan felt for you no love, whether whorish or mad.)

Iseut answers indirectly. Her reply appears to her audience only as a confirmation of her innocence (Jonin, 366). No man other than her husband and the leper entered between her thighs:

"— Seignors," fait el, "por Deu merci,
Saintes reliques voi ici.
Or escoutez que je ci jure,
De quoi le roi ce aseüre:
Si m'aït Dex et saint Ylaire,
Ces reliques, cest saintuaire,
Totes celes qui ci ne sont
Et tuit icil de par le mont,
Qu'entre mes cuises n'entra home,
Fors le ladre qui fist soi some,
Qui me porta outre les guez,
Et li rois Marc mes esposez.
Ces deus ost de mon soirement,
Ge n'en ost plus de tote gent.
De deus ne me pus escondire:
Du ladre, du roi Marc, mon sire.
Li ladres fu entre mes janbes
. . . .
Qui voudra que je plus en face,
Tote en sui preste en ceste place."

("Gentlemen," she says, "with God's mercy, I see here holy relics. Now listen to my oath, of which I assure the king: God and St. Hillary, these relics, this shrine, all the relics which are not here and all the shrines throughout the world, so may all help me as no man entered my thighs, except the leper who made a beast of burden of himself by carrying me over the fords, and King Mark, my husband. I exclude these two from my oath, but I exclude nobody else. I could refuse neither the leper, nor King Mark, my lord. The leper was between my thighs...

. . . .

If someone wants me to swear more, I am all ready on the spot.")

Iseut's position on the leper's back and the sexual nature of her oath give line 4205 two meanings. The first originates in the ordeal episode and describes Iseut, carried by the leper, with her legs around his body. The second refers to sexual intercourse. Since the leper and Tristan are one and the same, and since Tristan and Iseut did commit adultery, the second meaning applies not only to Mark, but also to the leper. However, as already shown, Tristan is supposed to be far away, and nobody recognizes him in his disguise. To the assembly, the leper had only one opportunity (which, by the way, involved no guilt) to enter between Iseut's thighs — namely, when he carried her on his back. Thus the witnesses rule out intercourse with the leper and assume that she could have slept only with her husband. Thus, although telling the truth and admitting her guilt, Iseut seems innocent to the assembly. In the opinion of those present, she actually asserted more than the three felons had requested:

> "Dex!" fet chascuns, "si fiere en jure:
> Tant en a fait après droiture!
> Plus i a mis que ne disoient
> Ne que li fel ne requeroient..."

("God!" says everyone, "she swears with such assurance! She did so much according to justice! She put into her oath more than the felons said or requested...")

Arthur himself promises Iseut his protection:

> Li rois Artus en piez leva,
> Li roi Marc a mis a raison,
> Que tuit l'oïrent li baron:
> "Rois, la deraisne avon veüe
> Et bien oïe et entendue.
> Or esgardent li troi felon,
> Donoalent et Guenelon,
> Et Goudoïne li mauvés,
> Qu'il ne parolent sol jamés.
> Ja ne seront en cele terre
> Que m'en tenist ne pais ne gerre,
> Des que j'orroie la novele
> De la roïne Yseut la bele,
> Que n'i allons a esperon
> Lui deraisnier par grant raison...."
> ....
> "Dame," fait il, "je vos asur:
> Ne troverez mais qui vos die,
> Tant con j'aie santé ne vie,
> Nis une rien se amor non."

(King Arthur stood up and called upon King Mark: "King, we saw, heard, and understood the ordeal. Now for the three felons, Donoalent, Ganelon, and the evil Goudoïne, they should never even speak against Iseut. As soon as I would hear news from Queen Iseut the Beautiful, neither peace nor war would prevent us from riding at full speed to wherever the felons may be...."

. . . .

"Milady", he says, "I assure you that as long as I have life and breath, you will no longer find anyone who will speak to you of anything but love.")

Line 4255 is ironic. People shall talk to Iseut of nothing but love. "Amor" may mean friendship or sexual love. The former meaning resolves the issue of the trial: Iseut is innocent and from now on nobody will bother her. The latter anticipates Iseut's following love escapades. The queen thus has a permanent certificate of innocence and a permanent mandate to sin.

The irony of line 4255 corresponds to irony in the entire ordeal scene. The general opinion and Arthur's comment assert Iseut's innocence. Since the opposite is true — she is actually guilty — the illusion of those present is incompatible with reality. Hence, the scene of the ordeal is ironic.

The ordeal is but one ironic episode in *Tristan*. The romance poses a perpetual question: have Tristan and Iseut committed adultery? While some characters think, and the reader knows that they have, Mark, unable to prove his wife's guilt, assumes her innocence. The irony of the ordeal corresponds to an ironic pattern throughout the romance.

In the various works discussed in this chapter, irony resulted from episodes of different length, sometimes close to each other, other times far apart. These episodes either were independently ironic or produced irony in combination with others. The longer and the more numerous they were, and the stronger their bearing on a given work, the more they approached works wholly ironic. As in the case of irony of words and episodic irony, the borderline between the latter and irony in wholly ironic works is often hard to establish. My purpose is not to separate one ironic context from another, but to show that irony may appear in contexts of any size. The following chapter will contain the discussion of two works which, in my opinion, are entirely ironic.

IV

WORKS WHOLLY IRONIC BY ONE AUTHOR

My discussion of *Aucassin et Nicolette* and Chrétien's *Chevalier au lion (Yvain)* will primarily concern irony as an overall structure of the narrative. This structure consists of a combination of episodes not necessarily ironic in themselves, which, placed against each other, generate irony and reveal the essentially ironic nature of these works. Episodic irony, treated in Chapter III, also resulted from a combination of usually non-ironic episodes, but did not involve an overall ironic structure. Smaller ironic contexts will receive mention here only if they are pertinent to the overall pattern.

Authorship plays an important part in the treatment of works by one author and again in the following chapter (*The Romance of the Rose*). Whereas Chapter IV treats irony as the literary achievement of one man, Chapter V will insist on the ironic tendencies in two authors, Guillaume de Lorris and Jean de Meun, who, consciously or not, joined efforts to create a single work. Since irony in the *Rose* reflects the perspectives of two men, its ironic context is wider than that of either *Aucassin* or *Yvain*.

Scholars generally agree that Chrétien wrote *Yvain* (See Frappier, *Chrétien de Troyes*, 11) but are uncertain of the author of *Aucassin*. Mario Roques summarizes the main theories on the origins of *Aucassin*. We learn in his survey that Gaston Paris attributes *Aucassin* to a *jongleur*. H. Suchier mentions a *clerc* who took up poetry. Bourdillon attributes the *chantefable* to a professional minstrel. Foerster sees, on the contrary, an aristocrat, too concise to be a professional. Finally Walther Suchier says that only a bourgeois could have liked realism as much as the author of *Aucassin*. But, as Roques points out, we know nothing of the real author and our ignorance gives way to conjecture.[1] There is however little doubt that this *chantefable* has only one author. Illuminating is Jodogne's recent

[1] Mario Roques, ed. "*Aucassin et Nicolette*", *chantefable du XIII*[e] *siècle*, 2nd edition (= *CFMA*, 41) (Paris: Champion, 1967), x-xi. All references to *Aucassin* are from this edition. Fragment and line numbers are inserted in the text.

article on *Aucassin et Nicolette* and *Clarisse et Florent*, where he sees the former work as one author's deliberate effort to parody the latter.[2]

Aucassin ridicules values frequent in chivalric romances, and in that respect contrasts with Chrétien's *Yvain*, as the *Voyage* does with the *Roland*. While *Aucassin* contains various types of irony not necessarily related to each other, in Chrétien the elements of the ironic context center on a few well-known recurring themes and motifs.[3]

Irony in *Aucassin* reflects a heterogeneous composition. Various elements of the epic and the lyric appear in the idyllic frame of the *chantefable*. The blend and the parody of the three genres still allow for a clear perception of poetry, nobility, prowess and especially love.[4] *Aucassin* contains many themes of medieval romance but attributes them to characters with whom they are not usually associated. Such thematic shifts are often ironic.

Irony in *Yvain* results from the leitmotif of the fountain set against the themes of love and adventure. The reader, who expects a development according to Arthurian tradition, must reinterpret all Arthurian values in terms set by Laudine, wife of Yvain. The conflict between these two sets of values is frequently expressed in the contrast between love and adventure, which connect Yvain to Laudine and to Arthur's court respectively.

The thematic duality of love and adventure appears in other Arthurian romances as well.[5] However, in the *Chevalier au lion* this duality has peculiar characteristics.

Generally speaking, irony in *Aucassin* and *Yvain* results from the incongruous use of certain themes appreciated by the medieval reader. Chivalry and religion, love and war, friendship and enmity were preoccupations whose ironic exploitation would not have remained unnoticed.

[2] Omer Jodogne, "*Aucassin et Nicolette, Clarisse et Florent*", *Mélanges... Frappier*, I, 478-481.

[3] Larry Martin Sklute, "The Ethical Structure of Courtly Romance: Chrétien de Troyes' *Yvain* and *Sir Gawain and the Green Knight*", Diss., Indiana, 1967, p. 85; Galen Richard Kline, "Humor in Chrétien de Troyes", Diss., Western Reserve, 1966.

[4] Jodogne, "La Parodie et le pastiche dans 'Aucassin et Nicolette'", *CAIEF*, 12 (1960), 64-65. Cf. Philippe Ménard, *Le Rire et le Sourire*, 518-519.

[5] E. Philipot, "Le Roman du *Chevalier au lion* de Crestien de Troyes", *Annales de Bretagne*, 8 (1892-1893), 323-324. See also Frappier, "Le Motif du 'don contraignant' dans la littérature du Moyen Age", *TLL*, 7. 2 (1969), 14 and *Le Roman breton: "Yvain ou Le Chevalier au lion"*, Les Cours de Sorbonne: Littérature française (Paris: Centre de documentation universitaire, 1952), 99-100; Erich Köhler, *Ideal und Wirklichkeit in der höfischen Epik: Studien zur Form der frühen Artus- und Graldichtung* (= *Beihefte zur Zeitschrift für romanische Philologie*, 97) (1956; rpt. Tübingen: Max Niemeyer, 1970), 66-88; Faith Lyons, "Sentiment et rhétorique dans l'*Yvain*", *Romania*, 83 (1962), 375-376.

1. *AUCASSIN ET NICOLETTE*

Irony in *Aucassin* consists of violating the chivalric code by a reversal of masculine and feminine roles. Inversion, particularly of character, is often associated with parody. Harden mentions various contrasts between expectation and fulfillment — such as great-small or small-great, solemn-absurd or absurd-solemn and ideal-ridiculous or ridiculous-ideal. Such contrasts result in exaggeration of the conduct of characters in the idyllic novel.[6] In addition, smaller ironic contexts, distributed throughout the *chantefable*, constitute a reminder of the ironic exchange. I shall show exchange first in such smaller contexts, then as a pattern throughout the work.

Aucassin contains innumerable isolated passages. Most important are the episodes where Aucassin fights against Bougar, the former's concept of Paradise and Hell, and "Torelore". Details on each group of episodes will bring out its ironic qualities and its bearing on the whole work.

Count Garin of Beaucaire asks Aucassin, his son, to fight against the army of Bougar de Valence. Aucassin, too preoccupied to defend his land, would join his father's army only if Garin allowed him after battle to see Nicolette, talk to her and kiss her once. The count finally agrees:

— Je prendrai les armes, s'irai a l'estor par tex covens que, se Dix me remaine sain et sauf, que vos me lairés Nicolete me douce amie tant veir que j'aie deux paroles u trois a li parlees et que je l'aie une seule fois baisie.

— Je l'otroi," fait li peres.

Il li creante et Aucassins fu lié. (VIII, ll. 33-38).

(— I will take up arms and go to battle. But you must agree that if God brings me back safe and sound, you will let me see Nicolette, my sweet friend, long enough to say two or three words to her and to kiss her once.

— Agreed," says the father. The father agrees, and Aucassin is happy.)

After the youth takes Bougar prisoner, Garin does not keep his promise:

... ja Dix ne m'aït, quant ja covens vos en tenrai: et s'ele estoit ja ci, je l'arderoie en un fu, et vos meismes porriés avoir tote paor. (X, 52-54).

(May God never help me if I keep such an agreement. In fact, if she were here, I would burn her at the stake, and you would have every reason to be afraid for your life.)

Supported by the feudal code of honor, the count's promise seemed in good faith. However, his attitude after Aucassin's victory is incompatible

[6] Robert Harden, "*Aucassin et Nicolette* as Parody", *SP*, 63 (1966), 3.

with that promise. Allowing Aucassin and Nicolette to meet and keeping them apart are incompatible opposites, which generate irony.

Aucassin subsequently frees his prisoner on the condition that the latter attack the count:

"Ce m'afiés vos, fait Aucassins, que, a nul jor que vos aiés a vivre, ne porrés men pere faire honte ne destorbier de sen cors ne de sen avoir que vos ne li faciés...."

....

Il li afie; et Aucassins le fait monter sor un ceval, et il monte sor un autre, si le conduist tant qu'il fu a sauveté. (X, 63-65 and 76-77).

("Promise me, says Aucassin, that as long as you live, you will never miss the opportunity of putting my father to shame or hurt his body and possessions...."

....

Bougar promises. Then Aucassin gives him a horse, mounts another and leads Bougar to safety.)

While the hero's unhappiness may justify his behavior, his deed still infringes upon the military alliance with his father. Bougar is first Aucassin's enemy, then his friend. Aucassin in turn is his father's ally, then his enemy. Reversal of position here generates irony.

In order to keep his son away from Nicolette, Garin requires his viscount, Nicolette's guardian, to lock her up. Inquiring about Nicolette, Aucassin reasserts his love: without her, his life is like death (VI, 8-13). The viscount replies that since he bought her from the Saracens, she is not the right girl for Aucassin, who should marry the daughter of a king or a count. If the hero ever sleeps with Nicolette, his soul will go to Hell rather than Paradise (VI, 14-23). However, the youth prefers the former — where intellectuals, knights and beautiful ladies, poets, musicians and the king himself get together — to the latter — the gathering place of old priests and cripples:

— En paradis qu'ai je a faire? Je n'i quier entrer, mais que j'aie Nicolete ma tresdouce amie que j'aim tant; c'en paradis ne vont fors tex gens con je vous dirai. Il i vont ci viel prestre et cil viel clop et cil manke qui tote jor et tote nuit cropent devant ces autex et en ces viés creutes, et cil a ces viés capes ereses et a ces viés taterelles vestues, qui sont nu et decauc et estrumelé, qui moeurent de faim et de soi et de froit et de mesaises; icil vont en paradis: aveuc ciax n'ai jou que faire. Mais en infer voil jou aler, car en infer vont li bel clerc, et li bel cevalier qui sont mort as tornois et as rices gueres, et li buen sergant et li franc home: aveuc ciax voil jou aler; et s'i vont les beles dames cortoises que eles ont deux amis ou trois avoc leur barons, et s'i va li ors et li argens, et li vairs et li gris, et si i vont herpeor et jogleor et li roi del siecle: avoc ciax voil jou aler, mais que j'aie Nicolete ma tresdouce amie aveuc mi. (VI, 24-39).

(— What would I do in Paradise? I do not seek entrance, I only seek to have Nicolette, my very sweet friend, whom I love so much. For only people such as I shall tell you go to Paradise. There go old priests, old cripples, and one-armed people, crouched day and night in front of the altars and in old crypts, those dressed in old threadbare coats and old rags, naked, barefooted, and dying of hunger, thirst, cold and misery: all those go to Paradise. I have nothing to do with them. But I want to go to Hell, because there go noble intellectuals, and noble knights who have died in tourneys and magnificent wars, good servants and courageous men: I want to go with them. There go the beautiful ladies of the court, for having two or three friends besides their barons, there go gold and silver, both light and grey, there go harpers and jongleurs and the king of the world. I want to go with them, providing that I take along Nicolette, my very sweet friend.)

Aucassin's preference for Hell contradicts the expectation of an audience in an age when catholicism and its striving for Paradise prevailed. Paradise, symbol of eternal happiness, and Hell, symbol of eternal pain, represent the poles which ultimately separate the just from the unjust. Incompatible opposites such as avoiding, instead of aiming toward Paradise, and preferring, instead of dreading Hell, produce irony.

A similar exchange occurs in the description of Nicolette's healing power. Aucassin claims that a mad pilgrim recovered completely after seeing her legs:

L'autre'ier vi un pelerin,
nes estoit de Limosin,
malades de l'esvertin,
si gisoit ens en un lit,
mout par estoit entrepris,
de grant mal amaladis;
tu passas devant son lit,
si soulevas ton traïn
et ton peliçon ermin,
la cemisse de blanc lin,
tant que ta ganbete vit:
garis fu li pelerins
e tos sains, ainc ne fu si;
si se leva de son lit,
si rala en son païs
sains et saus et tos garis. (XI).

(The other day I saw a pilgrim. He was born in Limousin and was sick with madness. He lay in bed, he was in a very bad state, seriously sick. You passed by his bed and raised your train, your ermine tunic and your white linen shirt so that he could see your leg: the pilgrim was cured and made altogether sane, more so than ever. He got out of bed and, safe and sound and completely cured, he returned to his country.)

This erotic cure may be a parody of Rivalen's healing (Thomas, *Tristan*). Seriously wounded in defending Mark's land, Rivalen comes back to life from Blancheflor's kisses. It is then that she conceived Tristan. Similarly, Lancelot made love to Guenièvre after hurting himself at the window of her prison.

The power to heal is usually a saint's prerogative. In the *chantefable*, Nicolette is therefore compared to a saint. This comparison is all the more striking that, after seeing her legs, the pilgrim returned to his country (l. 30) as if he had accomplished the purpose of his trip — praying at a saint's relics. Usually the sinner establishes contact with the saint by touching his robe. This physical contact cures the sinner and brings about pardon. Nicolette's clothing, like the saint's, cures the pilgrim. Unlike the saint's, however, it is not touched but lifted. Nicolette's bare legs suggest sin. Her deed implies a reversal of values which superimposes virtue and sin and thus creates irony similar to Aucassin's longing for Hell instead of Paradise.

Exchange is noticeable not only on a religious level. Men in *Aucassin* often behave like women and vice versa. The episode of Torelore expresses on a smaller scale the exchange of roles throughout the *chantefable*. When Aucassin and Nicolette arrive in the kingdom of Torelore,[7] whose values are upside-down, they find the king waiting to give birth, while the queen makes war:

> ... erra tant qu'il vint el castel; il demande u li rois estoit, et on li dist qu'il gissoit d'enfent.
> "Et u est dont se femme?"
> Et on li dist qu'ele est en l'ost et si i avoit mené tox ciax du païs... (XXVIII, 14-28).

> (... he wandered until he came to a castle. He asked where the king was, and was told that the king was in childbirth.
> "And where is his wife?"
> And he was told that she was in the army and had taken along everyone in the country.)

A woman, usually considered weak, performs deeds of prowess, while a man, usually considered strong, helplessly stays in bed.

The war itself also contains irony. Aucassin learns that a great war is in progress:

[7] For the narrative function of Torelore, see Myrrha Lot-Borodine, *Le Roman idyllique au moyen âge* (Paris: Picard, 1913), 81-82. Also helpful are F. Settegast, "Die Odysee oder die Sage vom heimkehrenden Gatten als Quelle mittelalterlicher Dichtung", *ZRP*, 39 (1917-1919), 282-290; Sister M. Faith McKean, "Torelore and courtoisie", *RomN*, 3 (1961-1962), 64-68.

... puis demanda quex hon c'estoit, ne s'il avoit gerre, et on li dist: "Oïl, grande." (XXVIII, 10-11).

(... then he asked what kind of man he was and if he was at war, and he was told: "Yes, a big war.")

However, the battle that he witnesses is merely a parody of war. Instead of killing each other, the enemies throw cheese, eggs, and mushrooms into a ditch filled with water. The person who most agitates the water is the winner:

XXXI....
Aucassins est arestés,
sor son arçon acoutés,
si coumence a regarder
ce plenier estor canpel:
il avoient aportés
des fromages fres assés
et puns de bos waumonés,
et grans canpegneus canpés;
cil qui mix torble les gués
est li plus sire clamés.[8]

(Aucassin stops, leaning on the bow of his saddle, and starts to look at the violent combat in the field: they had brought much fresh cheese, rotten apples, and large mushrooms from the field. The person who best agitates the fords is proclaimed the most valiant.)

This innocuous war contrasts to the destructive nature of war in general, and to its serious consequences, as anticipated in "Oïl, grande". The ironic context juxtaposes the serious and the comic, as well as expected force (normally associated with war) and actual harmlessness of attack and defense.

The few examples of episodic irony and irony of words already discussed in this chapter have in common the exchange of roles. Aucassin changed camps when he became his father's enemy after having fought in his army. The hero also reversed the traditional attitudes toward Paradise and Hell. Finally, in Torelore, men did women's jobs, while women acted like men. These episodes constantly point out a reversal of values and a broader ironic pattern according to which Aucassin often behaves like a lady, and Nicolette like a knight. In showing to what extent the work is a parody, Jodogne underlines the main ironic characteristics of the couple. Nicolette is courageous and ingenious. She escapes from her prison and finds the

[8] Micha, in his "En relisant 'Aucassin et Nicolette'", *MA*, 65 (1959), 283-284, draws several meaningful parallels between the war of Torelore and Rabelais.

way to Aucassin's. She escapes from Carthage, leaves for Beaucaire after learning to play the hurdy-gurdy and dressing as a man. Aucassin takes no initiative. He does not escape from his prison and does not try to find Nicolette. Once he finds her, he does not know what to do (Jodogne, "Parodie", 56-57). I shall now examine the function of these characteristics in the general context of the *chantefable*.

The work has a heroic beginning, in which the author introduces the protagonists:

> Qui vauroit bons vers oïr
> del deport du viel antif
> de deus biax enfans petis,
> Nicholete et Aucassins,
> des grans paines qu'il soufri
> et des proueces qu'il fist
> por s'amie o le cler vis... (I)

(Who would like to hear good verses from the pastime of the old jongleur, on two noble young persons, Nicolette and Aucassin, on the great pains that he suffered and on the valiant deeds that he performed for the sake of his fair friend...)

The above passage asserts that in order to win the woman he loved, Aucassin performed heroic deeds (l. 6). Such a feat commonly appears in courtly romances, where the knight uses his prowess to serve his beloved. Unlike the epic warrior, the hero's physical force is used at court, as he asserts his skill before his lady and peers. While both epic and courtly warriors believe in bravery, loyalty, and generosity, fighting in romances is often a test of courage, rather than a necessity of war.[9] Nevertheless, the *chantefable*, despite tradition, will systematically annihilate the assertions made in its first lines: Aucassin will perform few deeds of prowess.

Traditionally, love and military exploits go hand in hand. The knight fights even more valiantly when his lady watches or when she accepts him in her service. If the knight cannot reconcile love and war, he may become *recreant*, as in *Erec et Enide*, or mad, as in *Yvain*. There is constant tension between the Arthurian courtly values and those of the hero. Tension results from the attempt to express the hero's values in courtly terms, which are often inadequate for that purpose (Jackson, *Anatomy*, 29). Aucassin has all the qualifications of a good knight. However, love's influence on him is such that he does not desire to become a knight:

[9] W. T. H. Jackson, *The Anatomy of Love: The "Tristan" of Gottfried von Strassburg* (New York and London: Columbia Univ. Press, 1971), 16. See also Jackson's "Allegory and Allegorization", *RS*, 32 (1964), 167.

Biax estoit et gens et grans et bien tailliés de ganbes et de piés et de cors et de bras; il avoit les caviax blons et menus recercelés et les ex vairs et rians et le face clere et traitice et le nes haut et bien assis. Et si estoit enteciés de bones teces qu'en lui n'en avoit nule mauvaise se bone non; mais si estoit soupris d'Amor, qui tout vaint, qu'il ne voloit estre cevalers, ne les armes prendre, n'aler au tornoi, ne fare point quanque il deust. (II, 10-18)

(He was handsome, elegant, and big. His legs, his feet, his body, and his arms were well formed. He had curly blond hair, laughing green eyes, a fair oval face, a fine aquiline nose. He was so endowed with good qualities that he had no bad ones. But he was so taken by Amor, who conquers everything, that he did not want to be a knight, nor take arms, nor go to war, nor do what he should.)

Aucassin's knightly qualities, stressed by polysyndeton, call to mind the beginning of the *chantefable*. Both instances led us to believe that Aucassin would take up arms to win Nicolette, but his actual attitude shows the contrary. Incompatible opposites, military activity and passivity in the same circumstances are ironic.

Other contexts oppose expected valiance to actual military clumsiness, as when the hero, thinking of his beloved, twice misguides his horse. Once he fails to guide it as it carries him into the thick of the battle. The second time he falls from the horse and dislocates his shoulder.

The first time, he is fighting against Bougar's army. The enemies unhorse him and threaten him with death:

Aucassins fu armés sor son ceval, si con vos avés oï et entendu. Dix! con li sist li escus au col et li hiaumes u cief et li renge de s'espee sor le senestre hance! Et li vallés fu grans et fors et biax et bien fornis, et li cevaus sor quoi il sist rades et corans, et li vallés l'ot bien adrecié par mi la porte.

Or ne quidiés vous qu'il pensast n'a bués n'a vaces n'a civres prendre, ne qu'il ferist cevalier ne autres lui. Nenil nient! onques ne l'en sovint; ains pensa tant a Nicolete sa douce amie qu'il oublia ses resnes et quanques il dut faire; et li cevax que ot senti les esperons l'en porta par mi le presse, se se lance tres entre mi ses anemis; et il getent les mains de toutes pars, si le prendent, si le dessaisisent de l'escu et de le lance, si l'en mannent tot estrousement pris, et aloient ja porparlant de quel mort il feroient morir. (X, 1-15)

(Aucassin was armed on his horse, as you heard. God! how the shield suited his neck, the helmet his head and the sword handle his left hip! The young man was big, strong, handsome and well-built. His horse was quick and lively, and he led it well through the gate.

Now don't get the idea that he thought of taking either oxen, cows or goats, or that he struck a knight or that another struck him. Nothing of the sort. He never remembered that. Instead, he thought so much of Nicolette, his sweet friend, that he forgot his reins and everything that he had to do. The horse who had felt the spurs, carried him into the melee, where he dashed among his enemies. They raise their hands from everywhere, catch him, and take away his shield and spear. They take him prisoner, and already plan his death.)

Aucassin's portrait closely resembles that of a medieval knight. The poet praises the hero and every part of his *adoubement*. Similar praise appears in the following passage:

Garnemens demanda ciers
on li a aparelliés:
il vest un auberc dublier
et laça l'iaume en son cief,
çainst l'espee au poin d'or mier,
si monta sor son destrier
et prent l'escu et l'espiel;
regarda andex ses piés,
bien li sissent es estriers;
a mervelle se tint ciers. (XI)

(He requested rich equipment. It was made available. He put on a double-mailed hauberk and tied the helmet on his head, buckled on his sword with pommel made of pure gold, mounted his horse and took his shield and spear. He looked at both his feet. The stirrups suited him well. He was well pleased with his appearance.)

Such descriptions usually announce marvelous deeds. Aucassin goes to war not only because of his father's request, but also in order to win Nicolette. It is therefore in his interest to win the battle. In an earlier passage, the reader also saw the youth ready for battle:

De s'amie li sovient
s'esperona le destrier;
il li cort molt volentiers:
tot droit a le porte en vient
a la bataille. (IX)

(He remembers his sweetheart and spurs his horse. The horse starts running and comes straight to the gate, ready for battle.)

The second paragraph of the battle scene (*supra*, X) belies the first. Aucassin's conduct is thoroughly unknightly. Amorous ecstasy appears elsewhere in Old French literature, but does not imply defeat. For example, Perceval, associating Blancheflor's complexion with the three drops of blood on the snow, unhorses Saigremor and Keu, who challenge him. In search of adventure, Perceval saw a falcon follow and attack a wild goose. Three drops of blood fell on the snow from the goose's neck. Red on white enraptured Perceval, for they reminded him of the complexion of his beloved. Both Saigremor and Keu try to bring Perceval to Arthur. Their threatening requests result in combat and victory for Perceval.

The second time, Aucassin falls from his horse during, and because of, his quest for Nicolette:

Il mist le pié fors de l'estrier por descendre, et li cevaus fu grans et haus; il pensa tant a Nicolete se tresdouce amie qu'il caï si durement sor une piere que l'espaulle li vola hors du liu. Il se senti molt blecié, mais il s'efforça tant au mix qu'il peut et ataca son ceval a l'autre main a une espine, si se torna sor costé tant qu'il vint tos souvins en le loge... (XXIV, 82-87)

(He took his foot out of his stirrup in order to dismount. But the horse was big and tall. Thinking so much of Nicolette, his very sweet friend, he fell so hard on a stone that his shoulder flew out of place. He felt badly hurt, but forced himself as much as he could and, with his other hand, he tied his horse to a thorn tree and, leaning on his side, he dragged himself into the cabin...)

A characteristic of the man who performs deeds of prowess is mastery at horseback riding. Again, this time through clumsiness, our hero ironically violates the conduct of a perfect knight.

If Aucassin seldom acts like a knight, Nicolette often does. While the two lovers look for each other, it is always Nicolette who finds Aucassin, never the reverse. Thus, after he dislocates his shoulder, she finds him:

Quant Nicolete oï Aucassin, ele vint a lui, car ele n'estoit mie lonc; ele entra en la loge, si li jeta ses bras au col, si le baisa et acola. (XXVI, 1-3)

(When Nicolette heard Aucassin, she came to him, for she was not far. She entered the cabin, threw her arms around him, kissed and embraced him.)

The same is true at the end of the *chantefable*, when Aucassin becomes governor of Beaucaire after his father's death (XXXIV, 12-16). Nicolette, separated from her beloved, recognizes Carthage and recalls her origins (XXXVI, 9-12). Although lamenting the loss of his love and asserting his readiness to look for her anywhere, Aucassin makes no actual attempt to find her (XXXV). Nicolette, however, disguises herself as a jongleur. She returns to Beaucaire and, before making herself known, she sings the story of two lovers, Aucassin and Nicolette. Her preparation for the trip to Beaucaire is particularly significant:

Ele se porpensa par quel engien ele porroit Aucassin querre: ele quist une viele, s'aprist a vieler... Et ele s'enbla la nuit, si vint au port de mer, si se herbega ciés une povre fenme sor le rivage; si prist une herbe, si en oinst son cief et son visage, si qu'ele fu tote noire et tainte. Et ele fist faire cote et mantel et cemisse et braies, si s'atorna a guise de jogleor; si prist se viele, si vint a un marounier, se fist tant vers lui qu'il le mist en se nef. Il drecierent lor voile, si nagierent tant par haute mer qu'il ariverent en le terre de Provence. Et Nicolete issi fors, si prist se viele, si ala vielant par le païs tant qu'ele vint au castel de Biaucaire, la u Aucassins estoit. (XXXVIII, 11-23)

(She considered in what way she could look for Aucassin. She looked for a hurdy-gurdy and learned how to play... She escaped at night, arrived at the seaport, and lodged in the house of a poor woman on the shore. She took an herb, rubbed her head and face till she was all black and stained. She had a tunic, a coat, a shirt and breeches made, and she dressed as a *jongleur*. She took her hurdy-gurdy and went to a sailor. She managed to make him take her in his boat. They hoisted their sail and navigated on the high seas until they arrived in Provence. Nicolette disembarked, took her hurdy-gurdy and went playing throughout the country till the castle of Beaucaire, where Aucassin lived.)

Nicolette's behavior seems more appropriate for a man than for a woman. Her moral decisions (e.g., leaving her fatherland) contrast to the stereotype of the inactive lady in the ivory tower. Expected feminine weakness and actual masculine strength are at opposite poles and incompatible, and produce irony.

Typical of Aucassin's and Nicolette's behavior is the prison scene, which presents the lovers' chief characteristics. While the protagonists were in separate prisons, the girl escaped and contacted the young man. In devising the plan of escape, as she does later upon leaving Carthage, she demonstrated ingenuity as well as physical strength:

Nicolete jut une nuit en son lit, si vit la lune luire cler par une fenestre et si oï le lorseilnol center en garding, se li sovint d'Aucassin sen ami qu'ele tant amoit. Ele se comença a porpenser del conte Garin de Biaucaire qui de mort le haoit; si se pensa qu'ele ne remanroit plus ilec, que s'ele estoit acusee et li quens Garins le savoit, il le feroit de male mort morir. Ele senti que li vielle dormoit qui aveuc li estoit; ele se leva, si vesti un bliaut de drap de soie que ele avoit molt bon, si prist dras de lit et touailles, si noua l'un a l'autre, si fist une corde si longe conme ele pot, si le noua au piler de le fenestre; si s'avala contreval le gardin, et prist se vesture a l'une main devant et a l'autre deriere, si s'escorça por le rousee qu'ele vit grande sor l'erbe, si s'en ala aval le gardin....

....

Ele vint au postic, si le deffrema, si s'en isci par mi les rues de Biaucaire par devers l'onbre, car la lune luisoit molt clere, et erra tant qu'ele vint a le tor u ses amis estoit. Li tors estoit faelee de lius en lius; et ele se quatist delés l'un des pilers, si s'estraint en son mantel, si mist sen cief par mi une creveure de la tor qui vielle estoit et anciienne, si oï Aucassin qui la dedens plouroit et faisoit mot grant dol et regretoit se douce amie que tant amoit. (XII, 5-18 and 29-37)

(One night Nicolette lay in her bed, saw the moon shine through a window, and heard the nightingale sing in the garden. She remembered Aucassin, her sweetheart, whom she loved so much. She began to think of Count Garin of Beaucaire, who hated her to death. She decided that she should no longer stay there: if she were exposed and if Count Garin knew about it, he would make her die a horrible death. She felt that the old woman who was with her was sleeping. She got up, put on a very good silk tunic, took her sheets and towels, tied them to each other, made a rope as long as she could, and tied it to the column of the window.

On her way down, with one hand in front and the other in back, she tucked up her clothing to protect it from the abundant dew on the grass, and landed in the garden....

....

She came to the gate, opened it, and went out into the streets of Beaucaire in the shadow, for the moon was shining brightly. She walked to the tower where her sweetheart was. The tower was cracked here and there. So, she squatted near one of the columns, covered herself with her coat, and put her head through a crevice in the old tower. Then she heard Aucassin crying inside, displaying much sorrow, and regretting his sweet friend whom he loved so much.)

This passage violates a number of medieval clichés. With Aucassin locked up in the tower and Nicolette trying to reach him, the text reverses a typical situation resembling that of Lancelot and Guenièvre: the knight attempts to free the lady, who is prisoner. The young man is in a position of weakness, and the young lady in one of strength. Nicolette, who escapes from her prison, is active. Aucassin, who does nothing to obtain his freedom, is passive. Each position is ironic when placed against the expectation of the audience.

Irony in *Aucassin* results from an interchange which produces incongruous opposites. In some smaller ironic contexts of *Aucassin*, such interchange takes place between friendship and enmity, and between faith and heresy. In the overall pattern, characters often act in a manner fitting the opposite sex. The smaller ironic contexts also function as a key to, and reminder of, irony in the whole work.

Interchange makes irony in *Aucassin* particularly effective. Whereas other authors present one ironic context at a time, the author of *Aucassin* presents two: Aucassin describes not only Paradise in terms of Hell, but also Hell in terms of Paradise. In Torelore, men act like women, which is ironic in itself, but women also act like men. Aucassin behaves as Nicolette should, while she is as courageous as a knight. The author thus insists on irony by repetition of similar ironic contexts, each term of which is alternately expectation and reality.

2. THE *CHEVALIER AU LION* (*YVAIN*)

Irony in the *Chevalier au lion* results from the conflict between, and reconciliation of, love and adventure. After Yvain unhorses the presumptuous Keu, who challenged him at the Fountain of Barenton, our hero makes himself known to Arthur and his court, present at the fighting. Yvain is by then already married to Laudine, the lady of the fountain, whose husband he has slain. Happy to see his old friend, Gauvain urges him to reengage in adventure. Laudine agrees, although somewhat reluctantly, to grant her husband a leave of no more than one year. Absorbed in his knightly activities, Yvain exceeds the limit, and Laudine withdraws her love. For a time Yvain becomes mad with despair but is cured by the Lady of Norison's maids. He then engages in a series of adventures, in an attempt to become worthy of his wife's forgiveness. He and Laudine are finally reconciled.

Love and adventure, often complementary in medieval literature, conflict in the *Chevalier au lion*. The conflict of themes becomes ironic when it gives way to the lovers' reconciliation. Although Laudine hates Yvain for having abandoned her, her forgiveness results from the very adventures that she condemned.[10] Irony consists of her simultaneously loving and hating Yvain. As in *Aucassin*, the same ironic terms appear in contexts of varying complexity. Unlike *Aucassin*, where smaller episodes sometimes formed independent series, the ironic episode is an integral part of the ironic pattern in *Yvain*. The discussion of the *Chevalier au lion* will include first relevant episodic irony, then corresponding irony in the whole work.

After mortally wounding Laudine's husband, Esclados-le-Roux (ll. 862-875), Yvain escapes with his life, thanks to Lunete's ring, which makes him invisible:

> Lors li a l'anelet livré,
> si li dist qu'il avoit tel force
> com a, desus le fust, l'escorce
> qu'el le cuevre qu'an n'en voit point;
> mes il covient que l'en l'anpoint
> si qu'el poing soit la pierre anclose;
> puis n'a garde de nule chose
> cil qui l'anel an son doi a,
> que je veoir ne le porra
> nus hom, tant ait les ialz overz,
> ne que le fust qui est coverz
> de l'escorce, qu'an n'en voit point.[11]

(Then she gave him the ring and told him that it had the same power over him as the bark has over the tree trunk: the bark covers the trunk so that the trunk

[10] Interesting views of adventure appear in Thomas Artin, "The Allegory of Adventure: Meaning in Chrétien's *Yvain*", Diss., Princeton, 1968, and in John Finlayson, "*Yvain and Gawain* and the Meaning of Adventure", *Anglia*, 87 (1969), 313-337.

[11] Chrétien de Troyes, *Le Chevalier au lion* (*Yvain*), ed. Mario Roques, *Les Romans de Chrétien de Troyes*, IV (= *CFMA*, 89) (Paris: H. Champion, 1965), 32. All quotations are from this edition, and line numbers are inserted in the text.

is not at all visible. But he who has the ring must enclose it in his fist so as to hide the stone. Then he has nothing to worry about, because nobody, however open his eyes, will be able to see him, any more than the tree trunk covered by bark and completely invisible.)

Yvain thus makes futile Laudine's diligent search for the murderer. Two patterns characterize Laudine's attitude. On one hand, she deplores her husband's death. On the other, she must take care of her property.

She seems inconsolable as a widow. At the funeral, she faints, tears her hair, wrings her hands, and even wants to commit suicide:

> ... de duel feire estoit si fole
> qu'a po qu'ele ne s'ocioit
> a la foiee, si crioit
> si haut com ele pooit plus,
> et recheoit pasmee jus;
> et quant ele estoit relevee,
> ausi come fame desvee,
> se comançoit a dessirier
> et ses chevols a detranchier;
> ses mains detuert et ront ses dras,
> si se repasme a chascun pas
> ne riens ne la puet conforter,
> que son seignor en voit porter
> devant li, en la biere, mort,
> don ja ne cuide avoit confort;
> por ce crioit a haute voiz.

(She was so mad from her woe that she at times almost killed herself. She would shout as loud as she could, and she would fall down again in a swoon. Back on her feet, she, like a madwoman, would begin to tear her clothing and pull out her hair. She would twist her hands and rip her clothing, faint again at every step. Nothing could comfort her, for she saw her lord carried in his coffin; she thought she would never be comforted. This is why she cried out so loud.)

This passage contains an accumulation of terms showing Laudine's despair (l. 1161). Violent outbursts, vocal (ll. 1152-1153, 1165) or physical (ll. 1156-1159), contrast with complete inactivity (ll. 1154 and 1160). After the funeral she asserts that the murderer must be a cowardly ghost, for he dares not appear. He must have killed Esclados by treachery or have supernatural powers:

> Bien puis dire, quant je nel voi,
> que antre nos s'est ceanz mis
> ou fantosmes ou anemis;
> s'an sui anfantosmee tote;

ou il est coarz, si me dote.
Coarz est il, quant il me crient;
de grant coardise li vient,
quant devant moi mostrer ne s'ose.
Ha! fantosme, coarde chose,
por qu'ies vers moi acoardie,
quant vers mon seignor fus hardie?
Que ne t'ai ore an ma baillie?
Ta puissance fust ja faillie!
Por coi ne te puis or tenir?
Mes ce, comant pot avenir
que tu mon seignor oceïs,
se an traïson nel feïs?
Ja voir par toi conquis ne fust
mes sires, se veü t'eüst,
qu'el monde son paroil n'avoit,
ne Dex ne hom ne l'i savoit,
ne il n'en i a mes nul tex.
Certes, se tu fusses mortex,
n'osasses mon seignor atendre
qu'a lui ne se pooit nus prendre.

(I can surely say, since I do not see the killer, that either a ghost or the devil came between us. I must be all bewitched. Or he is a coward and is afraid of me. He is a coward, since he fears me. Because of his great cowardice, he dares not appear in front of me. Ah! ghost, cowardly being, why are you cowardly with me when you were fearless with my lord? Why do I not have you in my power now? Your power would already come to an end! Why can I not capture you? How else could you have killed my lord, if not treacherously? Truly, my lord would never have been conquered by you if he had seen you, for he was unequaled in this world. Neither God nor man knew of any such equal, nor is there such a man any longer. Certainly, had you been mortal, you would not have dared to pursue my lord, for no one could beat him.)

Laudine's grief, repeatedly stressed, justifies her desire to punish the murderer. In fact, Lunete fears her mistress' wrath against Yvain (l. 979). She says that Laudine and her company are almost ready to die of sorrow (ll. 984-986). If they catch Yvain, they will surely kill him (ll. 981, 990-992):

"Certes, fet ele, chevaliers,
Je criem que mal soiez venuz:
se vos estes ceanz tenuz
vos i seroiz toz depeciez,
que mes sire est a mort plaiez
et bien sai que vos l'avez mort.
Ma dame an fet un duel si fort
et ses genz an viron lui crïent,
que par po de duel ne s'ocïent;

si vos sevent il bien ceanz,
mes entr'ax est li diax si granz 988
que il n'i pueent or entandre,
si vos voelent ocirre ou pandre:
a ce ne pueent il faillir,
quant il vos voldront assaillir." 992

(She said: "Knight, I am certainly afraid that you have come at an unfortunate moment: if you were caught inside, you would be all cut to pieces, because my lord is mortally wounded, and I know for sure that you killed him. My lady is so woeful, and the men around grieve so much that they almost kill themselves. They know for sure that you are inside. Moreover, their woe is so great that they now cannot decide if you should be slain or hanged. They cannot fail to do either one or the other when they capture you.")

Despite Lunete's gloomy predictions, Laudine will suppress her anger at the thought of finding a new defender of the fountain. Persuaded by her maid, she decides to marry Yvain and make him defender of the fountain:

Se il est tex qu'a moi ateigne... 1805
....
je le ferai, ce vos otroi,
seignor de ma terre et de moi. 1808

(If he is suitable to me... I agree to make him lord of my land and of myself.)

Her impatience reaches its peak during a conversation with Lunete:

Mes ci por coi demorez vos? 1876
Alez! Ja plus ne delaiez!
Si faites tant que vos l'aiez,
et je remanderai mes genz.

(But why do you linger here? Go! Delay no longer! Do not stop until you get him. I shall consult with my people.)

Laudine's new attitude is understandable as a *raison d'état*. Although she may not love him, she needs a husband as strong as, or stronger than, her late one to protect her land. If not, says Lunete, no one could defend the land when King Arthur comes to the fountain in search of adventure:

vostre terre, qui desfandra
quant li rois Artus i vendra 1620
qui doit venir l'autre semainne
au perron et a la fontainne?
N'en avez vos eü message
de la dameisele sauvage 1624
qui letres vos en anvea?
Ahi! con bien les anplea!

Vos deüssiez or consoil prendre
de vostre fontaïnne desfandre,
et vos ne finez de plorer!

(Who will protect your land when King Arthur, who must come to the block of stone and the fountain in a week or so, arrives? Have you not received the message from the wild maiden who sent you a letter? Ah! how well she wrote it! Instead of seeking advice, as you should, on how to protect your fountain, you do not stop crying!)

Lunete points to the ironic incongruity in Laudine's position. The widow's tears result from love for her dead husband, sorrow for his death, fear or weakness. On one hand, she must find enough strength to look for a new defender of the fountain. On the other, because of her sorrow and tears, she is weak and unable to attend to her property. The *raison d'état* conflicts with her real feelings. Love for Esclados will contrast also with hatred against Yvain, when the latter becomes Lord of the Fountain. She is as reluctant to love Yvain when she marries him as she was to find a new husband. The irony of force vs. weakness is thus replaced by that of hatred vs. love.

Yvain qualifies as champion of the fountain, for he is obviously stronger than Esclados (ll. 1706-1713). Again, as Lunete says,

— Par foi, vos poez bien entandre
que je m'an vois par mi le voir,
et si vos pruef par estovoir
que mialz valut cil qui conquist
vostre seignor, que il ne fist:
il le conquist et sel chaça
par hardemant anjusque ça,
et si l'enclost an sa meison.

(— On my faith, you can really understand that I speak the whole truth. In addition, I will prove to you that the one who conquered your lord was necessarily more worthwhile: he conquered your lord, pursued him to his house, then fenced him in.)

Because of his adventures, Yvain is both indispensable and harmful to Laudine. He can protect her land, but he also contributed to ravaging it and killed its defender. Moreover, in search of adventure, Yvain will subsequently leave unguarded the land that he should protect. Laudine's behavior reflects her mixed feelings for Yvain — i.e., love and hate. If she were to marry him, she would probably forgive him. It is true that forgiveness of an enemy was common in Old French literature, particularly in the *Roman d'Alexandre*, but revenge was equally frequent. Besides, whereas in the *Roman d'Alexandre* a character officially forgives another, in the *Chevalier au lion* Laudine may have never forgiven Yvain. When, about to become her vassal, he admits his crime and asserts that nothing she would do could displease him, she suggests his own death as a possible way of displeasing him (l. 1981):

> "Dame, voir, ja ne vos querrai
> merci, einz vos mercïerai
> de quan que vos me voldroiz feire,
> que riens ne me porroit despleire.
> — Non, sire? Et se je vos oci?

("Lady, I will truly never seek mercy. Instead, I will be grateful to you for everything that you would do to me, for none of it could displease me. — Really, sir? And if I killed you?)

Laudine raises the possibility of having Yvain put to death after she has decided to marry him. As Sklute points out (pp. 134-135), the scene where Laudine meets Yvain seems ambiguous on account of the discrepancy between love and *raison d'état* and of Laudine's contradictory desires to kill and to forgive. If she did not love Esclados, she did not need to forgive. But if she loved him, could she forgive his murderer? In admitting his guilt, Yvain relies on a courtly convention that a man who yields to a lady is automatically forgiven. Laudine must choose between respecting that convention and punishing her husband's murderer. Although her dilemma may explain her attitude toward Yvain, marrying and killing the same person — i.e., rewarding an ally and punishing an enemy — are incompatible ironic opposites.

"Et se je vos oci" (l. 1981) confirms the fact that Laudine granted no official pardon, for she can still talk, though tentatively, of her enemy's death. This line calls to mind Laudine's old hatred and desire for revenge. These opposite and incongruous terms produce episodic irony. They cannot both be true. If alliance prevails, enmity seems only superficial. Such is probably the case in l. 1981, where Laudine merely tests Yvain and has no intention of killing him. Nevertheless, enmity occasionally takes over — e.g., when Yvain exceeds the time limit granted by his wife. The romance consists of the interplay of the elements of this ironic context. Until the conclusion of the story, the reader is never sure which element will predominate. One way to approach irony in the *Chevalier au lion* as a whole is to study the ironic relation of friendship and enmity, already illustrated on the episodic level. This relation centers on the recurrence of the Fountain of Barenton.

The fountain, associated with magic and marvelous deeds, is an old

Celtic *topos*. This *topos* acquires special value in the *Chevalier au lion* by its repetition and thematic associations, which together produce irony.[12] Like Arthur's court, the fountain is a unifying feature of the romance, where it appears as a leitmotif.[13] The associations of this motif include war and hatred as well as peace and love. Since the fountain episodes are central, the whole work is ironical. I shall discuss the four adventures performed at the fountain, the first by Calogrenant, the second and the fourth by Yvain, and the third by Keu. To bring out irony, I shall disregard the chronological order of the adventures, as I shall comment first on those of Calogrenant and Keu, then on those of Yvain.

At Pentecost, Calogrenant tells Arthur's court about his unfortunate adventure in the forest of Brocéliande. He found the fountain, threw water on a block of stone nearby, and thus produced a storm that devastated the land:

> La mervoille a veoir me plot
> de la tanpeste et de l'orage,
> don je ne me ting mie a sage;
> que volentiers m'an repantisse
> tot maintenant, se je poïsse,
> quant je oi le perron crosé
> de l'eve au bacin arosé.

[12] Frappier, *Etude sur "Yvain" ou le "Chevalier au lion" de Chrétein de Troyes* (Paris: Société d'édition d'enseignement supérieur, 1969), 85. For additional evidence of the exceptional qualities of the fountain, the following works are helpful: Félix Bellamy, *La Forêt de Bréchéliant, la fontaine de Bérenton, quelques lieux d'alentour, les principaux personnages qui s'y rapportent* (Rennes: J. Plihon and L. Hervé, 1896), I, 134-169, 463-594; Roger Sherman Loomis, *Arthurian Tradition & Chrétien de Troyes* (New York and London: Columbia Univ. Press, 1949), 292-293; George L. Hamilton, "Storm-Making Springs: Rings of Invisibility and Protection. — Studies on the Sources of *Yvain* of Chrétien de Troyes", *RR*, 2 (1911), 355-375; O. M. Johnston, "The Fountain Episode in Chrétien de Troyes's *Yvain*", *Transactions and Proceedings of the American Philological Association*, 38 (1902), lxxxiii-lxxxiv; Maxwell Sidney Luria, "The Christian Tempest: A Symbolic Motif in Medieval Literature", Diss., Princeton, 1965, pp. 135-136 and "The Storm-Making Spring and the Meaning of Chrétien's *Yvain*", *SP*, 64 (1967), 565; Louise B. Morgan, "The Source of the Fountain Story in the *Yvain*", *MP*, 6 (1908-1909), 332-333; W. A. Nitze, "The Fountain Defended", *MP*, 7 (1909), 160-161 and "*Yvain* and the Myth of the Fountain", *Speculum*, 30 (1955), 170 and 174; Margarete Rösler, "Die 'Fontainne perilleuse' in Chrestiens *Yvain*", *ZFSL*, 58 (1934), 232-235.

[13] Frappier, *Etudes sur "Yvain"*, 61. See also C. Foulon, "Le *Rou* de Wace, l'*Yvain* de Chrétien de Troyes et *Eon* de l'Etoile", *BBSIA*, 17 (1965), 93. Cf. Joseph J. Duggan, "Yvain's Good Name: The Unity of Chrétien de Troyes' Chevalier au lion'", *Orbis Litterarum*, 24 (1969), 112; W. Bruce Finnie, "A Structural Study of Six Medieval Romances", Diss., Ohio State, 1965, p. 109; Odette Snoy [d'Oppurers], *La Structure et le sens du "Chevalier au lion" de Chrétien de Troyes*, Diss. Univ. catholique de Louvain (Louvain: L. Wouters, 1959).

Mes trop en i verssai, ce dot;
que lors vi le ciel derot
que de plus de quatorze parz
me feroit es ialz li esparz;
et les nues tot mesle mesle
gitoient pluie, noif et gresle.
Tant fu li tans pesmes et forz
que cent foiz cuidai estre morz
des foudres qu'autour moi cheoient,
et des arbres qui peceoient.
Sachiez que molt fui esmaiez,
tant que li tans fu rapaiez.[14]

(I enjoyed seeing the miracle of the storm and the thunder: I heard the block, that I watered with the bowl, flood. But I poured too much, I am afraid, and do not consider myself wise for enjoying it. Now I would gladly repent, if I could. Afterwards, in the lightning, I saw the sky break in more than fourteen parts. The clouds cast off pell-mell rain, snow, and hail. The weather was so bad and severe that I thought a hundred times I was dead because of the thunder that fell around me and of the trees that were struck to the ground. Know that I was very frightened until the weather cleared.)

The magnitude of the meteorological cataclysm caused Calogrenant's fear, followed by his shameful adventure. Challenged and defeated by Esclados, he was lucky to remain alive:

... li chevaliers me feri
si durement que del cheval
par mi la crope, contre val,
me mist a la terre tot plat;
si me leissa honteus et mat,
c'onques mes ne me regarda.
Mon cheval prist et moi leissa;
si se mist arriere a la voie.
Et je, qui mon roi ne savoie,
remés angoisseus et pansis....

(The knight struck me so hard that he threw me on the horse's croup and then flat to the ground. He left me there ashamed and beaten, and no longer looked at me. He took my horse, left me, and he went back. I, stunned to the point of not recognizing my king, remained tormented and worried.)

Keu's adventure is less dramatic than Calogrenant's, but its outcome is similar. When Arthur and his court arrive at the fountain and produce a storm, Keu, unaware that Yvain is the new lord of Barenton, requests the honor of challenging the knight of that land:

14 See R. S. Loomis, "Calogrenanz and Crestien's Originality", *MLN*, 43 (1928), 215-222.

... mes sire Kex ot talant
qu'il demanderoit la bataille,
car, quiex que fust la definaille, 2232
il voloit comancier toz jorz
les meslees et les estorz
ou il i eüst grant corroz.

(Milord Keu desired to accept the challenge, for, whatever their outcome, he always wanted to begin grievous scuffles and tourneys.)

Just as Esclados unhorsed Calogrenant (ll. 538-543), Yvain unhorses Keu:

Mes sire Yvains cop si puissant 2256
li dona, que de sus la sele
a fet Kex la torneboele,
et li hiaumes an terre fiert.
Plus d'enui feire ne li quiert 2260
mes sire Yvains, ençois descent
a la terre, et son cheval prent.

(Milord Yvain gave him such a powerful blow that Keu tumbled from his saddle, and his helmet hit the ground. Milord Yvain seeks to harm him no more. Instead he dismounts and takes Keu's horse.)

Yvain takes advantage of this combat to reprimand Keu for his scornful attitude towards Calogrenant's unhappy adventure:

Ahi! ahi! con or gisiez 2265
vos qui les autres despisiez!

(Ha! ha! now lie there, you, who used to scorn others.)

Yvain's adventure has already been described in some detail. He repeats Calogrenant's combat, but unlike the latter, he wins by mortally wounding Esclados. The adventures of Yvain, Calogrenant, and Keu all consist of challenging the knight of the fountain by throwing water on the block of stone. Combat always ensues. In addition, Yvain must face not only the knight of the land, but also Laudine. The consequences of his combat are both military and sentimental. By killing Esclados, he can never hope to conquer Laudine, with whom he, protected by the ring, fell in love while she was still in mourning:

An ce voloir l'a Amors mis
qui a la fenestre l'a pris; 1428
mes de son voloir se despoire,
car il ne puet cuidier ne croire
que ses voloirs puisse avenir,
et dit: "Por fos me puis tenir, 1432
quant je vuel ce que ja n'avrai;

> son seignor a mort li navrai
> et je cuit a li pes avoir!
> Par foi, je ne cuit pas savoir,
> qu'ele me het plus or en droit
> que nule rien, et si a droit."

(Amor, who caught him at the window, gave him this desire. But he despairs because of his desire, for he can neither think nor believe that his wish could come true. He says: "I can consider myself mad, since I want what I can never have. I mortally wounded her lord, and I think of making peace with her! Indeed, I do not think I realize that she hates me more than anything, and rightly so.")

Yvain's position, like Laudine's, is ironic. He wants to make peace and love in a situation which allows only war and hatred. He calls to mind the abnormal state of the lover in "Je meurs de soif".

In considering Yvain's death (l. 1981), Laudine brings the enmity of the battlefield to the palace. After their marriage, she will still experience distaste and sometimes anger at the thought of her husband's military exploits. She reluctantly grants him permission to leave in pursuit of adventure. If he does not return after one year, her love for him will turn to hatred:

> ... "Je vos creant
> le congié jusqu'a un termine.
> Mes l'amors devanra haïne,
> que j'ai en vos, toz an soiez
> seürs, se vos trespassïez
> le terme que je vos dirai;
> sachiez que je n'en mantirai:
> se vos mantez, je dirai voir.
> Se vos volez m'amor avoir
> et de rien nule m'avez chiere,
> pansez de tost venir arriere
> a tot le moins jusqu'a un an
> huit jorz après la Saint Johan
> c'ui an cest jor sont les huitaves.
> De m'amor soiez maz et haves,
> se vos n'iestes jusqu'a ce jor
> ceanz avoec moi au retor."

("I grant you the leave till a certain date. But the love that I have for you will turn to hatred, you can be sure, if you go beyond the deadline that I shall indicate. Know that I shall never go against my word. Should you lie, I will still tell the truth. If you want to have my love and if you hold me dear, think of coming back soon, at the very latest a year from now, eight days after St. John, whose octave is today. May you lose my love if by that day you are not back with me.")

When Yvain exceeds the one-year limit, Lunete echoes Laudine's threats. The separation of the couple is final:

> Yvain, n'a mes cure de toi
> ma dame, ainz te mande par moi
> que ja mes vers li ne reveignes
> ne son anel plus ne reteignes.
> Par moi que ci an presant voiz
> te mande que tu li envoiz:
> rant li, qu'a randre le t'estuet.

(Yvain, my lady no longer cares for you. Rather she commands you through me never to come back to her, nor keep her ring. She commands you to give it back to her, through me, whom you see. Give it back to her, since you must.)

As will become apparent, Laudine is the enemy of not only Yvain but also adventure. The romance distinguishes between Arthurian values and hers. Adventure produces fame according to the former, and destruction according to the latter.

Laudine does not like the adventure of the fountain. What seems adventurous to others is detrimental to her, for the storm devastates her property. Similarly, Esclados reproached Calogrenant (ll. 502-503 and 606) for having destroyed his forest (ll. 499-501, 505, 508) and his castle (ll. 508-514) for no reason and without proper challenge (ll. 491-496):

> … Vassax, molt m'avez fet,
> sanz desfïance, honte et let.
> Desfïer me deüssiez vos,
> se il eüst reison an vos,
> ou au moins droiture requerre,
> einz que vos me meüssiez guerre.
> Mes se je puis, sire vasax,
> sor vos retornera cist max
> del domage qui est paranz;
> en viron moi est li garanz
> de mon bois qui est abatuz.
> Plaindre se doit qui est batuz;
> et je me plaing, si ai reison,
> que vos m'avez de ma meison
> fors chacié a foudre et a pluie;
> fet m'avez chose qui m'enuie,
> et dahez ait cui ce est bel,
> qu'an mon bois et an mon chastel
> m'avez feite tele envaïe,
> ou mestier ne m'eüst aïe
> ne de grant tor ne de haut mur.
> Onques n'i ot home asseür

an fortresce qui i fust
de dure pierre ne de fust.

(Noble sir, you did a lot of harm to me, without challenge, dishonor, and insult. You should have challenged me if you had had reason, or at least demanded justice before waging war. But, noble sir, the evil of this blatant damage will turn against you, if I have my way. The country around us bears witness to the destruction of my woods. The victim must complain. I therefore rightly complain that you violently chased me out of my house by thunder and rain and you harmed me. I'll be damned if I like such an attack on my woods and my castle. Neither a big tower nor a high wall could have helped me. No man was confident in the fortress of hard stone and wood.)

As for Laudine, she lost her first husband through Yvain's prowess, and her second, who, at Gauvain's advice, left her in search of adventure.

After Yvain reveals his identity to Arthur's court, Gauvain reminds Yvain of his knightly duties. Marriage should be a source of improvement, not of decadence. It is shameful to spend all one's life with women and give up military exploits. Yvain should accompany Gauvain in a life of tournaments and glory. Subsequently, Yvain and Gauvain participate in numerous adventures. When Laudine withdraws her love, Yvain first becomes mad, then, in order to rehabilitate himself and be worthy of his wife, performs deeds of prowess for the benefit of the helpless and unfortunate. He helps the Lady of Norison, who cured his madness, against the Count of Alier, who wants to conquer her country and marry her. He saves a lion attacked by a snake. The lion becomes Yvain's faithful servant and occasionally participates in his adventures. Yvain will thus be known as the "Chevalier au lion". He fights against the three knights who accused Lunete of unfaithfulness to her mistress, and against the giant Harpin. After killing the "fils de diable", he delivers three hundred girls from the castle of Pesme-Aventure, where, in miserable conditions, they wove textiles. Finally Yvain duels with Gauvain, in a feud between the two sisters of Noire-Epine, whose father died. Yvain represents the younger sister, to whom the older one denied her rightful heritage.

By urging Yvain to leave Laudine, Gauvain establishes a dichotomy of love and military exploits.[15] This dichotomy plays an important role in Chrétien's romances. Erec gives up his comfortable life with Enide to prove his prowess. Perceval leaves Blancheflor before his quest for the grail. Although valiant in battle, Alexander dares not express his love for Soredamor. Before admitting his love for Fénice, Cligès proves his

[15] Douglas Kelly, "Gauvain and *Fin'Amors* in the Poems of Chrétien de Troyes", *SP*, 67 (1970), 453-460.

valiance at Arthur's court. In the *Chevalier au lion*, the dichotomy becomes a conflict between Laudine and adventure.

The last adventure at the fountain breaks the pattern of combat established by the three previous ones. Yvain decides to force reconciliation with his wife by pouring water on the block of stone. Lunete's plea and the old *raison d'état* help Laudine make up her mind. However, the reconciliation still surprises the reader, aware of feudal and conjugal hostility. Curiously, Laudine appeals to Yvain for help for the same reason that she hates him. Because of the adventures that produced his wife's anger but made him famous, the knight with the lion inspires enough confidence in Laudine to become lord of the fountain.

The storm that Yvain started seems to destroy the whole forest, the castle, and the people in it. Laudine feels her last hour at hand. One would be better off captured in Persia than near Barenton:

> ... plovoir i firent.
> Ne cuidiez pas que je vos mante
> que si fu fiere la tormante
> que nus n'an conteroit le disme,
> qu'il sanbloit que jusqu'an abisme
> deüst fondre la forez tote!
> La dame de son chastel dote
> que il ne fonde toz ansanble;
> li mur croslent, et la torz tranble,
> si que par po qu'ele ne verse.
> Mialz volsist estre pris en Perse
> li plus hardiz antre les Turs,
> que leanz estre antre les murs.

(They made rain. In all truth, the uproar was so terrible that no one could recount a tenth of it. It seemed to have destroyed the whole forest! The lady in her castle is afraid that the uproar will destroy all of them. The walls and the tower are shaking and almost collapse. The most courageous of Turks would rather want to be captured in Persia than be inside these walls.)

In the context of such cataclysm, Laudine's reaction is plausible. She goes to ask for help from the knight with the lion, whom she does not at first recognize as Yvain[16] and whom she finds at the pine near the fountain:

[16] Yvain has changed not only in name, but also in character: "... the 'Chevalier au lion' undergoes a profound change: instead of submitting to his fate, as he did during the first part of the poem, he learns to master his destiny — to choose, according to a system of values he now fully understands. In contrast to epic heroism or saintliness, courtliness functions more exactly as an ideology than an a priori category." Karl D. Uitti, "Chrétien de Troyes' *Yvain:* Fiction and Sense", *RPh*, 22 (1969), 483.

... si s'an va,
tant que delez le pin trova
celui qu'ele ne cuidoit pas
trover a si petit de pas,
einz cuidoit qu'il li convenist
molt querre, einçois qu'a lui venist.
Par le lyeon l'a coneü
tantost com ele l'a veü;
si vint vers lui grant aleüre
et descent a la terre dure.

(... and she goes and finds near the pine the one whom she did not expect to find so close by. She thought that she would have to search for him rather than just come upon him. She recognized him by the lion as soon as she saw him. She quickly comes toward him and dismounts.)

As in the previous adventures, a knight starts a ravaging storm, and the owner of the land rides to meet him. Unlike those adventures, the owner is a woman, and no combat takes place. On the contrary, Yvain and Laudine are reconciled. In Laudine's words,

— Certes, fet ele, je voel bien,
por ce que parjure seroie
se tot mon pooir n'en feisoie,
la pes feire antre vos et moi;
s'il vos plest, je la vos otroi.

(She says: — I surely want to keep you as my husband, for I would perjure myself if I did not do everything in my power to make peace between you and me. If you so desire, I agree to it.)

Like their quarrel, their reconciliation is both military and conjugal, and ironically contrasts to their expected enmity. The ironic context consists of alliance and love opposed to combat and hatred. Yvain appears as Laudine's friend and enemy simultaneously. Thus irony in the romance has the same ironic context as Yvain's adventure, where patterns of forgiveness and revenge, or friendship and enmity conflicted. Episodic irony mirrors irony in the whole work.

Irony in works by one author may have numerous manifestations, which we can generally divide into two groups: accumulation of irony of words or episodic irony, so that the work appears as a cluster of ironic passages; juxtaposition throughout the work of sections not ironic in themselves but producing irony in combination with each other. The first group is not different in nature from the smaller-scale examples discussed in previous chapters. Moreover, irony in smaller contexts sometimes proved pertinent to the whole work. In *Aucassin* several passages contained the technique of exchange of roles, the main characteristic of irony in the overall pattern. In the *Chevalier au lion*, Yvain's first adventure at the fountain anticipated the irony produced by the combination of all the adventures. The smaller contexts served as a key to perceiving total irony. The same relations among contexts will apply to irony in works by two or more authors, of which *The Romance of the Rose* is the best example.

V

THE ROMANCE OF THE ROSE

The *Rose*, a work wholly ironic, offers a wider perspective of irony than *Aucassin* and *Yvain*. The perspective stems from the nature of the ironic context, from the length of the work, and from its dual authorship. The ironic context concerns various religious attitudes toward love, which result in conflicting views on virtue and vice.

From a religious viewpoint, love is a controversial subject in the Middle Ages. The word "amor" itself is ambiguous, as it may denote love of God, a virtue, or love of flesh, with mixed connotations. Kolb shows that love may point in opposite directions, toward the light of Heaven or the darkness of Hell. Moral love and love of God lead man to Heaven, whereas sexual love may lead him to Hell (*Begriff*, 17-18).

Carnal love presents a dilemma to medieval men. Although sinful in itself, intercourse is the only means by which people can multiply according to God's commandment. The Virgin Birth of Christ, removing Him from original sin, shows, among other things, that the visible cause of guilt in sexual matters in the Middle Ages was Christianity. This birth set a goal impossible to attain. On one hand, people were commanded to "increase and multiply", on the other, "they were told that the act which alone could produce this increase was sinful and indicative more than any other of man's fall from innocence and grace" (Jackson, *Anatomy*, 3). Medieval authorities on love suggested various solutions to this dilemma. Advocates of courtly love compromised between desire and dogma by accepting sex for the young and chastity for the old.[1]

Irony in the *Rose* originates in the simultaneous occurrence of virtuous and sinful love. The authors often equate lust to legitimate intercourse and even to love of God. As Fleming points out, the events of the *Rose*

[1] John Wilcox, "Defining Courtly Love", *PMASAL*, 12 (1930), 324. See also Félix Guillon, *Jean Clopinel dit de Meung: "Le Roman de la Rose" considéré comme document historique du règne de Philippe le Bel* (Paris: A. Picard and Orléans: J. Loddé, 1903), 127 and 141-142.

remind us of Eden: passion overthrows reason, and sin proves stronger than virtue. The hero accepts false courtesy, hypocrisy, and wicked counsel to seduce the Rose. His helpers, an old whore and Faus-Semblant among them, are not beyond the baseness of his purpose. The hero makes an enemy of Raison, whom he calls God's daughter.[2]

From the viewpoint of irony, the romance is a unified work, despite its dual authorship. Its unity results from narrative coherence as well as from Jean's acknowledged debt to Guillaume.

In the first part of the romance (ll. 1-4058), Guillaume the Lover has a dream of the beautiful Garden of Deduit. There Amor — the God of Love — and his court lead a happy life. After Lady Oiseuse introduces him into the garden, the narrator sees the Fountain of Narcisus and remembers the horrible way in which those who do not submit to Amor's command die. The Lover then falls in love with a Rosebud, whose reflection he saw at the bottom of this fountain. Near the fountain, the god wounds him, takes him in his service, and explains to him the pains and rewards of love.

To conquer the Rosebud, Guillaume has to dispose of her guardians — Chasteé, Dangier, Honte, Jalousie, and Male Bouche. He also has to fight hard to remain faithful to his lord despite a debate with Raison, God's daughter, who condemns Amor. The first part ends with the Lover's despair.

In the second part of the romance (ll. 4059-21780), by Jean de Meun, Raison reappears and elucidates her previous advice by opposing the Dreamer's foolish enterprise to superior types of love, such as charity. Although he wavers, the Dreamer remains faithful to his master. Amor gathers his barons, and together they decide to attack the castle sheltering the Rosebud. In order to insure success, he accepts, though reluctantly, Faus Semblant as his vassal. Among those who support Amor is Nature, God's helper. Before sending Genius, her confessor, to deliver an encouraging message to Amor's army, she complains about the laziness of

[2] John V. Fleming, *The "Roman de la Rose": A Study in Allegory and Iconography* (Princeton: Princeton Univ. Press, 1969), 50. On the conflict and reconciliation of courtly love and religion, the following titles by Alexander J. Denomy are helpful: *The Heresy of Courtly Love,* Introduction by William Lane Keleher, Boston College Candlemas Lectures on Christian Literature (1947; rpt. Gloucester, Mass.: Peter Smith, 1965), 18-19; "An Inquiry into the Origins of Courtly Love", *MS*, 6 (1944), 175-260; "*Fin' Amors:* The Pure Love of the Troubadours, Its Amorality, and Possible Source", *MS*, 7 (1945), 139-207; "*Jois* among Early Troubadours: Its Meaning and Possible Source", *MS*, 13 (1951), 177-217; "The Vocabulary of Jean de Meun's Translation of Boethius' *De Consolatione Philosophiae*", *MS*, 16 (1954), 19-34. See also Jean Fourquet, 'Littérature courtoise et théologie", EG, 12 (1957), 34-39; Jackson, "The *De Amore* of Andreas Capellanus and the Practice of Love at Court", *RR*, 49 (1958), 243-251.

man, who alone among creatures refuses to comply with Nature's and God's command to multiply. The God of Love and his men, supported by Venus, Nature, and Genius, are victorious, and the Lover wins the Rosebud.

When Amor explains to his barons why they should attack the castle, he identifies the Dreamer as Guillaume:

> Vez ci Guillaume de Lorriz,
> Cui Jalousie, sa contraire,
> Fait tant d'angoisse e de deul traire
> Qu'il est en perill de mourir
> Se je ne pens dou secourir.[3]

(Here is Guillaume de Lorris. Jalousie, his adversary, makes him suffer so much that he is in danger of death unless I decide to help him.)

The mention of Guillaume, author of, and character in, the first part, as a character in the second reinforces the unity of the romance. After a forty-year lapse, Jean will continue his predecessor's story:

> ... quant Guillaumes cessera,
> Johans le continuera,
> Emprès sa mort, que je ne mente,
> Anz trespassez plus de quarante...

(After Guillaume stops, in fact more than forty years after his death, Jean will continue the story.)

Collective authorship of the *Rose* points, as we shall see, to its richness in irony. Jean continues or develops certain ironic tendencies in Guillaume's works, and creates others. My subsequent discussion of irony accommodates two current diverging views on the structure of the *Rose*.[4]

According to one view, Guillaume's section would treat *fin'amor* exclusively, whereas Jean would use his predecessor's work as a pretext for satire on thirteenth-century people and institutions. This is by far the view most commonly held in contemporary criticism. The *Rose* would

[3] Guillaume de Lorris and Jean de Meun, *Le Roman de la Rose*, ed. Ernest Langlois, SATF, 63, 5 vols. (1914-1924; rpt. New York: Johnson, 1965), III, 164. All quotations are from this edition, and line numbers are inserted in the text. I have also consulted the following translations: André Mary, trans. *Le Roman de la Rose* (Paris: Gallimard, 1949); Harry W. Robbins, trans. *The Romance of the Rose*, ed. Charles W. Dunn, D 90 (New York: E. P. Dutton, 1962); Charles [R.] Dahlberg, trans. *The Romance of the Rose* (Princeton: Princeton Univ. Press, 1971).

[4] On the literary criticism of the *Rose*, see the excellent essay and bibliography by Marc-René Jung, "Der *Rosenroman* in der Kritik seit dem 18. Jahrhunderts", *RF*, 78 (1966), 203-252.

consist of two poems, the second of which would be the counterpart of the first. Guillaume's poem would reflect the views on love which were still flourishing at the beginning of the thirteenth century. Jean would replace his predecessor's somewhat affected development with a mixture of brutality, pedantry, and vigor.[5]

According to the other view, Jean carries out Guillaume's intentions completely by offering the reader a true art of love:

37 Ce est li Romanz de la Rose,
Ou l'Art d'Amors est toute enclose.

(This is the *Romance of the Rose*, where all the art of Amor is included.)

The most forceful subscriber to this view is Alan M. F. Gunn. Jean describes himself as a clerk of love and calls his work a treatise on the art. Jean "deliberately emphasized both the opposition and affinities in order to confirm the structure and define the meaning of the poem he was perfecting".[6] Both the continuation of, and the addition to, Guillaume's ironic tendencies make us aware of an ironic perspective.

My discussion of irony in the *Rose* will consist of three sections. The first will show how various kinds of love form a system of oppositions between virtue and vice and how by substituting one for the other the system becomes ironic. Section two will deal with the ironic conflict between Nature and Raison, which is chiefly Jean's invention but bears on the whole work. The conflict brings out the problem of *cupiditas* and virtuous physical love. Section three will analyze the ironic discrepancies

[5] J.-J. Ampère, "*Le Roman de la Rose*", *RDM*, 13, nouvelle série, 3 (1843), 542-543. Other critics include Edmond Faral, "*Le Roman de la Rose* et la pensée française au XIIIe siècle", *RDM*, 35 (1926), 439; Dorothy Marie Ralph, "Jean de Meun, the Voltaire of the Middle Ages", Diss., Illinois, 1940; Mary Morton Wood, *The Spirit of Protest in Old French Literature*, Columbia Univ. Studies in Romance Philology and Literature (New York: Columbia Univ. Press, 1917), 157-175; Arthur Keister Moore, *Studies in a Medieval Prejudice: Antifeminism*, Vanderbilt Univ. (Nashville, Tenn.: Joint Univ. Libraries, 1945), 10-15; Helmut Hatzfeld, "La Mistica naturalistica di Giovanni de Meung", trans. Ugo Piscopo, *Delta: Rivista di critica e di cultura*, 3rd series, 1 (July, 1962), 27, 35-36, and 47; Paul Strohm, "Guillaume as Narrator and Lover in the *Roman de la Rose*", *RR*, 59 (1968), 3-4.

[6] Alan M. F. Gunn, *The Mirror of Love: A Reinterpretation of the "The Romance of the Rose"* (Lubbock: Texas Tech. Press, 1952), 23-27 and 322. See also K. Sneyder de Vogel, "L'Unité du *Roman de la Rose*", *Neophil*, 37 (1953), 136; Eric C. Hicks, "Le Visage de l'antiquité dans le *Roman de la Rose:* Jean de Meung, savant et pédagogue", Diss., Yale, 1965, pp. 5-21; Gaston Gros, *L'Amour dans le "Roman de la Rose"*, Bibliothèque du lettré (Paris: Baudinière, 1925), 82; Lionel J. Friedman, "Jean de Meung, 'Antifeminism,' and 'Bourgeois Realism'", *MP*, 57 (1959-1960), 13-23; Paul B. Milan, "The Golden Age and the Political Theory of Jean de Meun: A Myth in *Rose* Scholarship", *Symposium*, 23 (1969), 137-149.

between *allegoria* and *littera,* which reflect the entire ironic system described in section one.

1. THE SOURCE OF IRONY IN *THE ROMANCE OF THE ROSE*

Irony in the *Rose* originates in the superposition of courtly and religious conceptions of love. Although in allegory one may stand for the other, their combination often unites incompatible opposites. In the *Rose,* where religion plays an important role, irony results from the expression of *fin'amor* in religious terms as a virtue and a vice simultaneously. Since virtue and vice are opposite by definition, their incongruous equation creates an ironic context.

This section will show the religious values which produce irony in the love story. Since the context consists mainly of mistaking virtues and vices, it will be useful to show this substitution on the level of word irony, more easily perceptible than irony as a continuous pattern throughout the work. After illustrating the technique of substitution, I shall discuss those elements of the romance which, expressed in religious terms and interchanged, produce irony.

The disguise of vices as virtues, and of malefactors as benefactors is common in medieval literature. In the Antichrist plays, for instance, Antichrist wants to be known as Messiah. A clear-cut example of disguise in the *Rose* is Faus Semblant's discourse.[7] About to become a member of Amor's army, he explains his treacherous character and his popularity by comparing himself to God. Faus Semblant is the son of Barat and Ypocrisie, who rule the world despite the Holy Ghost (ll. 11897-903):

> De tout le monde est empereres
> Baraz, mes sires e mes peres;
> Ma mere en est empereriz.
> Maugré qu'en ait Sainz Esperiz,
> Nostre poissanz lignages reine.
> Nous reinons ore en chascun reine,
> E bien est dreiz que nous reinons

[7] G. Ward Fennley, "Faus-Semblant, Fauvel and Renart le Contrefait: A Study in Kinship", *RR*, 23 (1932), 323-331; Sister M. Faith McKean, R.S.M., "The Role of Faux Semblant and Astenance Contrainte in the *Roman de la Rose*", in *Romance Studies in Memory of Edward Billings Ham*, ed. Urban Tigner Holmes (= *California State College Publications*, 2) (Hayward, Cal., 1967), 103-107; William W. Ryding, "Faus Semblant: Hero or Hypocrite?", *RR*, 60 (1969), 163-167.

Qui trestout le monde faisnons
E savons si les gens deceivre
Que nus ne s'en set aperceivre,
Ou qui le set aperceveir
N'en ose il descouvrir le veir....
. . . .
... l'eneur avons des omes.
Pour si bones genz tenu somes
Que de reprendre avons le pris
Senz estre d'ome nul repris.

(Barat ["Cheating"], my lord and father, is emperor of the whole world. My mother is empress. Our powerful lineage reigns despite the Holy Ghost. We now reign in every kingdom, and rightly so. We cheat the whole world and deceive people so that no one can notice it, or if someone can, he dares not uncover the truth....

. . . .

... we are honored by men. We are taken for such good people that we have the right to reprimand them without being reprimanded.)

If Faus Semblant tells the truth, his comments appear as a satire on medieval society. If he lies, he closely resembles Antichrist who, despite his boastful claims to be God, is finally defeated by Him. The *Rose* supports both interpretations, which resulted in a vigorous controversy in the fifteenth century and in numerous debates thereafter.

Barat, Ypocrisie, and Faus Semblant who, like Antichrist, deceive the world (*saeculum*), are God's enemies. Their defects, expressed in religious terms, appear as vices. The clause "Maugré qu'en ait Sainz Esperiz" (l. 11900) shows that vice exists despite virtue. "Trestout le monde faisnons" excludes God's influence on men, which would prevent the victory of vice over virtue. Lines 11912-20 reinforce the prosperity that Faus Semblant and his family enjoy and the preponderance of vice over virtue. Faus Semblant's assertion contradicts the Christian belief that God is always victorious. The assertion that Faus Semblant is more powerful than God when he actually is much weaker superimposes opposite, incompatible, and therefore ironic terms. Faus Semblant describes his defects as qualities that rightly belong to God, and, in so doing, receives support from Amor. When he accepts Faus Semblant in the army, the God of Love and his companions praise the new vassal and, implicitly, falsehood. Amor and his newly acquired subject sin against God equally. The concept of Amor as a sinner recurs time and again in the set of values established by Raison.

The distinction between love of God (*caritas*) and love of flesh, often associated with lust (*concupiscentia* or *cupiditas*), comes out most forcefully in Raison's speech to the Lover. She appears once in each part of the romance. Both times she discourages the Lover from conquering the Rosebud, condemns Amor, Oiseuse, and the whole garden. Thirteenth-century readers would hardly question the truth and wisdom of Raison's precepts, as, according to Guillaume, she is God's daughter. She must have been born in Paradise, for her majestic appearance reflects her divine origin:

2985 A son semblant e a son vis
Pert qu'el fu faite en parevis...

(According to her appearance and countenance, she seems to have been made in Paradise.)

God made her in His image (ll. 2990-91) and gave her power to protect human beings from their own madness (ll. 2992-95):

Sachiez, se la lettre ne ment,
Que Deus la fist demainement,
A sa semblance e a s'image,
2992 E li dona tel avantage
Qu'ele a pooir e seignorie
De garder ome de folie,
Por quoi il soit teus qu'il la croie.

(Know, if the letter does not lie, that God Himself made her in His own image and gave her the power to prevent man from madness. This is why man must believe her.)

In describing the impact that Raison probably had on the medieval audience, Badel reserves an important part for the Christian overtones of her speech. Besides evoking notions from antiquity, such as moderation, Raison has important Christian features. She calls to mind the divine Word and incarnates the ideal precepts of medieval life. Raison in the *Rose* never contradicts faith nor separates it from virtuous love.[8] Raison, God's offspring, parallels Christ, God's son according to Christianity. In addition, whereas senses are common to both men and animals, the faculty of reason belongs only to men. Ironically, the Lover will repeatedly contradict his assertion of line 2995. Amor's vassal, he will forsake Raison and, therefore, God.

At her second appearance, Raison instructs the Lover, at his request (ll. 4667-71), on various types of love (ll. 4676-78). She mentions disinterested friendship (ll. 4685-96), friendship for the sake of money (ll.

[8] P. Badel, "Raison 'fille de Dieu' et le rationalisme de Jean de Meun", *Mélanges... Frappier*, I, 42.

4769-74), charitable love (ll. 5503-05), and finally, love for the procreation of the species (ll. 5763-66) as opposed to lust. In describing each kind of love, she stresses the opposition between love of flesh and love of God. Such a distinction is noticeable in the Middle Ages, when treatises on both abound.[9]

The chief religious connotations of *amor* in the Middle Ages are well-directed and badly-directed love. Some texts use amor to describe both kinds of love, others to describe only one kind. Medieval audiences must have had mixed views and feelings on the subject. The foremost medieval authority on the religious value of love was St. Augustine. In *De Civitate Dei* he shows that love may be either good (*caritas*) or bad (*cupiditas*):

Nam cuius propositum est amare Deum et non secundum hominem, sed secundum amare proximum, sicut etiam se ipsum: procul dubio propter hunc amorem dicitur uoluntatis bonae, quae usitatius in scripturis sanctis caritas appellatur; sed amor quoque secundum easdem sacras Litteras dicitur....

....

Dicunt enim dilectionem accipiendam esse in bono, amorem in malo... Recta itaque uoluntas est bonus amor et uoluntas peruersa malus amor. Amor ergo inhians habere quod amatur, cupiditas est...

(He who resolves to love God, and to love his neighbour as himself, not according to man but according to God, is on account of this love said to be of good will; and this is in Scripture more commonly called charity, but it is also, even in the same books, called love....

....

They [those who think that charity or regard (*dilectio*) is one thing, love (*amor*) another] say that *dilectio* is used of a good affection, *amor* of an evil love....

The right will is, therefore, well-directed love, and the wrong will is ill-directed love. Love, then, yearning to have what is loved, is desire [*cupiditas*]...)[10]

[9] For the origins in Greek philosophy of various kinds of medieval love, see Johan Chydenius, *The Symbolism of Love in Medieval Thought* (= *Finska Vetenskapssocieteten, Commentationes humanarum litterarum*, 44. 1) (Helsinki-Helsingfors: Keskuskirjapaino-Centraltrykeriet, 1970), 7-9 ("*The Eros of Plato*"), 9-10 ("*The Philia of Aristotle*"), and 11-13 ("*The Agape of the New Testament*"). See also Raymond Klibanski, *The Continuity of the Platonic Tradition during the Middle Ages: Outlines of a Corpus Platonicum Medii Aevi* (London: Warburg Institute, 1939); Norman R. Shapiro, trans. and James B. Wadsworth, ed. *The Comedy of Eros: Medieval French Guides to the Art of Love* (Urbana: Univ. of Illinois Press, 1971); Gérard Paré, *Les Idées et les lettres au XIIIe siècle: "Le Roman de la Rose"* (= *Publications de l'Institut d'études médiévales Albert-le-Grand, Univ. de Montréal, Bibliothèque de philosophie*, 1) (Montréal: Centre de psychologie et de pédagogie, 1947), 82-98.

[10] St. Aurelius Augustine, *De Civitate Dei contra Paganos*, in *Opera Omnia*, ed. Bernard Dombart and Alphons Kalb (= *Corpvs Christianorum, Series Latina*, 47, vol. 14) (Turnholt: Brepols, 1955), 421-422. The translation is from Marcus Dods, trans.

In one of his sermons, St. Augustine associates love with movement:

Omnis amor aut adscendit, aut descendit. Desiderio enim bono leuamur ad Deum, et desiderio malo ad ima praecipitamur.[11]

(All love either ascends or descends. We are raised to God by a good wish and we are sent to Hell by a bad one.)

Love's movement upwards or downwards, representing *caritas* and *cupiditas* respectively, corresponds to the salvation of the just — i.e., rising to Paradise — and damnation of the evil — i.e., descending to Hell.

The *Rose* frequently exploits these contrary movements. Raison helps the Christian reader identify the set of values of his faith and distinguish good from bad. She connects friendship and love of God to *caritas*, a virtue, and love for the Rosebud, a woman, to vice (Jackson, *Anatomy*, 5-6).

Disinterested friendship derives from God's benevolence (l. 4688) to mankind (l. 4687) and manifests itself in charitable sharing of all goods (ll. 4689-90):

C'est bone volenté comune
De genz entr'aus senz descordance,
Selonc la Deu benivolence.
E seit entr'aus comunité
De touz leur biens en charité,
Si que par nule entencion
N'i puisse aveir excepcion.

(It is common good will among people, without disagreement, according to God's benevolence. Let them share, with no exception, their possessions according to charity.)

"Charité" (l. 4690) has clearly religious connotations, suggested by line 4688, which puts it in a Christian context.

---

and ed. *The City of God* (*Book XIV*), by St. Augustine (= *Hafner Library of Classics*, 4) (New York: Hafner, 1948), II, 10-11. See also Michael Müller, *Die Lehre des hl. Augustinus von der Paradiessehe und ihre Auswirkung in der Sexualethik des 12. und 13. Jahrhunderts bis Thomas van Aquin: Eine moralgeschichtliche Untersuchung* (= *Studien zur Geschichte der kath. Moraltheologie*, 1) (Regensburg: Friedrich Pustet, 1954), 9-10; 19-21.

11 Augustine, "In Psalmum CXXII Enarratio: Sermo ad Plebem", in *Enarrationes in Psalmos CI-CL* (= *Corpvs Christianorum, Series Latina*, 40, vol. 10. 3) (Turnholt: Brepols, 1956), 1814. See also Isidore of Seville, *Differentiarum sive De Proprietate Sermonum Libri Duo*, in *Opera Omnia* (= *PL*, 83) (Paris: J.-P. Migne, 1862), cols. 9-10 ("Inter *Amorem* et *Cupidinem*"). For a comparison between the pagan philosophers and the Church Fathers on natural love, see G. F. Jones, "Lov'd I Not Honour More", *CL*, 11 (1959), 136.

Raison's remarks on *caritas* become more and more precise, until she finally suggests herself as the Lover's ideal *amie*. Between the moment when she first talks to Guillaume and that when she offers him her love, she makes several remarks pertinent to *caritas*. For example, she attributes to Socratic love a variation of the golden rule:

> Fai tant que teus envers touz seies
> Con touz envers tei voudraies...

(Be toward others such as you would want them to be toward you.)

She further asserts that *caritas* is more essential than justice:

> Mais plus tient grant necessité
> Amour, qui vient de charité,
> Que joustice ne fait d'assez.

(But the love resulting from charity is by far more necessary than justice.)

Caritas is superior to Justice. Raison claims that *caritas* could by itself bring peace to the world, whereas, to attain the same purpose, Justice must use punishment. Justice becomes necessary only when *caritas* is lacking.[12]

Raison's offer to become the Lover's *amie* represents the culmination of virtuous love:

> Ci vueil t'amie devenir;
> E, se te veauz a mei tenir,
> Sez tu que m'amour te vaudra?
> Tant que jamais ne te faudra
> Nule chose qui te conviegne,
> Pour mescheance qui t'aviegne:
> Lors te verras si grant seigneur
> Qu'onc n'oïs paler de graigneur....
> ....
> Ci avras en cet avantage
> Amie de si haut lignage
> Qu'il n'est nule qui s'i compere,
> Fille de Dieu le souverain pere,
> Qui tele me fist e fourma.
> Regarde ci quele fourme a
> E te mire en mon cler visage.
> N'onques pucele de parage
> N'ot d'amer tel bandon con gié,
> Car j'ai de mon pere congié
> De faire ami e d'estre amee:

[12] Félix Lecoy, "Sur un passage délicat du *Roman de la Rose* (vers 5532 de l'édition Langlois)", *Romania*, 85 (1964), 372.

Je n'en serai, ce dit blasmee;
Ne de blasme n'avras tu garde,
Ainz t'avra mes peres en garde,
E nourrira nous deux ensemble.

(I want to become your sweetheart. Do you know how much my love will be worth to you if you want to share it? So much that, whatever misfortune may occur to you, you will never lack anything necessary. You will then become so great a lord that you have never heard of a greater one....

....

By this agreement you will have a sweetheart of such great lineage that no other friend is of a comparable one: daughter of God, the Sovereign Father, who made me so. Look at my fair complexion and its shape. Never has a noble maiden had as much power to love as I, for I have permission from my father to acquire a sweetheart and be loved. This means that I will not be blamed for loving. Nor will you worry about blame. Instead, my father will take care of you and will look after both of us.)

The association of the Lover with God's daughter (ll. 5813-17), explains his prospective grandeur (ll. 5804-08) and calls to mind virtuous love, which ascends ("Desiderio... bono leuamur ad Deum"). In the first part of the *Rose*, Raison came down from her tower to talk to Guillaume:

En cest point ai grant piece esté
Tant que me vit ensi maté
La dame de la haute angarde,
Qui de sa tor aval esgarde;
Raison fu la dame apelee.
Lors est de sa tor devalee,
Si est tot droit a moi venue.

(I was at this stage for a long time, until the lady called Raison, who looks down from her tower, from her observation post, saw me so defeated. Then she descended from her tower and came directly to me.)

In Part II, as we have seen, she wants to raise him to her level. Love of Raison thus implies *caritas*.

On the other hand, lust — i.e., love for the Rosebud — and subservience to Amor are sinful. Raison describes Amor as the devil who makes the Lover suffer:

Li vif deable, li maufé
T'ont ton athanor eschaufé,
Qui si fait tes eauz lermeier,
Qui de nule rien esmaier
Qui t'avenist ne te deüsses,
Se point d'entendement eüsses.
Ce fait li deus qui ci t'a mis,

Tes bons maistres, tes bons amis,
C'est Amours, qui soufle e atise
6400 La brese qu'il t'a ou cueur mise,
Qui fait aus eauz les lermes rendre.

(The living devils have heated your [alchemist] furnace which brings so many tears to your eyes. If you had a little understanding, you should not be tormented by anything that could occur. It is the god who brought you here, your good master, your good friend [that torments you]. It is Amor, who blows on, and fans the live charcoal that he put in your heart, who brings tears to your eyes.)

Raison equates love's sufferings to Hell, and their author to Amor. Tears (ll. 6393 and 6401) and heat (ll. 6392, 6399-6400) are expressions of amorous passion as well as torture. Amor is the devil (ll. 6391), who, like an alchemist, fans the flame that he put in the Lover's heart. Since Hell implies heat which, in turn, is related to Guillaume's passion, the narrator's feelings for the Rosebud constitute sinful descending love ("desiderio malo ad ima praecipitamur").

Amor, or according to the Rose, Cupido, is associated with lust. He is Venus' son (ll. 10827-28), as both authors repeatedly point out. "Cupido" calls to mind *cupiditas*, or *voluptas carnis* (Bernardus Silvestris) or *charnel delict* (*Echecs amoureux*). Any lecher is a worshipper of Venus and Cupid's man (Fleming, *Roman de la Rose*, 196). The opposition between *caritas* and *cupiditas* constitutes an important source of irony in the *Rose*. While these extremes can coexist — i.e., while the world is full of virtuous men and of sinners — the same character cannot display *caritas* and *cupiditas* simultaneously. Nevertheless, Amor is often described as a virtuous and sinful character simultaneously, and the love that he encourages goes in both directions.

Besides distinguishing *caritas* from *cupiditas*, Raison discriminates between sinful and virtuous love of flesh. In pointing to this medieval dilemma, she does not always attempt to solve it. In lines 6391-6401, "Tes bons maistres, tes bons amis" (l. 6398) creates irony of words. The ironic context consists of calling him a good master but describing him as the devil. The label and the description are opposite and incompatible.

At the beginning of her second appearance, Raison defined love by a series of ironic contradictions:

Amour ce est pais haïneuse,
Amour c'est haïne amoureuse;
C'est leiautez la desleiaus,
4296 C'est la desleiautez leiaus;
C'est peeur toute asseüree,
Esperance desesperee;

C'est raison toute forsenable;
C'est forsenerie raisnable;
C'est douz periz a sei neier...
. . . .
C'est langueur toute santeïve,
C'est santé toute maladive;
C'est fain saoule en abondance;
C'est couveiteuse soufisance...
. . . .
C'est faus deliz, c'est tristeur liee,
C'est leece la courrouciee;
Douz maus, douceur malicieuse,
Douce saveur mal savoureuse;
Entechiez de pardon pechiez,
De pechié pardons entechiez...
. . . .
Ce est enfers li doucereus,
C'est paradis li doulereus...

(Love is hateful peace, love is amorous hatred. It is unfaithful loyalty, it is faithful disloyalty. It is fear full of assurance, desperate hope. It is wholly mad reason, it is reasonable madness. It is sweet danger of drowning...

. . . .

It is sickness full of health, it is health full of sickness. It is hunger abundantly satisfied, it is greedy sufficiency...

. . . .

It is false pleasure, happy sadness, it is angry happiness; sweet evil, evil sweetness, sweet bad-tasting flavor; a sin touched by pardon, a pardon touched by sin...

. . . .

It is sweet Hell, it is sorrowful Paradise.)

The above paradoxes describe the lover's abnormal state (cf. "Je meurs de soif") and the controversy over sexual love in the Christian religion. Most of these paradoxes combine good and bad, or pleasant and unpleasant. Particularly important are lines 4315-16 and 4327-28, which transpose all preceding attributes of love into religious terms. "A sin touched by pardon" and "a pardon touched by sin" reflect the medieval dilemma of sexual love.[13] Hell and Paradise exchange their characteristics and so place love in an ironic context of simultaneous grace and damnation. The paradoxes indicate, besides the two directions of natural love, the incongruity of those directions.

Although she condemns sexual love, Raison sometimes says that it is bad only when enjoyed for its own sake rather than for procreation.[14]

13 Dahlberg, "Love and the *Roman de la Rose*", *Speculum*, 44 (1969), 573.

14 Stephen G. Nichols, Jr., "The Rhetoric and Sincerity in the *Roman de la Rose*", in *Romance Studies in Memory of Edward Billings Ham*, 124.

Raison gives several examples showing that condemnation of lust does not imply total abolition of sexual love (ll. 5732-33, 5741-43, and 5744-45). As avoiding one extreme is different from accepting the other (ll. 5738-40), as forbidding one foolishness does not mean allowing a greater one (ll. 5729-31), so forbidding foolish love (lust) does not imply forbidding love altogether:

> Sez tu pas qu'il ne s'ensuit mie,
> Se laissier vueil une folie,
> Que faire deie autel ou graindre?
> Ne pour ce, se je vueil esteindre
> La fole amour a quei tu bees,
> Comant je pour ce que tu hees?
> Ne te souvient il pas d'Horace,
> Qui tant ot de sen e de grace?
> Horaces dit, qui n'est pas nices:
> Quant li fol eschivent les vices,
> Si se tournent a leur contraires;
> Si n'en vaut pas meauz leur afaires.
> N'amour ne vueil je pas defendre
> Que l'en n'i deie bien entendre,
> Fors qu'a cele qui les genz blece.
> Pour ce, se je defent ivrece,
> Ne vueil je pas defendre a beivre.
> Ce ne vaudrait un grain de peivre.
> Se fole largece devee,
> L'en me tendrait bien pour desvee
> Se je comandaie avarice,
> Car l'une e l'autre est trop grand vice.

(Do you not know, it does not follow that, if I want to give up one madness, I have to make a similar or greater one? If I want to extinguish the mad love to which you aspire, do I command you to hate? Do you not remember Horace who had so much sense and charm? Horace, who is no fool, says: when the mad avoid vices, they turn to their opposites. Such change does not benefit their business. I do not want to forbid the understanding of love, except for that which hurts people. For, although I forbid drunkenness, I do not want to forbid drinking. If I did, my command would not be worth a grain of pepper. Although I forbid foolish generosity, I would be mad to command avarice, for one is as great a vice as the other.)

The word "vices" (l. 5738) in the paraphrase of Horace's "Satire I" (ii, 24) links religious condemnation to both lust and avoidance of sexual love. Love is acceptable unless it hurts people (ll. 5741-43).

Despite the reconciliation of both types of sexual love, their incompatibility constitutes a constant source of irony in the *Rose*. Like the opposition between *caritas* and *cupiditas*, these types of love generate an ironic pattern of virtue and vice. We have already seen this pattern in Raison's irony of words, which reflects the ironic mechanism of the whole romance.

Raison provides the theological context of two contrasts: sinful natural love vs. *caritas*, and sinful natural love vs. virtuous natural love. She speaks not only as a character of the romance but also as God's daughter. All that she asserts belongs to both the narrative context (*littera*) and its allegorization. She is essential in determining the literal and figurative meanings of the story, in whose context the two ironic contrasts originate.

It is significant that in the *Rose*, only characters closely linked to God, such as Raison and Nature, support *caritas* and virtuous physical love. Other characters often express *caritas* in terms of *cupiditas* or vice versa. Nature, God's helper, who usually supports Raison, nevertheless disagrees with her on Amor. He stands for virtuous natural love according to Nature, and for *cupiditas* according to Raison. In the narrative context, Amor appears sometimes as virtuous, other times as sinful. Irony originating in the disagreement or *conflictus* between Raison and Nature is one of Jean de Meun's contributions to the work. The author uses Guillaume's material but gives it a turn unforeseen in his predecessor's story.[15] The *conflictus* underlines the dilemma of natural love. In addition to the *conflictus*, the whole romance displays ironic discrepancies between *littera* and *allegoria*. These discrepancies bring out the contrasts of *cupiditas* to *caritas* and to virtuous natural love. Whether consciously or not, Guillaume and Jean brought out the same ironic pattern, which they associated with allegory, an important medieval rhetorical figure.

2. NATURE AND RAISON: THE IRONIC *CONFLICTUS*

The conflict between these two characters lies in their attitude toward Amor. While Raison repeatedly condemns him, Nature makes allies of him and Venus.[16] As mentioned, he represents lust according to Raison, and virtuous natural love according to Nature. The narrative conflict between these characters corresponds, allegorically, to the ironic clash between *cupiditas* and virtuous physical love. Many other discrepancies in the *Rose* point to the disagreement. Raison and Nature, God's daughter and minister respectively, should provide consistent criteria for the

15 Gérard Paré, *Les Idées et les lettres*, 203 and 207.

16 Fleming, "Natural and Unnatural Nature", in the *Roman de la Rose*, 189-190.

evaluation of matters of faith. However, unless the reader questions at least some of their assertions, he encounters logical contradictions in their arguments. If he does question their assertions, their authority is weakened, even though the poem appears to ascribe considerable value to their opinions in matters of religion. Whatever the reader's viewpoint, he cannot escape the ironic inconsistency of the *conflictus*, so common in the *Rose* and in medieval intellectual life in general. Disputation may have resulted from the conflict of values in the Middle Ages as well as from controversies in various university circles. The latter involved inconsistencies of dogma (Gunn, *Mirror*, 475). Nature's ironic treatment is made possible largely by her ambiguous position in the Middle Ages. Authors describe her on one hand as a force against evil, on the other as an ally of Satan. In general, the poets assumed that Nature is a goddess of good and life, whose laws everyone must obey. The demonic view of Nature persisted, however, throughout the Middle Ages and Renaissance. For some theologians, including Thomas Aquinas, Nature, degenerated with original sin, had reached Satan's domain.[17] Nature's favorable and unfavorable connotations explain her portrait as God's servant, yet Amor's ally.

In order to understand the conflict, it is useful to analyze the relationship between Nature and Genius, her confessor. Although very powerful, Nature appears less credible than Natura in Alanus' *De Planctu*, for example. When she complains to Genius about her misery and suffering, the latter compares her to other evil women and thus lowers her status. The speech of Genius has the same effect on Nature's image in the eyes of the reader as her conflict with Raison: Nature does not live up to the expectations created by the narrative context because, like other women, she has defects, and because her attitude toward Amor differs from Raison's. By its smaller number of lines and its closeness to the "Nature" episodes, the denigration of Nature by Genius is more easily perceptible than the implicit condemnation by Raison. But the conversation of Nature and Genius points to the *conflictus* between Nature and Raison.

When the conversation takes place, Nature has already been mentioned several times in the romance (see "Glossaire", *Rose*, V, p. 340, "Nature") and after her confession she assumes an active role in the conquest of the castle. Genius' carping attitude is surprising, for in this romance Nature is

[17] Edgar Colby Knowlton, "Natura as an Allegorical Figure", Diss., Harvard, 1918, pp. 40-41; "Nature in Old French", *MP*, 20 (1922-1923), 313; "The Goddess Nature in Early Periods", *JEGP*, 19 (1920), 232-233. For evidence of Nature's unfavorable connotations see Aldo Scaglione, *Nature and Love in the Late Middle Ages* (Berkeley and Los Angeles: Univ. of California Press, 1963), 8-9.

favorably regarded: Raison acknowledges natural love as divine, if it is inspired by the right motives; the context asserts time and again Nature's importance in the creation of the world; in her wretchedness, Nature also describes her role in the world; finally, Genius himself bows to Nature's authority by advising the knights about to attack the castle to comply with her divine command. All descriptions of Nature tend to link her to God.

Raison says that both she and Nature encourage pleasurable natural love (ll. 4412-20):

> Mais je sai bien, pas nou devin,
> Continuer l'estre devin
> A son poeir vouleir deüst
> Quiconques a fame geüst,
> E sei garder en son semblable,
> Pour ce qu'il sont tuit corrompable,
> Si que ja par succession
> Ne fausist generacion;
> Car, puis que pere e mere faillent,
> Nature veaut que li fill saillent,
> Pour recontinuer cete euvre,
> Si que par l'un l'autre recueuvre.
> Pour c'i mist Nature delit,
> Pour ce veaut que l'en s'i delit
> Que cil ouvrier ne s'en foïssent
> E que cete euvre ne haïssent,
> Car maint n'i trairaient ja trait
> Se n'iert deliz qui les atrait.

(But I know well (I am not guessing) that whoever lay with a woman should want with all his might to continue his divine self and maintain himself in his likeness. All men are subject to decay. They should want to maintain themselves so that perpetuation through succession would never fail. Since father and mother disappear, Nature wants the children to grow up and continue this work, so that one generation would replace the other. Nature put pleasure in procreation. She wants the participants to enjoy it in order for these workers not to run away and not to hate their work. Many would not touch their work if there were no pleasure to attract them.)

The narrative context too connects Nature with the perpetuation of the species and reinforces Raison's assertions:

> Nature, qui pensait des choses
> Qui sont desouz le ciel encloses,
> Dedenz sa forge entree estait,
> Ou toute s'entente metait
> En forgier singulieres pieces,
> Pour continuer les espieces...

(Nature, who was thinking of things contained below the Heavens, had entered her forge, where she used all her care to create individual pieces, for the continuation of the species.)

Furthermore, Nature, by her own admission, is God's constable and deputy (ll. 17781-82). She obtained that position because of God's esteem and affection (l. 16771):

> Cil Deux qui de beautez abonde,
> Quant il très beaus fist cet beau monde,
> Don il portait en sa pensee
> La bele fourme pourpensee...
> ....
> Cil Deus meïsmes, par sa grace,
> Quant il i ot par ses devises
> Ses autres creatures mises,
> Tant m'enoura, tant me tint chiere
> Qu'il m'en establi chamberiere...
> ....
> Pour chamberiere! certes veire
> Pour conestable e pour vicaire...

(God, who abounds in beauty, when He made very beautiful this beautiful world, whose shape He prefigured in his thought... God himself, through His grace, when He had placed his other creatures as he desired, He honored me so much and held me so dear that He made me His servant... Servant! Rather constable and deputy...)

When before the attack on the castle, he addresses the barons as Nature's messenger, Genius acknowledges her divine function:

> ... Nature
> ... de tout le monde a la cure,
> Come vicaire e conestable
> A l'empereur pardurable
> Qui siet en la tour souveraine
> De la noble cité mondaine,
> Don il fist Nature menistre,
> Qui touz les biens i amenistre...[18]

(Nature... is in charge of the whole world as deputy and constable of the Immortal Emperor, who sits in the Sovereign Tower of the noble worldly city whose minister He made Nature, who administers all its wealth.)

Considering Nature's high function and the divine grace bestowed upon her (l. 16768), Genius' reaction to her plight is insulting. Not noting his

[18] See Gérard Paré, "Le Message de Génius", in *Les Idées et les lettres*, 279-297.

insults; she will subsequently complain to him that among all creatures, man alone refuses to carry out her commands, although she equipped him with useful tools for that purpose and provided pleasure in the act of love. Man alone refuses to serve Amor. Failure to obey God's command to multiply grieves her more than all other human sins (ll. 19323-34), which she briefly enumerates (ll. 19225-37).

It is significant that Nature could make men carry out God's purpose without pleasure, if procreation were her only object. Although procreation and pleasure are not necessarily connected, in almost all treatments they are. Raison and Nature, like Andreas Capellanus and others, assume that sensual love (and its concomitants) is the kind that gives pleasure. They also assume that "good" love, such as *caritas*, gives virtue and a sense of spiritual well-being. However, the association of virtuous natural love with *caritas* is destroyed by the strong antifeminist passages in the *Rose*. Superposition of the high and the low connotations of love produces irony, in which some readers could see satire directed against idealized physical love or against *caritas*.

Before listening to Nature, Genius urges her to confess the reason for her unhappiness:

"— Ma dame, dou monde reïne,
Cui toute riens mondaine encline,
S'il est riens qui vous grieve en tant
Que vous en ailliez repentant,
Ou qui neïs vous plaise a dire,
De quiconques seit la matire,
Seit d'esjoïr ou de douleir,
Bien me poez vostre vouleir
Confessier trestout par leisir;
E je tout a vostre plaisir,"
Fait Genius, "metre i vourrai
Tout le conseil que je pourrai;
E celerai bien vostre afaire,
Se c'est chose qui face a taire."

("Milady, queen of the world, to whom all worldly things bow, if there is anything that grieves you to the point of making you repent or merely speak about it, you can leisurely confess your wish in me, whatever is the matter, whether joy or woe. I, in turn, says Genius, will readily give for your pleasure all the advice that I can give. In addition, I will hide your matter well if it is something to be kept silent.")

In attempting to console her, Genius says nothing about procreation and a lot about the fickleness of women (ll. 16325-28). Although Nature must have a good reason to weep so violently, women easily get angry and in fact are the root of all evil:

— Dame, touteveis vous conseille
Que vous voilliez ce pleur laissier,
Se bien vous voulez confessier,
E bien entendre a la matire
Que vous m'avez emprise a dire;
Car granz est, ce crei, li outrages,
Car bien sai que nobles courages
Ne s'esmeut pas de po de chose.
S'est mout fos qui troubler vous ose.
Mais, senz faille, il est veirs que fame
Legierement d'ire s'enflame.
Virgiles meïsmes tesmoigne,
Qui mout quenut de leur besoigne,
Que ja fame n'iert tant estable
Qu'il ne seit diverse e muable.
E si rest trop ireuse beste:
Salemons dit qu'onc ne fu teste
Seur teste de sarpent crueuse,
Ne riens de fame plus ireuse,
N'onc riens, ce dit, n'ot tant malice.
Briement en fame a tant de vice
Que nus ne peut ses moeurs parvers
Conter par rimes ne par vers.

(— Milady, I however advise you to give up this weeping, if you desire to confess and attend to the matter that you began to recount. The offense is great, I believe, since I know that a noble heart is not moved by trifles. And he who dares disturb you is very mad.

But it is certainly true that the woman is easily inflamed with wrath. Vergil himself, who knew their business very well, bears witness that there is no woman stable enough to leave no room for fickleness and instability. Besides, she is too wrathful a beast: Solomon says that there has never been a head more cruel than the head of a snake, nor has there been anything more wrathful than a woman, nor has anything had so much malice. In short, there is so much vice in a woman that nobody can recount her evil habits in rhyme or in verse.)

The irony of this passage results from Genius' denigration of Nature and her plight. "Legierement" (l. 16324), referring to a woman's hot temper, relates it to insignificant causes. As we later discover, Nature's discomfort is due to man's disobedience of God's command. Genius' implication that the unhappiness of Nature may be caused by a trifle contradicts not only his previous assertion on the seriousness of the plight, but also the seriousness of divine rule. The terms of the contradiction are incompatible opposites and create irony of words.

"Legierement" functions within the passage as the passage itself does among the episodes describing Nature's greatness. By comparing Nature to other women, Genius calls God's deputy fickle and vicious, thus infringing on the dignity of God's servant and perhaps even on that of God. Nature and the other women have in common their sex and all its defects. The first *exemplum* (ll. 16325-28) illustrates womanly fickleness, the second (ll. 16330-33) womanly anger and wickedness. Lines 16330-32 compare a woman's wrath to the cruelty of a snake. This comparison expresses Genius' previous assertion in biblical terms and explains the last three lines of the passage (ll. 16334-36): a woman has so many vices that no one can recount them in poetry. The snake calls to mind temptation and sin.

The strong ties between Nature, personified as a female, and the other members of her sex transform the derogatory description of women into an attack on Nature. Since she enjoys God's grace and is in His service, she is absolutely good. Genius, however, mentions her vices. Virtues and vices being incompatible and opposed, Nature's description is ironic.

As Nature cannot be both virtuous and vicious, either Genius commits heresy in associating Nature with vice,[19] or he is right, assuming Nature and the Christian religion are actually vicious.[20] He still would be right, if Nature's allegiance to God were false.[21] In the first case, Nature's divine qualities would represent reality, contradicted by Genius' lies. The blame would fall on Genius. However, his heresy would contradict his faithfulness to Nature. In the second case, the episode in question would become an attack on religion. Ironic contrast would take place between the favorable connotations of religion according to Christian theology and the unfavorable ones according to Jean de Meun. The third case may impute more to the romance as a whole than the preceding interpretations. On one hand, the assertion that Nature is not God's faithful servant is unlikely, for it contradicts everything that we know about her. It contradicts even Raison. On the other hand, Nature's behavior could support Genius' description. In encouraging Amor, she wrongly defies

19 Knowlton, "The Allegorical Figure Genius", *Classical Philology*, 15 (1920), 384. See also, by the same author, "Genius as an Allegorical Figure", *MLN*, 39 (1924), 89.

20 For example, fifteenth-century theologians saw in the *Rose* a satire on religion. For documents on the debate, see Charles Frederick Ward, *The Epistles in the "Romance of the Rose" and Other Documents in the Debate* (= *Transactions of the Royal Society of Canada*, 8) (Chicago: Univ. of Chicago Press, 1911), as well as note 33 of this chapter.

21 Guy Raynaud de Lage, "*Natura* et *Genius*, chez Jean de Meung et chez Jean Lemaire de Belges", *MA*, 58 (1952), 126.

Raison. Nature's vices, as described by Genius, may account for the hierarchy of powers, in which Nature takes second place to Raison.

The quarrel between Nature and Raison surpasses the limits of episodic irony, for it bears on the whole romance. The episodic irony produced by Genius' discourse directs the reader's attention to irony in Part II as well as in the whole romance. Raison and Nature differ in their position toward Amor. Raison's attacks against the God of Love become more violent in Part II but occur as early as Part I. Hence Nature's alliance with him contradicts the precepts of Raison in both parts of the romance, and the ironic context thus generated includes the whole work.

After showing the cause of her tears, Nature asks Genius to greet her friends, Amor, Venus, and their barons:

> Genius li bien empalez,
> En l'ost au deu d'Amours alez,
> Qui mout de mei servir se peine,
> E tant m'aime, j'en sui certaine,
> Que par son franc cueur debonaire
> Plus se veaut vers mes euvres traire
> Que ne fait fers vers aïmant;
> Dites lui que saluz li mant,
> E a dame Venus m'aime,
> Puis a toute la baronie...

(Eloquent Genius, go to the army of Amor, who takes pains to serve me well and loves me so much, I am sure, that, because of his noble amiable heart, he wants to draw close to my works more than iron to a magnet. Tell him that I send greetings to him and Lady Venus, my friend, as well as to all their baronage.)

Nature supports Amor because he encourages procreation of the species. Although, like Nature, Raison described physical love as a possible form of divine love, she considered Amor an enemy. So the conflict between Nature and Raison originates not in their views on natural love, but in their attitude toward Amor. Whereas to Raison he represents lust, Nature sees in him virtuous physical love. For Raison he is the devil — God's enemy. According to Nature he is God's friend and hers. Amor thus underlines the medieval dilemma of natural love: for encouraging the same action, he is considered both virtuous and sinful. While Nature and Raison have different functions and may stress different aspects of the Christian faith, they should accept the same hierarchy of values. Under God's guidance, what seems good to one must seem good to the other. However, their differing opinions on Amor show that he is both an ally and an enemy of God. Since alliance and enmity between the same parties in the same circumstances are incompatible opposites, the *conflictus* of

Nature and Raison produces irony, which underlines the dilemma of virtuous natural love and *cupiditas*.

Since according to medieval philosophers — Augustine among them — anything to do with the body is suspect, for the body often involves the lower nature of man, the God of Love could represent an elevation of what should be merely a natural process. He elaborates procreation into a ritual which diverts man from Raison. She opposes sexual love, essentially sensual and hence not of the higher nature of man. While Guillaume implies that sensuality can be elevated, Raison denies it. Thus the ironic contrast between the higher and the lower nature of man reinforces that between virtue and vice.

Nature and Raison cannot both be right about the God of Love. Raison probably offered more credibility to the medieval reader, for she conformed more readily to Christian precepts and the narrative context treats her more seriously than it does Nature. Denigrated by Genius, contradicting Raison, a Christian Nature would break a pattern universally accepted by the Christian world.

Some readers would take the opposite viewpoint. Raison is under constant attack from Amor and his barons as well as from the Lover. She could appear as an obstacle in conquering the Rosebud. Although this interpretation is equally valid on the literal level, it is unlikely on the allegorical one. Raison is a character in the romance, but as God's daughter, she has more power than the other characters. To a Christian audience, she provides the romance with a divine meaning and represents the norm.

3. IRONIC DISCREPANCIES BETWEEN *ALLEGORIA* AND *LITTERA* AND AMONG VARIOUS EXPRESSIONS OF *LITTERA*

This section will treat irony resulting from the violation of the relation between *allegoria* and *littera*. According to medieval theology, *allegoria* gives *littera* a higher meaning, or conversely, *littera* represents *allegoria*. However, Guillaume and Jean often destroy the parallelism between the allegorical levels by stressing differences rather than similarities. Conditioned by the allegorical techniques of his time and by the context of the romance, the medieval reader tends to think of *littera* and *allegoria* in the same terms. When the terms are opposed, the formula becomes impossible and the system ironic.[22]

[22] See Ellen Douglas Leyburn, *Satiric Allegory: Mirror of Man* (= *Yale Studies in English*, 130) (New Haven: Yale Univ. Press, 1956).

In a work as complex as the *Rose*, a word on allegory is necessary before attempting any study of irony related to it. Allegorization, which generates the ironic contrast between *caritas* and *cupiditas* and between *cupiditas* and virtuous natural love, differs from allegory, although both forms of representation are found in the *Rose*. Allegory as a genre stems from various rhetorical devices, especially personification. The personified abstractions become the only characters of the story, with the exception of the author or his persona (Jackson, "Allegory", 164). The brief summary of the *Rose*, provided earlier in this chapter, and a look at the names of characters clearly show the use of allegory as a genre. Such characters are Amor, Astenance Contrainte, Avarice, Bel Acueil, Biautez, Bien Celer, Chastée, Dangier, Deduit, Deliz, Douz Parler, Douz Penser, Faus Semblanz, Felonie, Fole Largece, Franchise, Haïne, Honte, Humilitez, Jalousie, Nature, Oiseuse, Papelardie, Raison, Richece, Tristece, Vieillece, Vilanie, Ypocrisie.

Allegorization is common practice in medieval literature and consists of interpreting one context in terms of another, usually of Christian revelation (Appendix II). While, as already shown, the story consists largely of personifications of abstractions, it has a counterpart in the Christian domain as well. Similar combinations also appear in Prudentius' *Psychomachia*, the earliest such work which survives, Boethius' *De Consolatione Philosophiae*, and Alanus' *De Planctu Naturae*. Although it is a pure allegory, the *Psychomachia* can also be viewed as an allegorization of the Old Testament, for Prudentius, in his prologue, describes Abraham as a prefiguration of Christ, and Abraham's struggle against the enemies of Israel as the combat between Christian virtues and vices. All characters in the *Psychomachia*, whose names are grammatically feminine, are abstractions and all are female, because of the tradition of feminine virtues and vices and because of feminine advisers such as Diotima in the *Symposium*. Although the characters in the *Psychomachia* are not exactly the same as the cardinal virtues and vices in later works, there is great resemblance (Jackson, "Allegory", 164-165).[23] *De Consolatione* and *De Planctu* not only personify abstractions but also attribute Christian values to them. Allegorization is all the more striking since Lady Natura is sometimes a pagan deity.[24]

[23] See Morton W. Bloomfield, *The Seven Deadly Sins: An Introduction to the History of a Religious Concept, with Special Reference to the Medieval English Literature* (1952; rpt. Michigan: Michigan State Univ. Press, 1967).

[24] I have used the following editions: Prudentius, *Psychomachia*, ed. and trans. H. J. Thomson, Loeb Class. Library (Cambridge, Mass.: Harvard Univ. Press, 1949-1952; rpt. 1961-1969), I, 274-283; Anicius Manlius Severinus Boethius, *Philosophiae Consola-*

Allegorization in the *Rose*, though less continuous than allegory, occurs frequently enough to insure perception by the reader. A theologian could consider the romance as the secular expression of Christian reality. To a courtier, at least as we know him from other medieval romances, love would acquire additional dignity through treatment in Christian terms. Regardless of the reader's individual tendencies, Guillaume and Jean refer time and again to the objects and characters of their romance according to both earthly and religious values. The authors establish parallel levels of reference — literal and allegorical.

The Rosebud, for example, has rich secular and religious traditions. It is the flower of Venus for the Romans, and a symbol of martyrdom for Christians. It may stand for beauty and virginity.[25] The garden where it grows originates in the combination of the same traditions and stands for the *locus amoenus* according to one, and for Paradise, according to the other (Appendix III).

The description of the birds in the Garden of Deduit again superimposes secular and Christian values:

Onc mais ne fu nus leus si riches
D'arbres ne d'oisillons chantanz,
Qu'il i avoit d'oisiaus trois tanz
Qu'en tot le reiaume de France.
Mout estoit bele l'acordance
De lor piteus chant a oïr;
Toz li monz s'en doit esjoïr.

(No place has ever been so rich in trees or in singing birds: the birds were three

---

tio, ed. Ludwig Bieler (= *Corpvs Christianorum, Series Latina*, 94); Alanus de Insulis, *Liber de Planctu Naturae*, in *Opera Omnia* (= *PL*, 210) (Paris: J.-P. Migne, 1855); Douglas M. Moffat, trans. *The Complaint of Nature*, by Alain de Lille (= *Yale Studies in English*, 36) (New York: Henry Holt, 1908). See also Pierre Courcelle, "*La Consolation de Philosophie*" *dans la tradition littéraire: Antécédents et postérité de Boèce* (Paris: Etudes augustiniennes, 1967).

[25] George [Wells] Ferguson, *Signs and Symbols in Christian Art*, 2nd edition (New York: Oxford Univ. Press, 1955), 47-48 ("Rose"). See also Félix Guillon, *Etude historique et biographique sur Guillaume de Lorris, auteur du "Roman de la Rose" d'après documents inédits & révision critique des textes des auteurs* (Orléans: H. Herluison and Paris: Dumoulin, 1881), 122-123; Charles Joret, *Les Plantes dans l'antiquité et au moyen âge: Histoire, usage et symbolisme*, 2 vols. (Paris: Emile Bouillon, 1897-1904) and "La Légende de la rose au moyen âge chez les nations romanes et germaniques", in *Etudes romanes dédiées à Gaston Paris... par ses élèves français et ses élèves étrangers des pays de langue française* (Paris: Emile Bouillon, 1891), 283 and 290-291. The most complete work on the subject is, to my knowledge, Joret's *La Rose dans l'antiquité et au moyen âge* (Paris: Bouillon, 1892), partic. 45, 50-52, 60, 231, 235, 237-238, 240, 307-308.

times more numerous than in the whole kingdom of France. The harmony of their sweet song, which everybody must enjoy, was beautiful to hear.)

"Piteux" (l. 485) means not only "sweet", but also "pious" and "merciful". The song "piteux... a oïr" may therefore indicate religious piety. Moreover, Guillaume the Lover compares the birds to angels (l. 664):

Trop par faisoient bel servise
Cil oisel que je vos devise.
Il chantoient un chant itel
Con fussent ange esperitel;
E bien sachiez, quant je l'oï,
Mout durement m'en esjoï;
Qu'onc mais si douce melodie
Ne fu d'ome mortel oïe.

(The birds which I describe to you performed a beautiful service. They sang like spiritual angels... Know well that when I heard their song, I heartily rejoiced. Never before had a mortal man heard such a sweet melody.)

"Servise" (ll. 661) describes not only feudal and amorous practice, but also religious services. The fact that no mortal ever heard such a sweet melody (ll. 667-68) brings out, on one hand the exquisiteness of the birds' song, on the other their belonging to an immortal world.

As the Lover enters the Garden of Deduit, its beauty makes him compare it to Paradise:[26]

Lors entrai, senz plus dire mot,
Par l'uis que Oiseuse overt m'ot,
Ou vergier, et quant je fui enz,
Je fui liez e bauz e joianz;
E sachiez que je cuidai estre
Por voir en parevis terrestre;
Tant estoit li leus delitables
Qu'il sembloit estre esperitables;
Car, si come lors m'iert avis,
Il ne fait en nul parevis
Si bon estre come il faisoit
Ou vergier qui tant me plaisoit.

(Then, without saying another word, I came into the garden through the door that Oiseuse had opened for me. Once inside, I felt full of joy and I truly thought I was in Earthly Paradise. The place was so delightful that it seemed spiritual. For, as it then seemed to me, no Paradise is so pleasant as the garden that I liked so much.)

[26] Cf. Robert Will, "Le Climat religieux de l'Hortus deliciarum d'Herrade de Landsberg", in *Recherches théologiques par les professeurs de la Faculté de théologie protestante de l'Université de Strasbourg, vol. II* (Paris: Félix Alcan, 1937), 122-166 [522-566].

The repetition of "parevis" (ll. 636 and 640) and the use of "esperitables" (l. 638) in relation to the garden indicate a religious vocabulary applied to a secular reality. The comparison between the Garden of Deduit and Paradise consists first of equating them (ll. 635-36), then of asserting the superiority of Deduit (ll. 639-42). The common denominator of the objects compared is pleasure (ll. 633-34, 637-38, 641-42), usually associated with both physical love and Paradise: the former is *littera*, the latter *allegoria*. In the comparison of equality, natural love, though different from *caritas*, does not denigrate Paradise and could appear as an illustration of the love of God. The comparison of superiority, however, surprises the reader. Although allegorization tolerates and uses earthly values, they are invariably inferior to the religious reality that they represent.[27] Yet this passage reverses the expected set of values. What is usually inferior becomes superior, and the superior in turn becomes inferior. The ironic context results from the repeated contrast between expectation and assertion — i.e., between opposite and incompatible values. Since the action of the *Rose* takes place in the Garden of Deduit, the ironic value of the garden becomes an ironic frame for the whole work.

As we have gathered from irony of words in the description of the garden, allegorization can bring out not only the common characteristics of supervening levels, but also their differences. Emphasis on differences and reinforcement of the preceding ironic context clearly come out in the episodes of the Fountain of Narcisus. This fountain first appears in Guillaume de Lorris. The Lover walks in the beautiful garden which he previously compared to Paradise and sees a fountain where Narcisus died for having seen himself in its waters:

En un trop bel leu arivai
Au derrenier, ou je trovai
Une fontaine soz un pin;
Mais puis Charle ne puis Pepin
Ne fu ausi biaus pins veüz;
E si estoit si haut creüz
Qu'ou vergier n'ot nul plus haut arbre.
Dedenz une pierre de marbre
Ot Nature par grant maistrise
Soz le pin la fontaine assise;

[27] Mircea Eliade, in his *The Sacred and Profane: The Nature of Religion*, trans. Willard R. Trask (= *Harvest*, *HB*, 144) (1957; New York: Harcourt, Brace & World, 1959), 10, stresses the difference between earthly and religious values: "The first possible definition of the sacred is that it is *the opposite of the profane*."

Si ot dedenz la pierre escrites,
Ou bort amont, letres petites,
Qui disoient qu'illuec desus
Se mori li biaus Narcisus.

(Finally, I arrived in a very beautiful place where I found a fountain under a pine. Such a beautiful pine had not been seen ever since Charles or Pepin. Nature had skillfully placed the fountain in a marble basin near the tree. On the upper edge of the basin, she wrote in small letters that the handsome Narcisus had died above there.)

Despite this favorable description of the fountain (ll. 1425, 1432-34), Genius, in Part II of the *Rose*, opposes it to the true Fountain in Paradise, and the Garden of Deduit to Paradise itself. Because of its length (ll. 20267-668), I will not quote Genius' comparison in full. Genius promises to reward the barons with Paradise, if they obey Nature's command. He previously showed the advantage of Paradise and its fountain, as compared to the Garden of Deduit and the Fountain of Narcisus. The difference between the gardens is like that between truth and fable (ll. 20287-88). Narcisus died for his foolishness. On the contrary, the Fountain in Paradise, in which fools do not believe (ll. 20525-26), gives life (l. 20521):

... qui dou bel jardin carré,
Clos au petit guichet barré,
Ou cil amanz vit la querole
Ou Deduiz o ses genz querole,
A ce beau parc que je devise,
Tant par est beaus a grant devise,
Faire voudrait comparaison,
Il ferait trop grant mespreison
S'il ne la fait tel ou semblable
Come il ferait de veir a fable...
....
"Ci cueurt la fontaine de vie
Par desouz l'olive foillie
Qui porte le fruit de salu."
Queus fu li pins qui l'a valu?
Si vous di qu'en cete fontaine,
Ce creront fole gent a peine...[28]

(Whoever would compare the beautiful square garden with a small locked gate, where the Lover saw Deduit and his people dance, to the beautiful park that I describe (it is as beautiful as can be imagined), would do great injustice if he did not make the comparison analogous to that between truth and fable...
....

[28] Frederick Goldin, *The Mirror of Narcissus in the Love Lyric* (Ithaca, N.Y.: Cornell Univ. Press, 1967), 55, 60-61, 63; Frappier, "Variations sur le thème du miroir, de Bernard de Ventadour à Maurice Scève", *CAIEF*, 11 (1959), 134-158.

"Here, under the leafy olive tree, which bears the fruit of salvation, flows the Fountain of Life." What pine has ever equaled its value? I am telling you that fools will hardly believe in this fountain.)

While Deduit's fountain caused Narcisus' death, Paradise possesses the Fountain of Life. The olive tree has various connotations, peace among them. In Genius' discourse, this tree also reaffirms life. According to the Bible (*Gen.*, VIII, 6-13), Noah released a dove from his ark. The dove found no place to settle and came back. Seven days later, he again released the dove, which this time came with a newly plucked olive leaf in its beak. Then Noah understood that the water had subsided. The olive is thus linked to life, to the salvation of Noah and of all beings. The fruit of salvation, which, according to Genius, grows above the Fountain of Life, contrasts with the fruit of temptation in the Garden of Eden — i.e., the Garden of Deduit.

Whereas the Lover insisted on the common ground between the garden and Paradise, Genius insists on their differences. By his association with God, Genius' description of the Garden commands more credibility than the Lover's. Despite the narrator's assertion, the Garden of Deduit is inferior to the Garden of Paradise. The irony resulting from Genius' comparison of the gardens reinforces the incongruity of considering superior that which is actually inferior. There is additional irony as Genius suggests that the Garden of Deduit is sinful, on one hand, and that the Lover should be helped to take full advantage of it, on the other.

The philosophical basis of the Lover's and Genius' views is to be found in Plato's "this-worldliness" and "otherworldliness", conflicting concepts which Lovejoy brilliantly traced throughout Western intellectual history. His explanations may help us understand the double function (reinforcement and negation) of allegory in the *Rose*.[29] "This-worldliness" and

[29] "To be concerned about what will happen to you after death, or to let your thought dwell much upon the joys which you hope will then await you, may obviously be the most extreme form of this-worldliness; and it is essentially such that life is conceived, not as profoundly different in kind from this, but only as more of the same sort of thing, a prolongation of the mode of being which we know in the world of change and sense and plurality and social fellowship, with merely the omission of the trivial or painful features of terrestrial existence...

By 'otherworldliness,' ... I mean the belief that both the genuinely 'real' and the truly good are radically antithetic in their essential characteristics to anything to be found in man's natural life, in the ordinary course of human experience, however normal, however intelligent, and however fortunate. The world we now and here know — various, mutable, a perpetual flux of states and relation of things, or an ever-shifting phantasmagoria of thoughts and sensations, each of them lapsing into nonentity in the very moment of its birth — seems to the otherworldly mind to have no substance in it; the objects of sense and even of empirical scientific knowledge are unstable, contingent, forever "otherworldliness" are particularly pertinent to allegorization, in which some medieval exegetes emphasize the common ground of *littera* and *allegoria*, while others dwell on their differences, even on their opposition. These concepts call to mind the relations between natural love and *caritas*: if their common ground is stressed, the former represents the latter; if their differences stand out, the former contrasts to the latter (Kolb, 120-22; Chydenius, *Symbolism*, 17). If, as is the case in the *Rose*, the two relations supervene, they produce irony.

The most striking example of irony in the *Rose* lies in the description of Amor. He has all the attributes of God as well as those of the devil.[30] The ironic discrepancies in Amor's attributes come out of the narrative context and, even more forcefully, of Raison's speeches and his own.

At the beginning of the romance, Amor seems to reign in the Garden of Deduit, just as God reigns in Paradise. In fact, because of the comparison of the garden to the Garden of Eden, the reader sees in Amor the literal representation of God, and in the love for the Rosebud the expression of *caritas*. Amor often uses religious terms to describe the Lover's subservience. He expects complete obedience from Guillaume and calls any cheating a sin:

Or vueil je, por ce que je t'ains,
De toi estre si bien certains,
E te vueil si a moi lier
Que tu ne me puisses nier
Ne promesse ne covenant,
Ne faire nul desavenant:
Pechiez seroit se tu trichoies,
Qu'il me semble que leiaus soies.

(Now, because I love you, I want to be so much sure of you, and I want to bind you to me so tightly that you could deny me neither promise nor covenant, nor do anything uncalled for. It seems to me that you are loyal, but it would be sinful to cheat.)

The word "pechiez" (l. 1975) gives the whole passage a religious significance in addition to its feudal one. Vassalage, conceived of in military and

---

breaking down logically into more relations of other things which when scrutinized prove equally relative and exclusive." Arthur O. Lovejoy, *The Great Chain of Being: A Study in the History of an Idea* (= *Academic Library, Harper Torchbooks, TB*, 1009) (1936; rpt. New York: Harper & Row, 1960), 24-25.

30 Professor Jackson, in his "The Politics of a Poet: The Archipoeta as Revealed by his Imagery", *Festschrift Kristeller* (in preparation), mentions a similar ironic context based on a mixture of secular and religious imagery. Like Amor in the *Rose*, Barbarossa equates himself to God (27-28).

amorous terms, may also refer to God's covenant with man (l. 1973). Loyalty to Amor (l. 1976) may stand for faith in God and for *caritas*. In that case, Amor's "je t'ains" (l. 1969) calls to mind Christ's love for humanity. Amor establishes a set of values ranging from virtue to sin. He associates loyalty to himself with virtue, and disloyalty with sin. The narrative context and Raison will subsequently reverse those values.

Amor further acts like God by giving the Lover ten commandments. They are formulated in Part I of the romance (ll. 2077-580) and repeated in Part II (ll. 10403-12). The Lover should obey them day and night (ll. 2039-42), if he wants his master to heal the wounds and pains of love (ll. 1777-81 and 2033-37):

> … je sai bien par quel poison
> Tu seras traiz a guerison.
> Se tu te tiens en leiauté,
> Je te donrai tel dëauté
> Qui de tes plaies te garra;
> Mais, par mon chief, or i parra
> Se tu de bon cuer serviras,
> E coment tu acompliras
> Nuit e jor les comandemenz
> Que je comant as fins amanz.

(I know well what potion will heal you. If you remain loyal, I will give you a marsh mallow ointment which will heal your wounds. But, by my head, I will now see whether you will sincerely serve me and how you will fulfill night and day the commandments that I give pure lovers.)

In Part II, Amor requests the Lover to repeat the commandments. Unlike Part I, where the commandments are too intricate to divide, Jean de Meun presents them as ten separate ideas and so brings out the biblical parallel:

> … [1] Vilenie
> Dei foïr; [2] e que ne mesdie;
> [3] Saluz dei tost doner e rendre;
> [4] A dire ordure ne dei tendre;
> [5] A toutes fames enourer
> M'esteut en touz tenz labourer;
> [6] Orgueil fuie; [7] cointes me tiegne,
> [8] Jolis e renveisiez deviegne;
> [9] A larges estre m'abandoigne;
> [10] En un seul leu tout mon cueur doigne.
> [The numbers in brackets are mine].

(I must run away from villainy. I must not slander. I must quickly give and answer greetings. I must not tend to speak filth. I must always work at honoring all women, avoid pride, be elegant, become gay and joyous, indulge in a generous existence, give my heart in only one place.)

Amor here plays the part of a confessor. Under Raison's influence, the Lover sinned by contemplating treason. After Raison's first appearance and her condemnation of Amor and Oiseuse, the Lover mortified himself (ll. 4131-33), blamed his guides in love (ll. 4133-46) and desired to repent (l. 4154):

> … fis grant folie e grant rage,
> Quant au deu d'Amours fis omage.
> Dame Oiseuse le me fist faire:
> Honi seit li e son afaire,
> Qui me fist ou joli vergier
> Par ma priere herbergier!
> Car s'ele eüst nul bien seü,
> El ne m'eüst onques creü:
> L'en ne deit pas creire fol ome
> De la value d'une pome;
> Blasmer le deit l'en e reprendre
> Ainz qu'en li laist folie emprendre;
> E je fui fos e el me crut.
> Onques par li biens ne me crut;
> El m'acompli trop mon vouleir,
> Si m'en esteut plaindre e douleir.
> Bien le m'avait Raison noté;
> Tenir m'en puis pour rassoté
> Quant des lors d'amer ne recrui
> E le conseil Raison ne crui.
> Dreit ot Raison de mei blasmer,
> Quant onques m'entremis d'amer;
> Trop griés maus m'en couvient sentir.
> Je m'en vueil, ce crei repentir.

(I showed great folly and madness when I gave homage to the god Amor. Lady Oiseuse made me do it. May she who, responding to my prayer, made me stay in the joyous garden, be disgraced, together with her business! If she had known anything good, she would not have believed me. A madman should command less belief than an apple's worth. He should be criticized and reprimanded rather than allowed to commit madness. But I was mad, and she believed me. She was no good to me. She fulfilled my will too readily, and, as a consequence, I must complain and suffer. Raison justly warned me. I can consider myself mad for not giving up love and for not taking Raison's advice.

Raison is right to reproach me for involving myself in love. It is fitting for me to feel grievous sorrow. I think I will repent.)

Repentance from love equates Amor with sin. Disloyalty to him is true faith, while loyalty is heresy. Although this equation is true according to Raison's values (ll. 4147-53), it is the reverse of Amor's precepts. According to those precepts, the Lover behaved badly (l. 10338) in foresaking his old master (ll. 10329-31), complaining about him and Oiseuse (ll. 10331-32), and listening to Raison (l. 10337). Amor asks the Lover to recite the ten commandments in lieu of confession:

10396 … en leu de confiteor,
Vueil, ainz que tu vers mei t'acordes,
Que touz mes comanz me recordes…

(Instead of a confiteor, I want you to recall all my commandments before we are reconciled.)

As Moses brought the ten commandments to the Jews, so the Lover will bring Amor's commandments to mortals. We know that he relates his dream at the command of Amor:

Or vueil cel songe rimeier,
32 Por voz cuers plus faire esgaier,
Qu'Amors le me prie e comande.... [:]
....
10548 [—] … pour ma grace deservir,
Deit il comencier le romant
Ou seront mis tuit mi comant…

(Now I want to put that dream in verse, in order to make your hearts rejoice, as Amor asks and commands… [:]
....
[—] In order to deserve my favor, he must begin the romance where all my commands will be included…)

Because of its strong ties with the Bible, the whole love story would appear as a literal expression of *caritas*. Natural love is virtuous, according to the set of values established by Amor and the narrative context.

However, neither Guillaume nor Jean clearly asserts that Amor represents God. In fact, despite Amor's association with God, the romance often attributes vices to the God of Love. Moreover, Oiseuse is Amor's strongest ally. When he gathers his vassals in order to attack the castle, she carries the largest banner ("Dame Oiseuse, la jardiniere, / I vint o la plus grant baniere…", ll. 10449-50). At the beginning of the romance, she admits the Lover to the Garden. She is not only extremely beautiful but also powerful in the Garden of Deduit (l. 584):

"Je me faz," ce dist ele, "Oiseuse
Apeler a mes connoissanz.

Riche fame sui e poissanz.
S'ai d'une chose mout bon tens,
Car a nule rien je n'entens
Qu'a moi joer e solacier,
E a moi pignier e trecier."

("My acquaintances call me Oiseuse," she said. "I am a rich and powerful woman. And I am very happy, for I have no other purpose than to enjoy and please myself, to comb and braid my hair.")

Because of her exclusive preoccupation with herself, Oiseuse "represents the leisure necessary for a courtly lover" (Gunn, *Mirror*, 105). She also appears in the religious allegorical context as a personification of *acedia*, the sin of sloth. *Otiositas* is a form of *acedia*,[31] which in turn "is by definition a mortal sin, since it opposes the virtue of *caritas* and its special aspect of spiritual joy" (Wenzel, 50). Oiseuse as a doorkeeper of Paradise instead of "some figure of the moral stature of St. Peter",[32] replaces expected virtue with vice. Her power thus resembles that of Faus Semblant and his parents, who are influential despite God. As an ally of Amor, she brings the god to her own level. The context thus provides an *analogia antithetica*, according to which the Garden of Deduit is simultaneously Paradise and Hell and Amor is both God and the devil. The various superpositions of virtue and vice create ironic contexts throughout the *Rose*.

Raison corroborates the denigration of Amor in the context of *otiositas*, by calling him "deable" and "maufé". She condemns Amor and Oiseuse from her first words in Part I. The Lover was wrong to become involved with them:

Biaus amis, folie e enfance
T'ont mis en poine e en esmai;
Mar veïs le bel tens de mai
Qui fist ton cuer trop esgaier;
Mar t'alas onques ombreier

[31] "Another innovation in the offspring of *acedia*, and a much more successful one, was made by Peraldus, who established sixteen 'vices belonging to *accidia*': *tepiditas, mollities, somnolentia, otiositas, dilatio, tarditas, negligentia, inconsummatio, remissio, dissolutio, incuria, ignavia, indevotio, tristitia in divino servito, taedium vitae, desperatio*." Siegfried Wenzel, *The Sin of Sloth: Acedia in Medieval Thought and Literature* (1960; rpt. Chapel Hill: Univ. of North Carolina Press, 1967), 79. See also p. 229, n. 72. Wenzel mentions Oiseuse on 122-123. Cf. Francesco Petrarca, *Il "De Otio Religioso"*, ed. Giuseppe Rotondi (= *Studi e testi*, 195) (Vatican: Biblioteca apostolica vaticana, 1958).

[32] Paul Piehler, *The Visionary Landscape: A Study in Medieval Allegory* (Montreal: McGill-Queen's Univ. Press, 1971), 102.

Ou vergier don Oiseuse porte
La clef don el t'ovri la porte;
Fos est qui s'acointe d'Oiseuse:
S'acointance est trop perilleuse.
El t'a traï deceü;
Amor ne t'eüst ja veü
S'Oiseuse ne t'eüst conduit
Ou bel bergier qui est Deduit.

(Handsome friend, madness and childishness brought you pain and anguish. In an evil hour you saw the beautiful May weather which made your heart rejoice too much. In an evil hour you went to shelter yourself in the shadow of the garden of which Oiseuse carries the key with which she opened the gate. Whoever befriends Oiseuse is mad: her friendship is too dangerous. She betrayed you. Amor would never have seen you if Oiseuse had not led you into Deduit's beautiful garden.)

Raison associates Oiseuse with the beautiful Garden of Deduit in May. The recurrence of this *locus amoenus* corresponds to the repetition of "mar" (ll. 3000 and 3002), which condemns love and, by implication, Amor.

The condemnation produces discrepancies on both levels of allegorization. Sinful love contradicts its previous image in the story and its favorable connotations in *allegoria*. On one hand, natural love is no longer virtuous, as we were led to believe, but sinful. The ironic contrast takes place between two kinds of natural love. On the other hand, sinful natural love contrasts to *caritas* which, due to the relation of *littera* to *allegoria*, it presumably represents. *Caritas* emerged from the description of Amor and the garden in paradisiac terms. Although *littera* represents *allegoria*, their meanings are opposed: the former describes *cupiditas*, the latter *caritas*. By the equation of the two levels, *caritas* and *cupiditas* would be synonymous, which is theologically impossible. So allegorization generates irony by equating virtue and sin.

The ambiguity of the ironic context could be interpreted in various ways. Theologians and Christians in general would accept Raison's set of values and perceive those of Amor as heretical. An atheist or a believer in *fin'amor* would tend to believe in Amor and reject Raison. The narrative context accommodates both interpretations, for it describes Amor and Raison as virtuous as well as sinful. The fifteenth century offered such representative readings of the romance: some readers saw in it criticism of women, others religious satire, others still an act of love.[33] Most

[33] For the fifteenth-century debate on the *Rose*, I have consulted the following works: Texts: Ward, *Epistles*; Christine de Pisan, "L'Epistre au dieu d'amours", in *Oeuvres poétiques*, ed. Maurice Roy, SATF, 22 (1886-1896; rpt. New York: Johnson, 1965),

interpretations center on love or religion because of ironic allegorization, which uses precisely those two themes as *littera* and *allegoria*. The *Rose* represents on a wide scale the medieval definition of *ironia*: an allegory whose terms are not only different, but also opposed.

The ironic context bears on the whole romance. Although not evident in Part I, the *conflictus* between Raison and Nature has its roots in Guillaume's work, where Raison condemns Amor for the first time. This ironic *conflictus* may well be Jean's invention. Both authors nevertheless concur on allegorical irony. Allegorization appears in both parts of the *Rose* and is often ironic. While *littera* relates Amor to *fin'amor*, *allegoria* often compares him to God. In the final analysis, irony in the *Rose* could be described as a gigantic debate between courtly and religious views on love. While viewpoints may differ throughout the romance depending on the characters involved or on the reader's interpretation, one term of the conflict is rarely seen without the other. Nobody can say for sure who wins the argument, but no one can deny that both adversaries put up a good fight.

II, 1-27; Jean Gerson, *Oeuvres complètes*, ed. Mgr. Glorieux (Paris: Desclée, 1960-1966), II, 65-70; Langlois, ed. "Le Traité de Gerson contre le *Roman de la Rose*", *Romania*, 45 (1918-1919), 23-48.

Secondary sources: Fleming, "The Moral Reputation of the *Roman de la Rose* before 1400", *RPh*, 18 (1964-1965), 430-435; Blanche H. Dow, *The Varying Attitude Toward Women in French Literature of the Fifteenth Century: The Opening Years* (New York: Publications of the Institute of French Studies, 1936), 128-222; André Combes, *Jean de Montreuil et le chancelier Gerson: Contribution à l'histoire des rapports de l'humanisme et de la théologie en France au début du XVe siècle* (= *Etudes de philosophie médiévale*, 32) (Paris: Vrin, 1942), 107-111, 113-115, 123-125, 129-131, 145-149, 151-155; Michel Defourny, "*Le Roman de la Rose* à travers l'histoire et la philosophie", *MRom*, 17 (1967), 54; Henri Jadart, *Jean Gerson* (*1363-1429*)*: Recherches sur son origine, son village natal et sa famille* (Reims: Deligne & Renart, 1881); A.-L. Masson, *Jean Gerson: Sa Vie, son temps, ses oeuvres* (Lejon: Emmanuel Vitte, 1894), 168-176; John B. Morrall, *Gerson and the Great Schism* (Manchester: Univ. Press, 1960), 12 and 17; Arthur Piaget, "Chronologie des epistres sur le *Roman de la Rose*", in *Etudes ... Gaston Paris*, 113-120.

CONCLUSION

This study has shown that irony in medieval literature is perceptible on various levels – word, episode, overall structure – and that our modern view of irony can be applied to any text, ancient or modern, regardless of author, audience or century. Irony as it is understood in nineteenth- and twentieth-century literary criticism attained degrees of subtlety absent from medieval treatises. However, the criteria to which it can be reduced find numerous convergent expressions in all periods.

This study has applied the modern and more complex criteria of irony to medieval contexts of varying size and extent. The criteria that underline irony of words, the only one mentioned in medieval treatises, also bring out episodic irony and irony as a structure in wholly ironic works. The works discussed illustrate, besides several ironic contexts, various genres and themes popular throughout the Middle Ages. Epic, romance, drama and poetry, concerning love, adventure, marriage, religion, war, friendship and enmity from the twelfth through the fifteenth century, exhibited irony. My purpose was not to enumerate all medieval ironic works, but to show that virtually any type of medieval work may be ironic on one level or another.

The size and extent of the ironic contexts that I have chosen are arbitrary. Although irony sometimes clearly belongs to a particular level, it often belongs to several. Moreover, in many instances irony on a smaller scale reflects wider patterns. Contexts thus linked sometimes form clusters which increase the reader's perception of the ironic structure of the work. Since the levels are often closely associated, it becomes more important to stress their similarity than their differences, although the perspective of contexts ranging from two words to a whole cycle is of no minor importance. While precise distinctions in size and extent are sometimes impossible to establish, we perceive a scale of contexts which may extend beyond literature and point to the extraordinary breadth of the concept of irony.

Several works stress ironic aspects important to the medieval audience. The whole concept of irony relates to this- and otherworldliness, which constitute a basic dichotomy in the views of the universe and which Lovejoy traced from Plato throughout the centuries. According to the first view, everything belongs to one Great Chain of Being. According to the second view, the nonsubstantiality of man's natural life is basically different from, and sometimes opposed to, the real and truly good nature of things. If these same views apply to the same system, they produce irony.

Extensive remarks on the relation between literature and other fields would go beyond my competence.[1] Nevertheless, I suspect that a thorough exploration of the implications of irony in all times and places would reveal it as a mode of thought and ultimately as an aspect of life.

[1] For such explorations in religion and history, see René Pintard, *Le Libertinage érudit dans la première moitié du XVIIe siècle* (Paris: Boivin, 1943), I, 121, 125-126; Reinhold Niebuhr, *The Irony of American History* (New York: Charles Scribner's Sons, 1954), pp. vii-viii, 1-16 and 151-174.

APPENDIX I: DEFINITIONS OF RHETORICAL IRONY

The words hardly vary from one definition to another. Here are a few taken from Latin grammarians and rhetoricians.

Grammarians. Volume and page references are to Heinrich Keil, ed. *Grammatici latini*, 8 vols. (Leipzig: Teubner, 1857-1864 and Hildesheim: Georg Olms, 1961). Flavius Sosipater Charisius, *Ars Grammaticae*, I, 276:

> "ironia est oratio pronuntiationis gravitate in contrarium deducens sensum verborum...: haec enim sententia, nisi graviter pronuntietur, non negantis erit sed confitentis..".

Diomedes, in *Ars Grammaticae*, I, 462, adds "non vituperantis erit sed laudantis..." See *Commentum Einsidlense in Donati Barbarismum*, VIII, 272; Donatus, *Ars Grammaticae*, IV, 401-402. Pompeius, *Commentum Artis Donati*, V, 310:

> "Ironia est, quotienscumque re vera aliud loquimur, et aliud significamus in verbis..."

Marius Plotius Sacerdos, *Artes Grammaticarum*, VI, 461:

> "Ironia est oratio cum inrisione, pronuntiatio dictionis in contrarium redigens intellectum... haec enim dictio nisi aliter pronuntietur, quam qualitas sua postulat, non erit voluntati dicentis apte positus intellectus."

All these grammarians consider irony a type of allegory. See Hugues de Saint-Victor, *De Grammatica*, ed. Jean Leclerq, *AHDLMA*, 18 (1943), 321; Paul Lehman, "Die *Institutio Oratoria* des Quintilianus im Mittelalter", *Philologus*, 89 (1934), 377; Richard McKeon, "Rhetoric in the Middle Ages", *Speculum*, 17 (1942), 1-32.

Rhetoricians. Page references are to Karl Felix von Halm, *Rhetores latini minores* (Leipzig: Teubner, 1863). Aquila Romanus, *De Figuris Sententiarum et Elocutionis Liber*, 24:

> "εἰρωνεία, simulatio, frequentissima apud oratores figura, ubi aliud verbis significamus aliud re sentimus.

Julius Rufinianus, *De Figuris Sententiarum et Elocutionis Liber*, pp. 28-39:

> "εἰρωνεία elocutiuncula sallustiana commodissime exprimatur, cum aliud in pectore reclusum, aliud in lingua promptum habemus, et sententia enuntiationis in contrarium verbis accipitur..."

See Martianus Capella, *Liber de Arte Rhetorica*, 478. Isidore of Seville, *Originum Libro Secundo capita quae sunt de rhetorica*, 521:

> "Ironia est, cum per simulationem diversum, quam dicit, intellegi cupit. Fit autem, aut cum laudamus eum, quem vituperare volumus, aut vituperamus, quem laudare volumus."

See the Venerable Beda, *Liber de Schematibus et Tropis*, p. 615.

For a useful list of grammarians and rhetoricians, see E. Dekkers and Aemilius A. Gaar, "Grammatici et Rhetores", *Clavis Patrum Latinorum*, 2nd edition (Bruges: C. Breyaert, 1961), 341-346.

According to Oscar Bloch and W. von Wartburg, *Dictionnaire étymologique de la langue française*, 4th edition (Paris: Presses univ. de France, 1964), 346, the term "irony" appears in French in 1370, in Oresme's translation of Aristotle. Oresme defines irony in a note to his translation:

> "Yronie est quant l'en dit une chose par quoi l'en veult donner a entendre le contraire. Si comme parleroit d'un sage homme notoirement et il diroit ainsi: 'il ne scet rien non.' Ou, 'il est plus sage qu'il ne cuide,' ou autre chose semblable."

Nicole Oresme, *Le Livre de Ethiques d'Aristote*, ed. Albert Douglas Menut (New York: G. E. Stechert, 1940), 255. Godefroy describes the meaning of irony in the Middle Ages as a "Raillerie particulière par laquelle on dit le contraire de ce que l'on veut faire entendre..." Frédéric Godefroy, *Dictionnaire de l'ancienne langue française et de tous ses dialectes du IXe au XVe siècle* (1880-1902; rpt. New York: Kraus, 1961), X, 31. See also *Dictionnaire de l'Académie française* (Lyon: Joseph Duplain, 1776), I, 666; Diderot, XIX, 83; Mortier, III, 2424.

APPENDIX II: WORKS ON ALLEGORY

On medieval exegesis, see Henri de Lubac's monumental work *Exégèse médiévale: Les Quatre Sens de l'Ecriture* (= *Théologie*, nos. 41, 42 & 59), 4 vols. (Aubier: Editions Montaigne, 1959-1964). Also helpful are Abraham Bezanker, "An Introduction to the Problem of Allegory in Literary Criticism", Diss., Michigan, 1954; Joseph Bonsirven, *Exégèse rabbinique et exégèse paulinienne*, Bibliothèque de théologie historique (Paris: Beauchesne, 1939), 211 and 351; Harry Caplan, "The Four Senses of Scriptural Interpretation and the Medieval Theory of Preaching", *Speculum*, 4 (1929), 229-290; Chydenius, *The Theory of Medieval Symbolism*, Finska Vetenskapssocieteten (Helsingfors: Academic Bookstore, 1960); Jean Daniélou, *From Shadows to Reality: Studies in the Biblical Typology of the Fathers*, trans. Dom Wulstan Hibberd (London: Burns & Pates, 1960), partic. 22-29; Gerard L. Ellspermann, *The Attitude of the Early Christian Latin Writers toward Pagan Literature and Learning* (= *Catholic Univ. of America Patristic Studies*, 82) (Washington, D. C.: Catholic Univ. of America Press, 1949); Robert Worth Frank, Jr., "The Art of Reading Medieval Personification-Allegory", *ELH*, 20 (1953), 237-250; Edwin Honig, *Dark Conceit: The Making of Allegory*, Boar's Head Book (1959; rpt. Cambridge: Walker-de Berry, 1960), 20-21, 31-33; R. L. P. Milburn, *Early Christian Interpretations of History*, Bampton Lectures of 1952 (London: Adam & Charles Black, 1954), partic. 38-53; Charles Muscatine, "The Emergence of Psychological Allegory in Old French Romance", *PMLA*, 68 (1953), 1179; Jean Pépin, *Mythe et allégorie: Les Origines grecques et les contestations judéo-chrétiennes*, Philosophie de l'esprit (Aubier: Editions Montaigne, 1958); P. C. Spiq, *Esquisse d'une histoire de l'exégèse latine au moyen âge*, Bibliothèque thomiste, 26 (Paris: Vrin, 1944).

On allegory and the *Rose*, see Karl Heisig, "Arabische Astrologie und christliche Apologetik im Rosenroman", *RF*, 71 (1959), 414-419; Gérard Paré, *Le "Roman de la Rose" et la scolastique courtoise* (= *Publications de l'Institut d'études médiévales d'Ottawa*, no. 10) (Paris: Vrin, 1941); Arnold Williams, "Medieval Allegory: An Operational Approach", *Poetic Theory/Poetic Practice: Papers of the Midwest Modern Language Association* (*1968; Ed. Robert Scholes*), 1 (1969), 83.

The following works will also be of service: Rosemond Tuve, *Allegorical Imagery: Some Medieval Books and Their Posterity* (Princeton: Princeton Univ. Press, 1966), 233-283; Don Cameron Allen, *Mysteriously Meant: The Rediscovery of Pagan Symbolism and Allegorical Interpretation in the Renaissance* (Baltimore & London: Johns Hopkins Press, 1970); Ph. Aug. Becker, "Clément Marot und der *Rosenroman*", *GRM*, 4 (1912), 684-687; K. Sneyders de Vogel, "Marot et le *Roman de la Rose*", *Neophil.*, 17 (1931-1932), 269-271; Félix Lecoy, "Une Mention du *Roman de la Rose* au XVIe siècle", *Romania*, 87 (1960), 119-120; Jean Seznec, *La Survivance des dieux antiques: Essai sur le rôle de la tradition mythologique dans l'humanisme et dans l'art de la Renaissance* (= *Studies of the Warburg Institute*, 11) (London: Warburg Institute,

1940); Nicole Zingarelli, "L'*Allegoria* del *Roman de la Rose*", in *Studi dedicati a Francesco Torraca nel XXXVI anniversario della sua laurea* (Naples: Francesco Perrella, 1912), 495-524.

Of secondary interest are: Paul Alphandéry, "L'Evhémérisme et les débuts de l'histoire des religions au moyen âge", *Revue de l'histoire des religions*, 103 (1934), 5-27; John Daniel Cooke, "Euhemerism: A Medieval Interpretation of Classical Paganism", *Speculum*, 2 (1927), 396-410; Gaston Boissier, *La Fin du paganisme: Etude sur les dernières luttes religieuses en Occident au quatrième siècle*, 7th edition, Bibliothèque d'histoire (Paris: Hachette, 1891), II, 203-204; Lester K. Born, "Ovid and Allegory", *Speculum*, 9 (1934), 362-379; M. -M. Davy, *Essai sur la symbolique romane* (*XII*[e] *siècle*), Homo-Sapiens (Paris: Flammarion, 1955), 51-52; Mircea Eliade, *Images et symboles* (Paris: Gallimard, 1952); Gilbert E. A. Grindle, *The Destruction of Paganism in the Roman Empire from Constantine to Justinian* (Oxford: Blackwell, 1892); E[arl] Baldwin Smith, *Architectural Symbolism of Imperial Rome and the Middle Ages* (= *Princeton Monographs in Art and Archaeology*, 30) (Princeton: Princeton Univ. Press, 1956).

APPENDIX III: MEDIEVAL GARDENS

The following titles place the medieval garden in the secular or the religious tradition, or both. The abbreviations in brackets — i.e., [s], [r] and [sr] — indicate the tradition outlined by a particular work.

Medieval authorities: Alanus de Insulis, *Compendiosa in Cantica Canticorum ad Laudem Dei Parae Virginis Mariae Elucidatio*, *PL*, 210, col. 65-67 [r] and *Liber in Distinctionibus Dictionum Theologicalium*, *PL*, 210, col. 890-891 ("*Paradisus*") [r]; Honorius d'Autun, *De Imagine Mundi Libri Tres*, *Opera Omnia* (= *PL*, 172) (Paris: J.-P. Migne, 1854), col. 123 [r] and *Elucidarium sive Dialogus de Summa Lotius Christianae Theologiae* (= *PL*, 172), col. 1117-1118 [r]; Hugues de Saint-Victor, *In Salomonis Ecclesiastem Homiliae XIX* (= *PL*, 175) (Paris: Garnier, 1879), col. 169-170.

Modern authorities: Sir Frank Crisp, *Mediaeval Gardens: 'Flowery Medes' and Other Arrangements of Herbs, Flowers and Shrubs Grown in the Middle Ages, with Some Account of Tudor, Elizabethan and Stuart Gardens*, ed. Catherine Childs Patterson, 2 vols. (London: John Lane the Bodley Head, 1924), I, 30-31 [s], 114 [r]; Paule Demats, "*D'Amoenitas* à *Déduit:* André le Chapelain et Guillaume de Lorris", *Mélanges... Frappier*, I, 217-233 [s]; George D. Economou, "Januarie's Sin Against Nature: The *Merchant's Tale* and the *Roman de la Rose*", *CL*, 17 (1965), 254 [sr]; Stanley Leman Galpin, "Influence of the Mediaeval Christian Visions on Jean de Meun's Notions of Hell", *RR*, 2 (1911), 55 [r]; A. Bartlett Giamatti, *The Earthly Paradise and the Renaissance Epic* (Princeton: Princeton Univ. Press, 1966), 11-13, 33, 62-63, 66, 87, 90-91 [sr]; Adolf Katzenellenbogen, *Allegories of the Virtues and Vices in Medieval Art from Early Christian Times to the Thirteenth Century* (= *Norton Library*, N 243) (1939; rpt. New York: Norton, 1964), 10 [r]; C. S. Lewis, *The Allegory of Love: A Study in Medieval Tradition* (= *Galaxy*, *GB* 17) (1936; rpt. London: Oxford Univ. Press, 1968), 119-120 [sr]; Howard Rollin Patch, *The Other World According to Descriptions in Medieval Literature* (= *Smith College Studies in Modern Languages, New Series*, 1) (Cambridge, Mass.: Harvard Univ. Press, 1950), 134, 136-137 [r]; Paul Piehler, *The Visionary Landscape: A Study in Medieval Allegory* (Montreal: McGill-Queen's Univ. Press, 1971), 77-79, 99 [sr]; D. W. Robertson, Jr., "The Doctrine of Charity in Medieval Literary Gardens", *Speculum*, 26 (1951), 24-29 [r]; F. R. Webber, *Church Symbolism: An Explanation of the More Important Symbols of the Old and New Testament, the Primitive, the Medieval and the Modern Church*, Introd. by Ralph Adams Cram (Cleveland: J. H. Hansen, 1927), 351 ("Garden") [r]; Arnold Williams, *The Common Expositor: An Account of the Commentaries on Genesis, 1527-1633* (Chapel Hill: Univ. of North Carolina Press, 1948), 94-95 [sr].

SELECTED BIBLIOGRAPHY

DEFINITION OF IRONY

1. *Before 1800*

Aquila Romanus, *De Figuris Sententiarum et Elocutionis Liber*. See Halm, 22-37.

Aristotle, *Nichomachean Ethics*, trans. Martin Oswald (= *Library of Liberal Arts*, no. 75) (Indianapolis and New York: Bobbs-Merrill, 1962).

——, *Poetics*. See Else.

Arnauld, Antoine and Pierre Nicole, *La Logique ou l'art de penser contenant, outre les règles communes, plusieurs observations nouvelles, propres à former le jugement*, ed. Pierre Clair and François Girbal, Le Mouvement des idées au XVIIe siècle (Paris: Presses univ. de France, 1965).

Atkins, J. W. H., *Literary Criticism in Antiquity: A Sketch of Its Development, Vol. I*: *Greek* (Gloucester, Mass.: Peter Smith, 1961).

Baldwin, Charles Sears, *Ancient Rhetoric and Poetic Interpreted from Representative Works* (New York: MacMillan, 1924).

Beda, the Venerable, *De Schematis et Tropis Sacrae Scripturae*. In *Opera Omnia*, I (= *Patrologiae Cursus completus... series latina*, vol. 90, ed. J.-P. Migne) (Paris: 1862).

Boileau-Despréaux, Nicolas, *L'Art poétique*, ed. Charles-H. Boudhors, Les Textes français (Paris: Belles Lettres, 1939).

Bornecque, Henri, ed. and trans., *Ad C. Herennium de Ratione Dicendi* (*Rhétorique à Hérennius*), *ouvrage longtemps attribué à Cicéron* (Paris: Garnier, 1932).

Charisius, Flavius Sosipater, *Ars Grammaticae*. See Keil, I, 1-296.

Cicero, *De Oratore*, ed. H. Rackham, Loeb Classical Library, 2 vols. (Cambridge, Mass.: Harvard Univ. Press, 1942).

Cooper, Lane, *An Aristotelian Theory of Comedy with an Adaptation of the Poetics and a Translation of the "Tractatus Coislinianus"* (New York: Harcourt, Brace, 1922).

Cousin, Jean, *Etudes sur Quintilien*, 2 vols. (Paris: Boivin, 1935).

Curtius, Ernst Robert, "Mittelalterliche Literaturtheorien", *Zeitschrift für romanische Philologie*, 62 (1942), 417-491.

Diomedes, *Ars Grammaticae*. See Keil, I, 297-529.

Donatus, *Ars Grammatica*. See Keil, IV, 353-402.

——, *Commentum Einsidlense in Donati Barbarismum*. See Keil, VIII, 267-274.

Draper, John W., "The Theory of the Comic in Eighteenth-Century England", *Journal of English and Germanic Philology*, 37 (1938), 207-223.

Else, Gerald F., ed., *Aristotle's "Poetics": The Argument* (Cambridge, Mass.: Harvard Univ. Press, 1963).

Evrard l'Allemand, *Laborintus*. See Faral, *Les Arts poétiques*, 336-377.

Grant, Mary A., *The Ancient Rhetorical Theories of the Laughable* (= *Univ. of Wisconsin Studies in Language and Literature*, 21) (Madison: Univ. of Wisconsin Press, 1924).

Grosser, Dorothy Evelyn, *Studies in the Influence of the "Rhetorica ad Herennium" and Cicero's "De Inventione"*.

Halm, Karl Felix von, *Rhetores latini minores* (Leipzig: Teubner, 1863).

Harrick, Marvin T., *Comic Theory in the Sixteenth Century* (= *Illinois Studies in Language and Literature*, 34, 1-2) (Urbana: Univ. of Illinois Press, 1950).

Hugues de Saint-Victor, *De Grammatica*. In *Archives d'histoire doctrinale et littéraire du moyen âge*, 18 (1943), 263-322.

Isidore of Seville, *Etymologiae*, ed. Rudolphus Beer (Leiden: A. W. Sijthoff, 1909).

——, *Originum Libro Secundo Capita quae sunt de Rhetorica*. See Halm, 505-522.

Julius Rufinianus, *De Figuris Sententiarum et Elocutionis Liber*. See Halm, 38-62.

Keil, Heinrich, ed., *Grammatici Latini*, 8 vols. (Leipzig: Teubner, 1857-1864; Hildesheim: Georg Olms, 1961).

Kennedy, George, *The Art of Persuasion in Greece* (Princeton: Princeton Univ. Press, 1963).

——, *The Art of Rhetoric in the Roman World (300 B.C. - A.D. 300)* (Princeton: Princeton Univ. Press, 1972).

La Bruyère, Jean, *Oeuvres*, ed. G[ustave] Servois, Les Grands Ecrivains de la France, 3 vols. (Paris: Hachette, 1865-1878).

Lehmann, Paul, "Die *Institutio Oratoria* des Quintilianus im Mittelalter", *Philologus*, 89 (1934), 349-383.

McCall, Marsh H., Jr., *Ancient Rhetorical Theories of Simile and Comparison*, Loeb Classical Monographs (Cambridge, Mass.: Harvard Univ. Press, 1969).

Marrou, Henri-Irénée, *A History of Education in Antiquity*, trans. George Lamb, after *Histoire de l'Education dans l'Antiquité*, 3rd edition (= *Mentor*, *MQ* 552) (New York: New American Library, 1964).

Martianus Capella, *Liber de Arte Rhetorica*. See Halm, 449-492.

Mollard, A., "La Diffusion de l'*Institution oratoire* au XIIe siècle", *Moyen Age*, 44, 3rd series, v (1934), 161-175 and 45, 3rd series, vi (1935), 1-9.

Murphy, James J., ed. and trans., *Three Medieval Rhetorical Arts* (Berkeley: Univ. of California Press, 1971).

Oresme, Nicole, *Le Livre de Ethiques d'Aristote*, ed. Albert Douglas Menut (New York: G. E. Stechert, 1940).

Plato, *Collected Dialogues*, ed. Edith Hamilton and Huntington Cairns (= *Bollingen Series*, 71) (Princeton: Princeton Univ. Press, 1961).

Pompeius, *Commentum Artis Donati*. See Keil, V, 81-312.

Rashdall, Hastings, *The Universities of Europe in the Middle Ages*, new edition, 3 vols. (London: Oxford Univ. Press, 1958).

Sacerdos, Marius Plotius, *Artes Grammaticarum*. See Keil, VI, 415-546.

Voltaire, "Remarques sur Médée", *Commentaires sur Corneille*, 2 vols., in *Oeuvres*, ed. Beuchot, Vols. XXXV-XXXVI (Paris: Lefèvre and Werdet et Lequien, 1829).

Weinberg, Bernard, ed., *Critical Prefaces of the Renaissance* (= *Northwestern Univ. Humanities Series*, vol. 20) (1950; rpt. New York: AMS Press, 1970).

2. *After 1800*

Books

Adams, Joey, *Strictly for Laughs* (New York: Frederick Fell, 1955).

Auerbach, Erich, *Literary Language & Its Public in the Middle Ages*, trans. Ralph Manheim (= *Bollingen Series*, 74) (1958; trans. New York: Pantheon, 1965).

Babbitt, Irving, *Rousseau and Romanticism* (Boston and New York: Houghton Mifflin, 1919).

Bakhtin(e), Mikhaïl M., *Rabelais and His World*, trans. Helene Iswolsky (Cambridge, Mass. and London: MIT Press, 1968).

——, *Problèmes de la poétique de Dostoïevski*, trans. Guy Verret, Slavica (1963; Lausanne: L'Age d'Homme, 1970).

Baudelaire, Charles, *De l'essence du rire et généralement du comique dans les arts plastiques*, in *Oeuvres complètes*, ed. Jacques Crépet (Paris: Louis Conard, 1923), I, 369-396.

Bénichou, Paul, *Morales du grand siècle* (Paris: Gallimard, 1948).

Bergson, Henri, *Le Rire: Essai sur la signification du comique*, 273rd edition, Bibliothèque de philosophie contemporaine (Paris: Presses univ. de France, 1969).

Biller, Gunnar, *Etude sur le style des premiers romans français en vers* (*1150-1175*) (= *Göteborgs Högskolas Arsskrift* 1916, no. IV) (Göteborg: Wettergren and Kerber, 1916).

Boehner, Philotheus, *Medieval Logic: An Outline of Its Development from 1250 to c. 1400* (Chicago: Univ. of Chicago Press, 1952).

Booth, Wayne C., *The Rhetoric of Fiction*, P 267 (Chicago and London: Univ. of Chicago Press, 1961).

Bowen, Barbara C., *The Age of Bluff: Paradox and Ambiguity in Rabelais & Montaigne* (= *Illinois Studies in Language and Literature*, 62) (Urbana: Univ. of Illinois Press, 1972).

Brereton, Geoffrey, *Principles of Tragedy: A Rational Examination of the Tragic Concept in Life and Literature* (Coral Gables: Univ. of Miami Press, 1968).

Brooks, Cleanth, *The Well Wrought Urn: Studies in the Structure of Poetry* (=*Harvest, HB* 11) (New York: Harcourt, Brace, 1947).

Brooks, Cleanth, ed., *Tragic Themes in Western Literature*, Y-25 (New Haven: Yale Univ. Press, 1955).

Bruyne, Edgar de, *Etudes d'esthétique médiévale*, 3 vols. (= *Rijksuniversiteit te Gent. Werken uitgegeven door de Faculteit van de Wijsbegeerte en letteren*, 97-99) (Bruges: De Tempel, 1946).

Burke, Kenneth, *A Grammar of Motives* (New York: Prentice-Hall, 1945).

Cèbe, Jean-Pierre, *La Caricature et la parodie dans le monde romain antique des origines à Juvénal* (= *Bibliothèque des écoles françaises d'Athènes et de Rome*, fasc. 206) (Paris: E. de Boccard, 1966).

Chapiro, Marc, *L'Illusion comique*, Université de Genève, Faculté des lettres, Thèse no. 92 (Paris: Presses univ. de France, 1940).

Coleman, Dorothy Gabe, *Rabelais: A Critical Study in Prose Fiction* (Cambridge, England: Cambridge Univ. Press, 1971).

Cox, Harvey, *The Feast of Fools: A Theological Essay on Festivity and Fantasy* (= *Harper Colophon Books*, CN 212) (1969; rpt. New York: Harper & Row, 1970).

Dyson, A. E., *The Crazy Fabric: Essays in Irony* (London: Macmillan and New York: St. Martin's Press, 1965).

Eastman, Max, *The Sense of Humor* (New York: Charles Scribner's Sons, 1922).

Elliott, Robert, C., *The Power of Satire: Magic, Ritual, Art* (Princeton: Princeton Univ. Press, 1960).

Empson, William, *Seven Types of Ambiguity* (New York: New Directions, 1930).

Enck, John J., Elisabeth T. Forter, Alvin Whitley, eds., *The Comic in Theory and Practice* (New York: Appleton-Century-Crofts, 1960).

Ernst, Fritz, *Die romantische Ironie* (Zürich: Schultess, 1915).

Falk, Eugene H., *Renunciation as a Tragic Focus: A Study of Five Plays*, introd. by Norman J. DeWitt (Minneapolis: Univ. of Minnesota Press, 1954).

Feibleman, James, *In Praise of Comedy: A Study in Its Theory and Practice* (London: Georg Allen & Unwin, 1939).

Felheim, Marvin, ed., *Comedy: Plays, Theory and Criticism*, Harbrace Sourcebooks, ed. David Levin (New York: Harcourt, Brace & World, 1962).

Fischer, David Hackett, *Historians' Fallacies: Toward a Logic of Historical Thought* (= *Harper Torchbooks, TB* 1545) (New York and Evanston: Harper & Row, 1970).

Freud, Sigmund, *Wit and Its Relation to the Unconscious*, in *The Basic Writings of Sigmund Freud*, trans. A. A. Brill (= *Giant*, 39) (New York: Modern Library, 1938), 631-803.

Frye, Northrop, *Anatomy of Criticism: Four Essays* (Princeton: Princeton Univ. Press, 1957).

Gaiffe, Félix, *Le Rire et la scène française*, Bibliothèque de la Revue des cours et conférences (Paris: Boivin, 1931).

Glicksberg, Charles I., *The Ironic Vision in Modern Literature* (The Hague: Martinus Nijhoff, 1969).

Goldmann, Lucien, *Le Dieu caché: Etude sur la vision tragique dans les "Pensées" de Pascal et dans le théâtre de Racine*, Bibliothèque des idées (Paris: Gallimard, 1959).

Goodell, Thomas Dwight, *Athenian Tragedy: A Study in Popular Art* (New Haven: Yale Univ. Press, 1920).

Greig, J. Y. T., *The Psychology of Laughter and Comedy* (New York: Dodd, Mead, 1923).

Gurevitch, Morton, "European Romantic Irony", Diss., Columbia, 1957.

Hathorn, Richmond Y., *Tragedy, Myth, and Mystery* (= *Midland, MB* 92) (Bloomington and London: Indiana Univ. Press, 1962).

Haury, Auguste, *L'Ironie et l'humour chez Cicéron* (Leiden: E. J. Brill, 1955).

Hertzler, Joyce O., *Laughter: A Socio-Scientific Analysis* (Jericho, N. Y.: Exposition Press, 1970).

Highet, Gilbert, *The Anatomy of Satire* (Princeton: Princeton Univ. Press, 1962).

Hodgart, Matthew, *Satire*, World Univ. Library (New York and Toronto: McGraw-Hill, 1969).

Hugues, Peter and David Williams, eds., *The Varied Pattern: Studies in the 18th Century* (= *Publications of the McMaster Univ. Association for 18th-Century Studies*, 1) (Toronto: A. M. Hakkert, 1971).

Jancke, Rudolf, *Das Wesen der Ironie: Eine Strukturanalyse ihrer Erscheinungsformen* (Leipzig: Johann Ambrosius Barth, 1929).

Jankélévitch, Vladimir, *L'Ironie*, Nouvelle Bibliothèque scientifique (Paris: Flammarion, 1964).

Kaiser, Walter, *Praisers of Folly: Erasmus, Rabelais, Shakespeare* (= *Harvard Studies in Comparative Literature*, no. 25) (Cambridge, Mass.: Harvard Univ. Press, 1963).

Kernan, Alvin B., *The Cankered Muse: Satire of the English Renaissance* (= *Yale Studies in English*, 142) (New Haven: Yale Univ. Press, 1959).

Kernan, Alvin B., ed., *Modern Satire*, Harbrace Sourcebooks, ed. David Levin (New York: Harcourt, Brace & World, 1962).

Kierkegaard, Søren, *Concluding Unscientific Postscript*, trans. David F. Swenson and Walter Lowrle (Princeton: Princeton Univ. Press, 1941).

——, *The Concept of Irony, with Constant Reference to Socrates*, trans. and ed. Lee M. Capel (= *Midland*, MB 111) (Bloomington and London: Indiana Univ. Press, 1965).

Kitto, H. D. F., *Greek Tragedy*, 2nd edition (London: Methuen, 1950).

——, *Form and Meaning in Drama*, 2nd edition (London: Methuen, 1964).

Knox, Norman, *The Word "Irony" and Its Context, 1500-1755* (Durham: Duke Univ. Press, 1961).

Koestler, Arthur, *Insight and Outlook: An Inquiry into the Common Foundations of Science, Art and Social Ethics* (New York: Macmillan, 1949).

Lalo, Charles, *Esthétique du rire*, Bibliothèque de philosophie scientifique (Paris: Flammarion, 1949).

Lenient, C[harles] [Félix], *La Satire en France au moyen âge* (Paris: Hachette, 1859).

Levin, Harry, ed., *Veins of Humor* (= *Harvard English Studies*, 3) (Cambridge, Mass.: Harvard Univ. Press, 1972).

Lipps, Theodor, *Komik und Humor: Eine psychologisch-ästhetische Untersuchung* (= *Beiträge zur Ästhetik*, VI) (Leipzig: Leopold Voss, 1922).

Ludovic, Anthony M., *The Secret of Laughter* (New York: The Viking Press, 1933).

Mandel, Oscar, *A Definition of Tragedy*, Gotham Library (1961; rpt. New York: New York Univ. Press, 1968).

Mauron, Charles, *Psychocritique du genre comique* (Paris: José Corti, 1964).

Monnerot, Jules, *Les Lois du tragique*, Bibliothèque de philosophie contemporaine (Paris: Presses univ. de France, 1969).

Monro, D. H., *Argument of Laughter* (Univ. of Notre Dame Press, 1963).

Muecke, D[ouglas] C., *The Compass of Irony* (London: Methuen, 1969).

Muller, Herbert J., *The Spirit of Tragedy* (New York: Alfred A. Knopf, 1956).

Myers, Henry Alonzo, *Tragedy: A View of Life* (Ithaca: Cornell Univ. Press, 1956).

Niebuhr, Reinhold, *The Irony of American History* (New York: Charles Scribner's Sons, 1954).

Olson, Elder, *Tragedy and the Theory of Drama* (= *Wayne*, *WB* 22) (1961; rpt. Detroit: Wayne State Univ. Press, 1966).

Paulhan, Fr[édéric], *La Morale de l'ironie*, Bibliothèque de philosophie contemporaine (Paris: Félix Alcan, 1909).

Paulson, Ronald, *The Fictions of Satire* (Baltimore: Johns Hopkins Press, 1967).

Paulson, Ronald, ed., *Satire: Modern Essays in Criticism*, Prentice-Hall English Literature Series (Englewood Cliffs: Prentice-Hall, 1971).

Piddington, Ralph, *The Psychology of Laughter: A Study in Social Adaptation* (London: Figurehead, 1933).

Pintard, René, *Le Libertinage érudit dans la première moitié du XVIIe siècle*, 2 vols. (Paris: Boivin, 1943).

Plessner, Helmuth, *Lachen und Weinen: Eine Untersuchung nach den Grenzen menschlichen Verhaltens* (Bern: Francke, 1950).

Potts, L. J., *Comedy* (= *Hutchinson's Univ. Library*, no. 41) (London: Cheltenham and London, 1948).

Riffaterre, Michael, *Le Style des "Pléiades" de Gobineau: Essai d'application d'une méthode stylistique* (New York: Columbia Univ. Press, 1957).

——, *Essais de stylistique structurale*, ed. and trans. Daniel Delas, Nouvelle Bibliothèque scientifique (Paris: Flammarion, 1971).

Saint-Denis, E. de., *Essais sur le rire et le sourire des Latins* (*Publication de l'Univ. de Dijon*, 32) (Paris: Belles Lettres, 1965).

Saulnier, Claude, *Le Sens du comique: Essai sur le caractère esthétique du rire* (Paris: Vrin, 1940).

Scherer, Jacques, *La Dramaturgie classique en France* (Paris: Nizet, [1950]).

Schopenhauer, Arthur, *The World as Will and Idea*, trans. R. B. Haldane and J. Kemp, 3 vols. (London: Kegan Paul, Trench, Trübner, 1866-1907).

Sedgewick, C. G., "Dramatic Irony: Studies in Its History, Its Definition and Its Use Especially in Shakespere and Sophocles", Diss., Harvard, 1913.

——, *Of Irony, Especially in Drama* (Toronto: Univ. of Toronto Press, 1948).

Sharpe, Robert Boies, *Irony in the Drama: An Essay on Impersonation, Shock, and Catharsis* (Chapel Hill: Univ. of North Carolina Press, 1959).

Shestov, Lev, *La Philosophie de la tragédie: Dostoïevsky et Nietzsche*, trans. Boris de Schloezer (Paris: Flammarion, 1966).

Spamer, Hermann, *Die Ironie im altfranzösischen Nationalepos* (Strassburg: M. DuMont Schauberg, 1914).

States, Bert, O., *Irony and Drama: A Poetics* (Ithaca, N.Y. and London: Cornell Univ. Press, 1971).

Strohschneider-Kohrs, Ingrid, *Die romantische Ironie in Theorie und Gestaltung*, in *Hermaea*, VI (Tübingen: Max Niemeyer, 1960).

Sully, James, *An Essay on Laughter: Its Forms, Its Causes, Its Development and Its Value* (New York and Bombay: Longmans, Green, 1902).

Swabey, Marie Collins, *Comic Laughter: A Philosophical Essay* (New Haven and London: Yale Univ. Press, 1961).

Sypher, Wylie, ed., *Comedy* (= *Doubleday Anchor Books*, A87) (Garden City: Doubleday, 1956).

Tave, Stuart M., *The Amiable Humorist: A Study in the Comic Theory of the Eighteenth and Early Nineteenth Centuries* (Chicago: Univ. of Chicago Press, 1960).

Theodor, Hugo, *Die komischen Elemente der altfranzösischen chansons de geste* (= *Beheifte zur Zeitschrift für romanische Philologie*, no. 48) (Halle: Max Niemeyer, 1913).

Thompson, Alan Reynolds, *The Anatomy of Drama* (Berkeley and Los Angeles: Univ. of California Press, 1946).

Thompson, J. A. K., *Irony: An Historical Introduction* (London: George Allen & Unwin, 1926).

Thomson, Robert, *The Psychology of Thinking* (= *Pelican*, A 453) (1959; rpt. Baltimore: Penguin, 1963).

Turner, F. McD. C., *The Element of Irony in English Literature* (Cambridge, England: Cambridge Univ. Press, 1926).

Ueberhorst, Karl, *Das Komische*, 2 vols. (Leipzig: Georg Wigand, 1896-1900).

Unamuno, Miguel de, *The Tragic Sense of Life in Men and in Peoples*, trans. J. E. Crawford Flitch, introd. by Salvador de Madariaga (London: Macmillan, 1931).

Worcester, David, *The Art of Satire* (= *Norton Library*, N 472) (New York: Norton, 1969).

Zumthor, Paul, *Essai de poétique médiévale*, Coll. "Poétique" (Paris: Seuil, 1972).

Articles

Aden, John M., "Towards a Uniform Satiric Terminology", *Satire Newsletter*, 1, ii (1964), 30-32.

Adolf, Helen, "On Medieval Laughter", *Speculum*, 22 (1947), 251-253.

Aubouin, E., "Humour et transfert", *Revue d'esthétique*, 3 (1950), 369-387.

Auerbach, Erich, "The Western Public and Its Language", in Auerbach, *Literary Language in Late Antiquity and in the Middle Ages*, 235-338.

Baldensperger, F., "Les Définitions de l'humour", *Annales de l'Est*, 14 (1900), 177-200.

Baumgarten, Sandor, "Une Figure soi-disant comique: Le Snob", *Revue d'esthétique*, 3 (1950), 343-348.

Bawden, H. Heath, "The Comic as Illustrating the Summation-Irradiation Theory of Pleasure-Pain", *Psychological Review*, 17 (1910), 336-346.

Bayer, Raymond, "L'Humour: Conférence", *Revue d'esthétique*, 2 (1949), 319-322.

Birney, Earle, "English Irony before Chaucer", *University* of *Toronto Quarterly*, 6 (1936-1937), 538-557.

Boskoff, Priscilla S., "Quintilian in the Late Middle Ages", *Speculum*, 27 (1952), 71-78.

Brewer, Edward V., "The Influence of Jean Paul Richter on George Meredith's Conception of the Comic", *Journal of English and Germanic Philology*, 29 (1930), 243-256.

Brooks, Cleanth, "Irony and 'Ironic' Poetry", *College English*, 9 (1947-1948), 231-237.

——, "Irony as a Principle of Structure", in *Literary Opinion in America: Essays Illustrating the Status, Methods, and Problems of Criticism in the United States in the Twentieth Century*, ed. Morton Dauwen Zabel, 3rd edition, revised (= *Harper*

Torchbooks, The University Library, TB 3013) (1937; New York and Evanston: Harper & Row, 1962), 729-741.

Carnochan, W. B., "Satire, Sublimity, and Sentiment: Theory and Practice in Post-Augustan Satire", *PMLA*, 85 (1970), 260-267.

Carritt, E. F., "A Theory of the Ludicrous: A Footnote to Croce's Aesthetic", *Hibbert Journal*, 21 (1922-1923), 552-564.

Cazamian, L., "Pourquoi nous ne pouvons définir l'humour", *Revue germanique*, 2 (1906), 601-634.

Chaix-Ruy, J., "L'Essence du rire", *Revue d'esthétique*, 3 (1950), 229-264.

Chambers, Lehard H., "Irony in the Final Chapter of the *Quijote*", *Romanic Review*, 61 (1970), 14-22.

Champigny, Robert, "Implicitness in Narrative Fiction", *PMLA*, 85 (1970), 988-991.

Chantavoine, Henri, "De l'ironie en littérature: M. Anatole France", *Le Correspondant*, 187, nouvelle série, 151 (1897), 181-189.

Clough, Wilson O., "Irony: A French Approach", *Sewanee Review*, 47 (1939), 175-183.

Curtius, Ernst Robert, "Jest and Earnest in Medieval Literature". See Curtus, *European Literature*, 417-435.

Datain, Jean, "Le Sourire grammatical", *Vie et langage*, 220 (1970), 362-368.

DeMott, Benjamin, "The New Irony: Sicknicks and Others", *American Scholar*, 31 (1961-1962), 108-119.

Doumic, René, "Les Inconvénients de l'ironie", and "Les Avantages de l'ironie", in *La Vie et les moeurs au jour le jour* (Paris: Perrin, 1895), 87-104.

Emerson, Ralph Waldo, "The Comic", *Letters and Social Aims*, in *Complete Works, Vol. VIII* (Boston: Houghton, Mifflin, 1883), 149-166.

Empson, William, "Wit in the Essay on Criticism", *Hudson Review*, 2 (1949-1950), 559-577.

Fernagu, Marguerite, "Le Rire tragique", *Revue d'esthétique*, 3 (1950), 398-419.

Fluck, Hanns, "Der Risus Paschalis: Ein Beitrag zur religiösen Volkskunde", *Archiv für Religionswissenschaft*, 31 (1934), 188-212.

Gabriel, A. L., "The Preparatory Teaching in the Parisian Colleges during the XIVth Century", *Revue de l'Univ. d'Ottawa*, 31 (1951), 449-483.

Ginestier, Paul, "L'Humour, expression sociologique", *Revue d'esthétique*, 3 (1950), 349-368.

——, "La Logique de l'humour", *Revue d'esthétique*, 2 (1949), 86-95.

Gouhier, Henri, "Condition du comique", *Revue d'esthétique*, 3 (1950), 301-309.

Green, D. H., "Irony and Medieval Romance", in *Arthurian Romance: Seven Essays*, ed. D. D. R. Owen (Edinburgh and London: Scottish Academic Press, 1970), 49-64.

Guite, Harold, "An 18th-Century View of Roman Satire". See Hugues, Peter and David Williams, eds., 113-120.

Harvey, Lawrence E., "Corneille's *Horace:* A Study in Tragic and Artistic Ambivalence", in *Studies in Seventeenth-Century French Literature*, ed. Jean-Jacques Demorest (= *Anchor Books*, A 503) (1952; rpt. Garden City: Doubleday, 1966), 65-96.

Hendrickson, G. L., "Satura tota nostra est", *Classical Philology*, 22 (1927), 46-60.

Hollingworth, H. L., "Experimental Studies in Judgment: Judgments of the Comic", *Psychological Review*, 18 (1911), 132-156.

Hutchens, Eleanor N., "The Identification of Irony", *ELH*, 27 (1960), 352-363.

Kahn, Gustave, "L'Ironie dans le roman français (à propos du centenaire de Mérimée)", *La Nouvelle Revue*, 24 (1903), 528-534.

Knight, Alan E., "The Medieval Theater of the Absurd", *PMLA*, 86 (1971), 183-189.

Lacombe, P., "Du comique et du spirituel", *Revue de métaphysique et de morale*, 5 (1897), 571-590.

Lalo, Charles, "Le Rire esthétique: Conférence", *Revue d'esthétique*, 2 (1949), 313-315.

——, "Le Comique et le spirituel", *Revue d'esthétique*, 3 (1950), 310-327.

Legman, G., "Toward a Motif-Index of Erotic Humor", *Journal of American Folklore*, 75 (1962), 227-248.

Lewicka, Halina, "Un Procédé comique de l'ancienne farce: La Fausse Compréhension du langage". See *Mélanges... Frappier*, II, 653-658.

Lipps, Th., "Psychologie des Komik", *Philosophische Monatshefte*, 24 (1888), 385-422, 513-529, and 25 (1889), 28-50, 129-160, 408-433.

Lucas, F. L., "The Reverse of Aristotle", *Classical Review*, 37 (1923), 98-104.

Macey, Samuel, "Theatrical Satire: A Protest from the Stage against Poor Taste in Theatrical Entertainment". See Hugues, Peter, and David Williams, eds., 121-129.

Mack, Maynard, "The Muse of Satire". See Paulson, ed., 190-201.

McKeon, Richard, "Rhetoric in the Middle Ages", *Speculum*, 17 (1942), 1-32.

McMahon, A. Philip, "Seven Questions on Aristotelian Definitions of Tragedy and Comedy", *Harvard Studies in Classical Philology*, 40 (1929), 97-198.

Malloch, A. E., "The Techniques and Function of the Renaissance Paradox", *Studies in Philology*, 53 (1965), 191-203.

Mélinand, Camille, "Pourqoui rit-on? Etude sur la cause psychologique du rire", *Revue des Deux Mondes*, 65 (1895), 612-630.

Meredith, George, "An Essay on Comedy". See Sypher, ed., 3-57.

Morin, Violette, "L'Histoire drôle", *Communications*, 8 (1966), 102-119.

Navarre, Octave, "Théophraste et La Bruyère", *Revue des études grecques*, 27 (1914), 384-440.

Ong, Walter J., S. J., "Swift on the Mind: Satire in a Closed Field", in *Rhetoric, Romance and Technology: Studies in the Interaction of Expression and Culture* (Ithaca and London: Cornell Univ. Press, 1971), 190-212.

Palante, Georges, "L'Ironie: Etude psychologique", *Revue philosophique de la France et de l'étranger*, 61 (1906), 147-163.

Penjon, A., "Le Rire et la liberté", *Revue philosophique de la France et de l'étranger*, 36 (1893), 113-140.

Randolph, Mary Claire, "The Structural Design of the Formal Verse Satire", *Philological Quarterly*, 21 (1942), 368-384.

Sarton, May, "The Shield of Irony", *The Nation*, 182, 14 April, 1956, 314-316.

Schaerer, René, "Le Méchanisme de l'ironie dans ses rapports avec la dialectique", *Revue de métaphysique et de morale*, 48 (1941), 181-209.

Souriau, Etienne, "L'Humour surcontré", *Revue d'esthétique*, 3 (1950), 388-397.

Spencer, Herbert, "The Physiology of Laughter", in *Essays: Scientific, Political and Speculative* (New York: Appleton, 1892), II, 452-466.

Snuggs, Henry L., "The Comic Humours: A New Interpretation", *PMLA*, 62 (1947), 114-122.

Tatlock, J. S. P., "Medieval Laughter", *Speculum*, 21 (1946), 289-294.

Ustick, W. Lee and Hoyt H. Hudson, "Wit, 'Mixt Wit', and the Bee in Amber", *Huntington Library Bulletin*, 8 (Oct., 1935), 103-130.

Victoria, Marcos, "Notes sur la dévaluation comique", *Revue d'esthétique*, 3 (1950), 328-332.

Victoroff, D[avid], "De la fonction sociale du rire", *Revue d'esthétique*, 2 (1949), 34-47.

——, "Le Rire et le rêve", *Revue d'esthétique*, 3 (1950), 265-273.

Wright, Andrew H., "Irony and Fiction", *Journal of Aesthetics & Art Criticism*, 12 (1953-1954), 111-118.

IRONY IN MEDIEVAL LITERATURE

1. *Texts*

Aebischer, Paul, ed., *Le Voyage de Charlemagne à Jérusalem et à Constantinople* (= *Textes littéraires français*, 115) (Geneva: Droz, 1965).

Alanus de Insulis, *Anticlaudianus*, in *Opera Omnia*, cols. 481-576.

——, *Compendiosa in Cantica Canticorum ad Laudem Deiparas Virginis Mariae Elucidatio*. See *Opera Omnia*, cols. 51-110.

——, *The Complaint of Nature*, trans. Douglas M. Moffat (= *Yale Studies in English*, no. 36) (New York: Henry Holt, 1908).

——, *Liber de Planctu Naturae*. See *Opera Omnia*, cols. 429-482.

——, *Liber in Distinctionibus Dictionum Theologicalium*. See *Opera Omnia*, cols. 685-1012.

——, *Opera Omnia* (= *Patrologiae Cursus Completus... Series Latina*, Vol. 210, ed. J. -P. Migne) (Paris: 1855).

André de la Vigne, *Moralité de l'Aveugle et du Boiteux*, in *Le Théâtre français avant la Renaissance (1450-1550): Mystères, moralités et farces*, ed. Edouard Fournier, 2nd edition (Paris: Laplace, Sanchez, 1872), 155-161.

Andreas Capellanus, *The Art of Courtly Love*, trans. John Jay Parry (New York: Ungar, 1959).

Augustinus, St. Aurelius, *De Civitate Dei*, ed. Bernard Dombert and Alphons Kalb (= *Corpvs Christianorum, Series latina*, 47, vol. XIV) (Turnholt: Brepols, 1955).

——, "In Psalmum CXII Enarratio: Sermo ad Plebem", in *Enarrationes in Psalmos CI-CL* (= *Corpvs Christianorum. Series latina*, 40, vol. X.3.) (Turnholt: Brepols, 1956).

——, See Dods, Marcus, trans. and ed.

Bédier, Joseph, ed. and trans., *La Chanson de Roland, publiée d'après le manuscrit d'Oxford*, 237th edition (Paris: H. Piazza, 1937).

Béroul, *Le Roman de Tristan*, ed. Ernest Muret, 4th edition, revised by L. M. Defourques (= *Classiques français du moyen âge*, 12) (Paris: H. Champion, 1962).

Bodel, Jean, *Le Jeu de Saint Nicolas*, ed. Albert Henry, 2nd edition (= *Université libre de Bruxelles. Travaux de la Faculté de philosophie et lettres*, 21) (Brussels: Presses univ. de Bruxelles, 1965).

Boethius, Anicius Manlius Severinus, *Philosophiae Consolatio*, ed. Ludwig Bieler (= *Corpvs Christianorum, Series latina*, 94).

Butler, H. E., trans., *The "Institutio Oratoria" of Quintilian, Vol. III*, Loeb Classical Library (London: William Heinemann and New York: G. P. Putnam's Sons, 1922).

Chaucer, Geoffrey, *The Romance of the Rose*, in *Works*, ed. F. N. Robinson, 2nd edition (1933; rpt. Boston: Houghton Mifflin, 1961), 564-637.

Charles d'Orléans, *Poésies*, ed. Pierre Champion (= *Classiques français du moyen âge*, 89) (Paris: H. Champion, 1965).

Chrétien de Troyes, *Cligés*, ed. Alexandre Micha, *Les Romans de Chrétien de Troyes*, II (= *Classiques français du moyen âge*, 84) (Paris: H. Champion, 1957).

——, *Erec et Enide*, ed. Mario Roques, *Les Romans de Chrétien de Troyes*, I (=*Classiques français du moyen âge*, 80) (Paris: Champion, 1963).

——, *Le Roman de Perceval ou Le Conte du graal*, ed. William Roach, 2nd edition (= *Textes littéraires français*, 71) (Geneva: Droz and Paris: Minard, 1959).

——, *Le Chevalier au lion* (*Yvain*), ed. Mario Roques, *Les Romans de Chrétien de Troyes*, IV (= *Classiques français du moyen âge*, 89) (Paris: H. Champion, 1965).

——, *Le Chevalier de la charrete*, ed. Mario Roques, *Les Romans de Chrétien de Troyes*, III (= *Classiques français du moyen âge*, 86) (Paris: H. Champion, 1965).

Christine de Pisan, *Oeuvres poétiques*, ed. Maurice Roy (= *Société des anciens textes français*, 22), 3 vols. (Paris: Didot, 1886-1896; rpt. New York: Johnson, 1965).

Dahlberg, Charles [R.], trans., *The Romance of the Rose*, by Guillaume de Lorris and Jean de Meun (Princeton: Princeton Univ. Press, 1971). See also Guillaume de Lorris.

Dods, Marcus, trans, and ed., *The City of God*, by St. Augustine, 2 vols. (=*Hafner Library of Classics*, 4) (New York: Hafner, 1948).

Dunn, Charles W., ed. See Guillaume de Lorris.

Galpin, Stanley Leman, "*Les Eschez amoureux:* A Complete Synopsis with Unpublished Extracts", *Romanic Review*, 11 (1920), 283-307.

Gerson, Jean, *Oeuvres complètes*, ed. Mgr. Glorieux, 7 vols. (Paris: Desclée, 1960-1966).

Guillaume de Lorris and Jean de Meun, *Le Roman de la Rose*, ed. Ernest Langlois (= *Société des anciens textes français*, 63), 5 vols. (1914-1924; rpt. New York: Johnson, 1965). See also Dahlberg, Charles, trans.; Mary, André, trans.; Robbins, Harry W., trans.

——, *The Romance of the Rose*, trans. Harry W. Robbins, ed. Charles W. Dunn, D 90 (New York: E. P. Dutton, 1962).

Isidore of Seville, Saint, *Differentiarum, sive De Proprietate Sermonum, Libri Duo*, in *Opera Omnia* (= *Patrologiae Cursus Completus... Series Latina Prior*, 83, Ed. J. -P. Migne) (Paris: 1862).

Jenkins, T. Atkinson, ed., *La Chanson de Roland: Oxford Version*, revised edition, Heath's Modern Language Series (Boston: Heath, 1924).

Lecompte, I. C., ed., "Le Fablel dou Dieu d'Amors", *Modern Philology*, 8 (1910-1911), 63-86.

Macrobius, Ambrosius Theodosius, *Commentarii in Somnium Scipionis*, in *Opera*, 2 vols. (Quedlinburg and Leipzig: Gottfried Ban, 1848), I, 1-216.

Mary, André, trans., *Le Roman de la Rose*, by Guillaume de Lorris and Jean de Meun (Paris: Gallimard, 1949). See also Guillaume de Lorris.

Ovid, *The Art of Love and Other Poems*, ed. and trans. J. H. Mozley, Loeb Classical Library (Cambridge, Mass.: Harvard Univ. Press, 1962).

Pelan, M. M. and N. C. W. Spence, ed., *Narcisus* (= *Publications de la Faculté des lettres de l'Univ. de Strasbourg*, 147) (Paris: Belles Lettres, 1964).

Prudentius, Aurelius, *Psychomachia*, ed. and trans. H. J. Thomson, Loeb Classical Library, 2 vols. (Cambridge, Mass.: Harvard Univ. Press, 1949-1953; rpt. 1961-1969), I, 274-343.

Quintilianus, *Institutio Oratoria*, ed. Ludwig Radermacher, revised by Vinzenz Buchheit, Academia Scientiarum Germanica Berolinensis. Bibliotheca Scriptorum Graecorum et Romanorum Teubneriana (Berlin: Teubner, 1965).

Roques, Mario, ed., *Aucassin et Nicolette: Chantefable du XIIIe siècle*, 2nd edition (=*Classiques français du moyen âge*, 41) (Paris: Champion, 1967).

Rutebeuf, *Oeuvres complètes*, ed. Edmond Faral and Julia Bastin, Fondation Singer-Polignac, 2 vols. (Paris: A. et J. Picard, 1959-1960).

Shapiro, Norman R., trans. and James B. Wadsworth, ed., *The Comedy of Eros: Medieval French Guides to the Art of Love* (Urbana: Univ. of Illinois Press, 1971).

Thomas, *Les Fragments du "Roman de Tristan"*, ed. Bartina H. Wind (=*Textes littéraires français*, 92) (Geneva: Droz, 1960).

Villon, François, *Oeuvres*, ed. Auguste Longnon, 4th edition, revised by Lucien Foulet (=*Classiques français du moyen âge*, 2) (Paris: Champion, 1961).

——, *Oeuvres*, ed. Louis Thuasne, 3 vols. (Rpt. Geneva: Slatkine, 1967).

Ward, Charles Frederick, *The Epistles on the "Romance of the Rose" and Other Documents in the Debate* (=*Transactions of the Royal Society of Canada*, 8) (Chicago: Univ. of Chicago Press, 1911).

2. *Critical works*

Books

Allen, Don Cameron, *Mysteriously Meant: The Rediscovery of Pagan Symbolism and Allegorical Interpretation in the Renaissance* (Baltimore and London: Johns Hopkins Press, 1970).

Auerbach, Erich, *Typologische Motive in der mittelalterlichen Literatur* (=*Schriften und Vorträge des Petrarca-Instituts Köln*, 2) (Krefeld: Scherpe, 1953).

Bayrav, Süheylâ, *Symbolisme médiéval*: *Béroul, Marie, Chrétien* (Paris: Presses universitaires de France, 1957).

Bédier, Joseph, *Les Légendes épiques: Recherches sur la formation des chansons de geste, vols. III and IV*, 3rd edition (Paris: Champion, 1929).

Bell, Dora M., *L'Idéal éthique de la royauté en France au moyen âge d'après quelques moralistes de ce temps* (Geneva: Droz, 1962).

Bellamy, Félix, *La Forêt de Bréchéliant, la fontaine de Bérenton, quelques lieux d'alentour, les principaux personnages qui s'y rapportent*, 2 vols. (Rennes: J. Plihon and L. Hervé, 1896).

Benedetto, Luigi di, ed., *La Leggenda di Tristano* (Bari: Gius. Laterza, 1942).

Bernheimer, Richard, *Wild Men in the Middle Ages: A Study in Art, Sentiment, and Demonology* (Cambridge, Mass.: Harvard Univ. Press, 1952).

Bezzola, Reto R., *Les Origines et la formation de la littérature courtoise en Occident* (*500-1200*) (= *Bibliothèque de l'Ecole des Hautes Etudes*, 286) (Paris: H. Champion, 1944).

——, *Le Sens de l'aventure et de l'amour* (*Chrétien de Troyes*) (Paris: Jeune Parque, 1947).

Bloch, Marc, *French Rural History: An Essay on Its Basic Characteristics*, trans. Janet Sondheimer, introd. by Bryce Lyon (Berkeley and Los Angeles: Univ. of California Press, 1966).

——, *La Société féodale* (=*Evolution de l'humanité*, 8) (Paris: Albin Michel, 1968).

Bloomfield, Morton W., *The Seven Deadly Sins: An Introduction to the History of a Religious Concept, with Special Reference to Medieval English Literature* (1952; rpt. Michigan: Michigan Univ. Press, 1967).

Boissier, Gaston, *La Fin du paganisme: Etude sur les dernières luttes religieuses en occident au quatrième siècle*, 7th edition, Bibliothèque d'histoire (Paris: Hachette, 1891).

Bonsirven, Joseph, *Exégèse rabbinique et exégèse paulinienne*, Bibliothèque de théologie historique (Paris: Beauchesne, 1939).

Campaux, Antoine, *François Villon, sa vie et ses oeuvres* (Paris: A. Durand, 1859).

Champion, Pierre, *Vie de Charles d'Orléans* (*1394-1465*) (Paris: H. Champion, 1911).

——, *François Villon: Sa Vie et son temps*, 2nd edition, 2 vols. (= *Bibliothèque du XVe siècle*, 20-21) (Paris: Champion, 1967).

Chapters in Western Civilization, Vol. I, 3rd edition (New York: Columbia Univ. Press, 1961).

Chiri, Giuseppe, *L'Epica latina medioevale e la "Chanson de Roland"* (Genova: Emiliano degli Orfini, 1936).

Chydenius, Johan, *The Theory of Medieval Symbolism*, Finska Vetenskapssocieteten (Societas Scientiarum Finnica) (Helsingfors: Academic Bookstore, 1960).

——, *The Symbolism of Love in Medieval Thought*, Finska Vetenskapssocieteten (Societas Scientiarum Finnica) (= *Commentationes humanarum litterarum*, Vol. 44.1) (Helsinki-Helsingfors: Keskuskirjapaino-Centraltrykeriet, 1970).

Cigada, Sergio, *L'Opera poetica di Charles d'Orléans* (=*Università cattolica del Sacro*

Cuore. Saggi e ricerche, serie 3: *Scienze filologiche e letteratura*, I) (Milan: Società editrice "Vita e pensiero", 1960).

Clédat, Léon, *Rutebeuf*, Les Grands Ecrivains français (Paris: Hachette, 1891).

——, *La Poésie lyrique et satirique en France au moyen âge*, Coll. des classiques populaires (Paris: Société française d'imprimerie et de librairie, 1932).

Cohen, Gustave, *Le Roman de la Rose*, Cours de Sorbonne (Paris: Centre de documentation universitaire).

Combes, André, *Jean de Montreuil et le chancelier Gerson: Contribution à l'histoire des rapports de l'humanisme et de la théologie en France au début du XVe siècle* (= *Etudes de philosophie médiévale*, 32) (Paris: Vrin, 1942).

Combridge, Rosemary Norah, *Das Recht im 'Tristan' Gottfrieds von Strassburg* (= *Philologische Studien und Quellen*, 15) (Berlin: Erich Schmidt, 1964).

Cons, Louis, *Etat présent des études sur Villon* (= *Etudes françaises*, 37) (Paris: Belles Lettres, 1936).

Corti, Alfonso, *François Villon, su vida y su obra* (Buenos Aires: Talleres graficos sudamericanos, 1931).

Cosman, Madeleine Pelner, *The Education of the Hero in Arthurian Romance* (Chapel Hill: Univ. of North Carolina Press, 1965).

Coulet, Jules, *Etudes sur l'ancien poème français du "Voyage de Charlemagne en Orient"* (Montpellier: Coulet, 1907).

Courcelle, Pierre, *"La Consolation de Philosophie" dans la tradition littéraire: Antécédents et postérité de Boèce* (Paris: Etudes augustiniennes, 1967).

Crawley, Ernest, *The Mystic Rose: A Study of Primitive Marriage and of Primitive Thought in Its Bearing on Marriage*, revised by Theodore Besterman, 2nd edition, 2 vols. (1927; rpt. New York: Meridian Books, 1960).

Curtius, Ernst Robert, *European Literature and the Latin Middle Ages*, trans. Willard R. Trask (= *Harper Torchbooks*, TB 2015, *Bollingen Library*, 36) (New York and Evanston: Harper & Row, 1953).

Daniélou, Jean, *From Shadows to Reality: Studies in the Biblical Typology of the Fathers*, trans. Dom Wulstan Hibberd (London: Burns & Oates, 1960).

Davy, M. -M., *Essai sur la symbolique romane* (*XIIe siècle*), Homo-Sapiens (Paris: Flammarion, 1955).

Dehm, Christian, *Studien zu Rutebeuf* (Würzburg: P. Kilian, 1935).

Demarolle, Pierre, *L'Esprit de Villon: Etude de style*, Coll. "Style et esprit français" (Paris: Nizet, 1968).

Denomy, Alexander J., *The Heresy of Courtly Love*, introd. by William Lane Keleher, Boston College Candlemas Lectures on Christian Literature (1947; rpt. Gloucester, Mass.: Peter Smith, 1965).

Dorfman, Eugene, *The Narreme in Medieval Romance Epic: An Introduction to Narrative Structures* (= *Univ. of Toronto Romance Series*, 13) (Toronto: Univ. of Toronto Press, 1969).

Dow, Blanch Hinman, *The Varying Attitude toward Women in French Literature of the Fifteenth Century: The Opening Years* (New York: Publications of the Institute of French Studies, 1935).

Dubruck, Edelgard, *The Theme of Death in French Poetry of the Middle Ages and the Renaissance* (= *Studies in French Literature*, I) (The Hague: Mouton, 1964).

Dunbar, Helen Flanders, *Symbolism in Medieval Thought and Its Consummation in the Divine Comedy* (1929; rpt. New York: Russell, 1961).

Eisner, Sigmund, *The Tristan Legend: A Study in Sources* (Evanston, Ill.: Northwestern Univ. Press, 1969).

Eliade, Mircea, *Images et symboles* (Paris: Gallimard, 1952).

——, *The Sacred and the Profane: The Nature of Religion*, trans. Willard R. Trask (= *Harvest*, *HB* 144) (1957; New York: Harvest, Brace & World, 1959).

——, *Myths, Dreams and Mysteries: The Encounter between Contemporary Faiths and Archaic Realities*, trans. Philip Mairet (= *Harper Torchbooks*, TB 1320) (1957; New York and Evanston: Harper & Row, 1960).

Ellspermann, Gerard L., *The Attitude of the Early Christian Latin Writers toward Pagan Literature and Learning* (= *Catholic Univ. of America Patristic Studies*, 82) (Washington, D. C.: Catholic Univ. of America Press, 1949).

Ettmayer, Karl Ritter von, *Der "Rosenroman" (Erster Teil): Stilistische, grammatische und literarhistorische Erläuterungen zum Studium und zur Privatlektüre des Textes*, Repertorien zum Studium altfranzösischer Literaturdenkmäler (Heidelberg: Carl Winter, 1919).

Fansler, Dean Spruill, *Chaucer and the "Roman de la Rose"* (New York: Columbia Univ. Press, 1914).

Faral, Edmond, *Recherches sur les sources latines des contes et romans courtois du moyen âge* (Paris: Champion, 1913).

——, *"La Chanson de Roland": Etude et analyse*, Chefs-d'oeuvre de la littérature expliqués (Paris: Melltoée, 1932).

——, *Les Arts poétiques du XIIe et du XIIIe siècle: Recherches et documents sur la technique littéraire du Moyen Age* (Paris: Champion, 1962).

Ferguson, George [Wells], *Signs and Symbols in Christian Art*, 2nd edition (New York: Oxford Univ. Press, 1955).

Feuillerat, Albert, ed., *Studies by Members of the French Department of Yale University: Decennial Volume* (= *Yale Romanic Studies*, no. 18) (New Haven: Yale Univ. Press, 1941).

Fleming, John V., *The "Roman de la Rose": A Study in Allegory and Iconography* (Princeton: Princeton Univ. Press, 1969).

Fletcher, Angus, *Allegory: The Theory of a Symbolic Mode* (Ithaca, N.Y.: Cornell Univ. Press, 1964).

Fourrier, Anthime, *Le Courant réaliste dans le roman courtois en France au Moyen-Age: Les Débuts (XIIe s.)*, Univ. de Paris, Faculté des lettres (Paris: Nizet, 1960).

Fox, John, *The Poetry of Villon* (London: Thomas Nelson, 1962).

——, *The Lyric Poetry of Charles d'Orléans* (Oxford: Clarendon Press, 1969).

Frank, Grace, *The Medieval French Drama* (1954; rpt. London: Oxford Univ. Press at Clarendon Press, 1967).

Frappier, Jean, *La Poésie lyrique française aux XIIe et XIIIe siècles: Les Auteurs et les genres*, Cours de Sorbonne: Littérature française (Paris: Centre de documentation universitaire).

——, *Le Roman breton, Chrétien de Troyes: "Cligès"*, Cours de Sorbonne: Littérature française (Paris: Centre de documentation universitaire, 1951).

——, *Le Roman breton*: *"Yvain ou le Chevalier au lion"*, Cours de Sorbonne: Littérature française (Paris: Centre de documentation universitaire, 1952).

——, *Etude sur "Yvain" ou le "Chevalier au lion" de Chretien de Troyes* (Paris: Société d'édition d'enseignement supérieur, 1969).

Fundenburg, George Baer, *Feudal France in the French Epic: A Study of Feudal French Institutions in History and Poetry* (1919; rpt. Port Washington, N.Y.: Kennikat Press, 1966).

Garvey, Sister M. Calixta, *The Syntax of the Declinable Words in the "Roman de la Rose"* (Washington, D.C.: Catholic Univ. of America, 1936).

Giamatti, A. Bartlett, *The Earthly Paradise and the Renaissance Epic* (Princeton: Princeton Univ. Press, 1966).

Gilson, Etienne, *Reason and Revelation in the Middle Ages* (New York: Charles Scribner's Sons, 1938).

Goldin, Frederick, *The Mirror of Narcissus in the Courtly Love Lyric* (Ithaca, N.Y.: Cornell Univ. Press, 1967).

Golther, Wolfgang, *Tristan und Isolde in den Dichtungen des Mittelalters und der neuen Zeit* (Leipzig: S. Hirzel, 1907).

Goodrich, N. L., *Charles of Orleans: A Study of Themes in His French and in His English Poetry* (Geneva: Droz, 1967).

Graevell, Dr., *Die Characteristik der Personen im Rolandsliede: Ein Beitrag zur Kenntniss seiner poetischen Technik* (Heilbronn: Gebrüder Henniger, 1880).

Gray, J. Glenn, *The Warriors: Reflections on Men in Battle* (= *Harper Torchbooks: The Academy Library, TB* 1294) (1959; rpt. New York and Evanston: Harper & Row, 1967).

Gros, Gaston, *L'Amour dans le "Roman de la Rose"*, Bibliothèque du lettre (Paris: Baudinière, 1925).

Guerrieri Crocetti, C[amillo], *La Leggenda di Tristano nei più antichi poemi francesi* (Genova: Di Stefano and Milan: Rodolfo Malfasi, [1950]).

Guillon, Félix, *Etude historique et biographique sur Guillaume de Lorris, auteur du "Roman de la Rose", d'après documents inédits & révision critique des textes des auteurs* (Orléans: H. Herluison and Paris: Dumoulin, 1881).

——, *Jean Clopinel dit de Meung: "Le Roman de la Rose" considéré comme document historique du règne de Philippe le Bel* (Paris: A. Picard and Orléans: J. Loddé, 1903).

Gunn, Alan M. F., *The Mirror of Love: A Reinterpretation of "The Romance of the Rose"* (Lubbock: Texas Tech. Press, 1952).

Guyer, Foster Erwin, *Chrétien de Troyes: Inventor of the Modern Novel* (New York: Bookman Associates, 1957).

Györi, Jean, *Etude sur la "Chanson de Roland"* (Paris: Droz, 1936).

Haidu, Peter, *Aesthetic Distance in Chrétien de Troyes: Irony and Comedy in "Cligès" and "Perceval"* (Geneva: Droz, 1968).

——, *Lion-Queue-Coupée: L'Ecart symbolique chez Chrétien de Troyes* (= *Histoire des idées et critique littéraire*, 123) (Geneva: Droz, 1972).

Halphen, Louis, *Etudes critiques sur l'histoire de Charlemagne* (Paris: Félix Alcan, 1921).

Heinrich, Fritz, *Über den Stil von Guillaume de Lorris und Jean de Meung* (= *Ausgaben und Abhandlungen aus dem Gebiete der romanischen Philologie*, 29 (Marburg: N. G. Elwert'sche, 1885).

Heitmann, Klaus, *Fortuna und Virtus: Eine Studie zu Petrarcas Lebensweisheit* (= *Studi italiani*, I) (Köln and Graz: Böhlau, 1958).

Holmes, Urban Tigner, ed., *Romance Studies in Memory of Edward Billings Ham* (= *California State College Publications*, 2) (Hayward, California, 1967).

L'Homme devant Dieu: Mélanges offerts au Père Henri de Lubac, 3 vols. (Théologie, 56) (Paris: Aubier-Montaigne, 1963-1964).

Honig, Edwin, *Dark Conceit: The Making of Allegory*, Boar's Head Book (1959; rpt. Cambridge: Walker-de Berry, 1960).

Horrent, Jules, *Le Pèlerinage de Charlemagne: Essai d'explication littéraire avec des notes de critique textuelle* (= *Bibliothèque de la Faculté de philosophie et lettres de l'Univ. de Liège, fasc.* 158) (Paris: Belles Lettres, 1961).

Huizinga, Johan, *The Waning of the Middle Ages: A Study of the Forms of Life, Thought and Art in France and the Netherlands in the XIVth and XVth Centuries*, trans. F. Hopman (= *Doubleday Anchor Books*, A 42) (1949; rpt. Garden City: Doubleday, 1954).

Huot, P[aul], *Etude sur le "Roman de la Rose"* (Orléans: Alex Jacob, 1853).

Jackson, W. T. H., *The Anatomy of Love: The "Tristan" of Gottfried von Strassburg* (New York and London: Columbia Univ. Press, 1971).

Jadart, Henri, *Jean de Gerson (1363-1429): Recherches sur son origine, son village natal et sa famille* (Reims: Deligne & Renart, 1881).

Jarrett, Bede, *Social Theories of the Middle Ages, 1200-1500* (Westminster, Maryland: Newman Book Shop, 1942).

Jeanroy, Alfred, *Les Origines de la poésie lyrique en France au moyen âge: Etudes de littérature française et comparée suivies de textes inédits*, 3rd edition (Paris: Champion, 1925).

Jones, George Fenwick, *The Ethos of the Song of Roland* (Baltimore: Johns Hopkins Press, 1963).

Jonin, Pierre, *Les Personnages féminins dans les romans français de Tristan au XII*^e^ *siècle: Etude des influences contemporaines* (*Publication des Annales de la Faculté des lettres Aix-en-Provence, Nouvelle série* 22) (Aix-en-Provence: Ophrys, 1958).

Jordan, Ludwig, *Metrik und Sprache Rutebeufs* (Wolfenbüttel [Götingen?]: Otto Wollermann, 1888).

Joret, Charles, *La Rose dans l'antiquité et au moyen âge* (Paris: Emile Bouillon, 1892).

——, *Les Plantes dans l'antiquité et au moyen âge: Histoire, usages et symbolisme*, 2 vols. (Paris: Emile Bouillon, 1897-1904).

Katzenellenbogen, Adolf, *Allegories of the Virtues and Vices in Medieval Art from Early Christian Times to the Thirteenth Century* (= *Norton Library, N* 243) (1939; rpt. New York: Norton, 1964).

Kerdaniel, Edouard L. de, *Un Rhétoriqueur: André de la Vigne* (Paris: Champion, 1919).

——, *Un Auteur dramatique du quinzième siècle: André de la Vigne* (Paris: Champion, 1923).

Klibanski, Raymond, *The Continuity of the Platonic Tradition during the Middle Ages: Outlines of a Corpus Platonicum Medii Aevi* (London: Warburg Institute, 1939).

Köhler, Erich, *Ideal und Wirklichkeit in der höfischen Epik: Studien zur Form der frühen Artus- und Graldichtung* (= *Beiheifte zur Zeitschrift für romanische Philologie*, 97) (1956; rpt. Tübingen: Max Niemeyer, 1970).

Kolb, Herbert, *Der Begriff der Minne und das Entstehen der höfischen Lyrik* (= *Hermaea: Germanistische Forschungen, neue Folge*, 4) (Tübingen: Max Niemeyer, 1958).

Koschwitz, Eduard, *Ueberlieferung und Sprache der Chanson du Voyage de Charlemagne à Jérusalem et à Constantinople* (Heilbronn: Gebr. Henninger, 1876).

Kuhn, Alfred, *Die Illustration des Rosenromans* (Freiburg im Breisgau: C. A. Wagner, 1911).

Kuhn, David, *La Poétique de François Villon* (Paris: Armand Colin, 1967).

Kupka, Paul, *Zur Chronologie und Genesis des "Roman de la Rose"* (Gardelegen: Julius Könecke, 1901).

Labriolle, Pierre de, *La Réaction païenne: Etude sur la polémique antichrétienne du I*^er^ *au VI*^e^ *siècle* (Paris: Artisan du livre, 1934).

Langlois, Ernest, *Origines et sources du "Roman de la Rose"*, Bibliothèque des Ecoles françaises d'Athènes et de Rome (Paris: Ernest Thorin, 1891).

Lazar, Moshé, *Amour courtois et "fin' amors" dans la littérature du XII*^e^ *siècle* (= *Bibliothèque française et romane, série* C: *Etudes littéraires*, VIII) (Paris: C. Klincksieck, 1964).

Lea, Henry Charles, *History of Sacerdotal Celibacy in the Christian Church*, 4th edition, revised (University Books, 1966).

Le Gentil, P[ierre], *La Chanson de Roland* (= *Connaissance des lettres*, 43) (Paris: Hatier, 1955).

Lejeune, Rita, *Mélanges*. See *Mélanges... Rita Lejeune*.

Lewicka, Halina, *La Langue et le style du théâtre comique français des XV*^e^ *et XVI*^e^ *siècles: La Dérivation* (Warsaw: Państwowe Wydawnictwo Naukowe [Editions scientifiques de Pologne] and Paris: Klincksieck, 1960).

Lewis, C. S., *The Allegory of Love: A Study in Medieval Tradition* (= *Galaxy, GB* 17) (1936; rpt. London: Oxford Univ. Press, 1968).

Leyburn, Ellen Douglass, *Satiric Allegory: Mirror of Man* (= *Yale Studies in English*, 130) (New Haven: Yale Univ. Press, 1956).

Loomis, Roger Sherman, *Arthurian Tradition & Chrétien de Troyes* (New York and London: Columbia Univ. Press, 1941).

Loomis, Roger Sherman, ed. *Arthurian Literature in the Middle Ages: A Collaborative History* (1959; rpt. Oxford: Clarendon Press, 1961).

Lot-Borodine, Myrrha, *Le Roman idyllique au moyen âge* (Paris: Picard, 1913).

Lovejoy, Arthur O., *The Great Chain of Being: A Study in the History of an Idea* (= *Harper Torchbooks: The Academic Library*, TB 1009) (1936; rpt. New York: Harper & Row, 1960).

Lubac, Henri de, *Exégèse médiévale: Les Quatre Sens de l'Ecriture*, 4 vols. (= *Théologie*, nos. 41, 42, and 59) (Aubier: Editions Montaigne, 1959-1964).

Lucas, Harry, *Les Poésies personnelles de Rutebeuf: Etude linguistique et littéraire suivie d'une édition critique du texte avec commentaire et glossaire* (Strassburg: Faculté des lettres de l'Univ. de Strasbourg, 1938).

McLeod, Enid, *Charles of Orleans: Prince and Poet* (London: Chatto & Windus, 1969).

Marrou, Henri-Irénée, *Saint Augustin et la fin de la culture antique* (= *Bibliothèque des écoles françaises d'Athènes et de Rome*, 45) (Paris: E. de Boccard, 1938).

Masson, A.-L., *Jean Gerson: Sa Vie, son temps, ses oeuvres* (Lyons: Emmanuel Vitte, 1894).

Mélanges de langue et de littérature du moyen âge et de la Renaissance offerts à Jean Frappier... par ses collègues, ses élèves et ses amis, 2 vols. (= *Publications romanes et françaises*, 112) (Geneva: Droz, 1970).

Mélanges offerts à Rita Lejeune, 2 vols. (Gembloux: Duculot, 1969).

Ménard, Philippe, *Le Rire et le sourire dans le roman courtois en France au Moyen Age (1150-1250)* (= *Publications romanes et françaises*, 105) (Geneva: Droz, 1969).

Menendes Pidal, Ramón, "*La Chanson de Roland*" *et la tradition épique des Francs*, 2nd edition, revised by René Louis, trans. Irénée-Marcel Cluzel (Paris: A. & J. Picard, 1960).

Michaud, Guy, *Message poétique du symbolisme* (Paris: Nizet, 1966).

Milburn, R. L. P., *Early Christian Interpretations of History*, Bampton Lectures of 1952 (London: Adam & Charles Black, 1954).

Mojsisovics, Edgar von, *Metrik und Sprache Rustebuef's* (Heidelberg: Carl Winter, 1906).

Moore, Arthur Keister, *Studies in a Medieval Prejudice: Antifeminism*, Vanderbilt Univ. (Nashville, Tennessee: Joint Univ. Libraries, 1945).

Morrall, John B., *Gerson and the Great Schism* (Manchester: Univ. Press, 1960).

Müller, Franz Walter, *Der "Rosenroman" und der lateinische Averroismus des 13. Jahrhunderts* (Frankfurt am Main: Vittorio Klostermann, 1947).

Müller, Michael, *Die Lehre des hl. Augustinus von der Paradiessehe und ihre Auswirkung in der Sexualethik des 12. und 13. Jahrhunderts bis Thomas von Aquin: Eine moralgeschichtliche Untersuchung* (= *Studien zur Geschichte der kath. Moraltheologie*, 1) (Regensburg: Friedrich Pustet, 1954).

Munari, Franco, *Ovid im Mittelalter* (Zürich and Stuttgart: Artemis, 1960).

Nichols, Stephen G., Jr., *Formulaic Diction and Thematic Composition in the "Chanson de Roland"* (= *Univ. of North Carolina Studies in the Romance Languages and Literatures*, 36) (Chapel Hill: Univ. of North Carolina Press, 1961).

Otto, Rudolf, *The Idea of the Holy: An Inquiry into the Non-Rational Factor in the Idea of the Divine and Its Relation to the Rational*, trans. John W. Harvey, 2nd edition (= *Galaxy*, *GB* 14) (1950; rpt. London: Oxford Univ. Press, 1971).

Oulmont, Charles, *Les Débats du clerc et du chevalier dans la littérature poétique du moyen-âge: Etude historique et littéraire suivie de l'édition critique des textes* (Paris: Champion, 1911).

Owen, D. D. R., ed., *Arthurian Romance: Seven Essays* (Edinburgh and London: Scottish Academic Press, 1970).

Panvini, Bruno, *La Legenda di Tristano e Isotta*, introd. by Salvatore Santangelo (= *Biblioteca dell' Archivum Romanicum*, 32) (Florence: Leo S. Olschki, 1951).

Paré, Gérard, *Le "Roman de la Rose" et la scolastique courtoise* (= *Publications de l'Institut d'études médiévales d'Ottawa*, 10) (Paris: Vrin, 1941).

——, *Les Idées et les lettres au XIIIe siècle: "Le Roman de la Rose"* (= *Publications de l'Institut d'études médiévales Albert-le-Grand, Univ. de Montréal, Bibliothèque de philosophie*, 1) (Montréal: Centre de psychologie et de pédagogie, 1947).

Paris, Gaston, *Histoire poétique de Charlemagne* (Paris: A. Franck, 1865).

——, *Tristan & Iseut* (Paris: Emile Bouillon, 1894).

Patch, Howard R., *The Other World according to Descriptions in Medieval Literature* (= *Smith College Studies in Modern Languages, New Series*, I) (Cambridge, Mass.: Harvard Univ. Press, 1950).

——, *The Goddess Fortuna in Medieval Literature* (1927; rpt. New York: Octagon, 1967).

Pellegrini, Silvio, *Studi rolandiani e trobadorici* (= *Biblioteca di filologia romanza*, 8) (Bari: Adriatica, 1964).

Pépin, Jean, *Mythe et allégorie: Les Origines grecques et les contestations judéo-chrétiennes*, Philosophie de l'esprit (Aubier: Editions Montaigne, 1958).

Petit de Julleville, Louis, *Répertoire du théâtre comique en France au moyen-âge*, Histoire du théâtre en France (Paris: Léopold Cerf, 1886).

——, *La Comédie et les moeurs en France au moyen âge*, 4th edition, Histoire du théâtre en France (Paris: Léopold Cerf, 1910).

Piehler, Paul, *The Visionary Landscape: A Study in Medieval Allegory* (Montreal: McGill-Queen's Univ. Press, 1971).

Recherches théologiques par les professeurs de la Faculté de théologie protestante de l'Université de Strasbourg, 3 vols. (Paris: Félix Alcan, 1936-1938).

Regalado, Nancy Freeman, *Poetic Patterns in Rutebeuf: A Study in Noncourtly Poetic Modes of the Thirteenth Century* (= *Yale Romanic Studies, 2nd series*, 21) (New Haven and London: Yale Univ. Press, 1970).

Rice, Winthrop Huntington, *The European Ancestry of Villon's Satirical Testaments* (= *Syracuse Univ. Monographs*, 1) (New York: Corporate Press, 1941).

Riedel, F. Carl, *Crime and Punishment in the Old French Romances* (= *Columbia Univ. Studies in English and Comparative Literature*, 135) (New York: Columbia Univ. Press, 1938).

Riquer, Martin de, *Los Cantares de gesta franceses* (*su problemas, su relacion con España*), Biblioteca romanica hispanica (Madrid: Gredos, 1952).

Ruggieri, Ruggero M., *Il Processo di Gano nella "Chanson de Roland"* (= *Publicazioni della Scuola di filologia moderna della R. Università di Roma*, III) (Florence: G. C. Sansoni, 1936).

Rychner, Jean, *La Chanson de geste: Essai sur l'art épique des jongleurs* (= *Société de publications romanes et françaises*, 53) (Geneva: Droz, 1955).

Savage, Edward B., *The Rose and the Wine: A Study of the Evolution of the Tristan and Isolt Tale in Drama* (Cairo: American Univ. at Cairo Press, 1961).

Scaglione, Aldo D., *Nature and Love in the Late Middle Ages* (Berkeley and Los Angeles: Univ. of California Press, 1963).

Schoepperle, Gertrude, *Tristan and Isolt: A Study of the Sources of the Romance*, 2nd edition, ed. Roger Sherman Loomis, 2 vols. (New York: Burt Franklin, 1960).

Schwab, Johann Baptist, *Johannes Gerson, Professor der Theologie und Kanzler der Universität Paris: Eine Monographie* (Würzburg: Stahel'schen, 1858).

Seaton, [Mary] Ethel, *Studies in Villon, Vaillant and Charles d'Orléans* (Oxford: B. H. Blackwell, 1957).

Serper, Arié, *La Manière satirique de Rutebeuf: Le Ton et le style* (Naples: Liguori, 1972).

Seznec, Jean, *La Survivance des dieux antiques: Essai sur le rôle de la tradition mythologique dans l'humanisme et dans l'art de la Renaissance* (= *Studies of the Warburg Institute*, XI) (London: Warburg Institute, 1940).

Siciliano, Italo, *François Villon et les thèmes poétiques du moyen âge* (1933; rpt. Paris: Nizet, 1967).

Spiq, P. C., *Esquisse d'une histoire de l'exégèse latine au moyen âge* (= *Bibliothèque thomiste*, 26) (Paris: Vrin, 1944).

Spitzer, Leo, *L'Amour lointain de Jaufré Rudel et le sens de la poésie des troubadours* (= *Univ. of North Carolina Studies in the Romance Languages and Literatures*, 5) (Chapel Hill: Univ. of North Carolina, 1944).

Studi in onore di Italo Siciliano (= *Biblioteca dell' Archivum Romanicum*, 86) (Florence: Leo S. Olschki, 1966).

Thuasne, Louis, *Villon et Rabelais: Notes et commentaires* (1911; rpt. Geneva: Slatkine, 1969).

Tindall, William York, *The Literary Symbol* (= *Midland, MB* 7) (Bloomington: Indiana Univ. Press, 1955).

Traver, Hope, *The Four Daughters of God: A Study of the Versions of this Allegory with Special Reference to Those in Latin, French, and English* (= *Bryn Mawr College Monographs, Monograph Series*, VI) (Bryn Mawr: Bryn Mawr College, 1909).

Tuve, Rosemond, *Allegorical Imagery: Some Medieval Books and Their Posterity* (Princeton: Princeton Univ. Press, 1966).

Tuzet, Hélène, *Le Cosmos et l'imagination* (Paris: José Corti, 1965).

Valency, Maurice, *In Praise of Love: An Introduction to the Love-Poetry of the Renaissance* (= *Macmillan Paperbacks, MP* 58) (1958; New York: Macmillan, 1961).

Vàrvaro, Alberto, *Il "Roman de Tristan" di Béroul* (= *Università di Pisa, Studi di filologia moderna, Nuova serie*, 3) (Torino: Bottega d'Erasmo, 1963).

——, *Struttura e forme della letteratura romanza del medioevo, vol I* (Naples: Liguori, 1968).

Vinaver, Eugène, *The Rise of Romance* (New York and Oxford: Oxford Univ. Press, 1971).

Webber, F. R., *Church Symbolism: An Explanation of the More Important Symbols of the Old and New Testament, the Primitive, the Mediaeval and the Modern Church*, introd. by Ralph Adams Cram (Cleveland: J. H. Hansen, 1927).

Welther, J.-Th., *L'Exemple dans la littérature religieuse et didactique du moyen âge* (Paris: Guitard, 1927).

Wenzel, Siegfried, *The Sin of Sloth: Acedia in Medieval Thought and Literature* (1960; rpt. Chapel Hill: Univ. of North Carolina Press, 1967).

Wetherbee, Winthrop, *Platonism and Poetry in the Twelfth Century: The Literary Influence of the School of Chartres* (Princeton: Princeton Univ. Press, 1972).

Whitehead, F. A. H. Diverres and F. E. Sutcliffe, ed., *Medieval Miscellany Presented to Eugène Vinaver by Pupils, Colleagues and Friends* (Manchester Univ. Press; New York: Barnes & Noble, 1965).

Whittaker, Thomas, *Macrobius or Philosophy, Science and Letters in the Year 400* (Cambridge, England: Univ. Press, 1923).

Wilder, Amos N., *Early Christian Rhetoric: The Language of the Gospel* (Cambridge, Mass.: Harvard Univ. Press, 1971).

Williams, Arnold, *The Common Expositor: An Account of the Commentaries on Genesis, 1527-1633* (Chapel Hill: Univ. of North Carolina Press, 1948).

Wood, Mary Morton, *The Spirit of Protest in Old French Literature*, Columbia Univ. Studies in Romance Philology and Literature (New York: Columbia Univ. Press, 1917).

Wyndham Lewis, D. B., *François Villon: A Documented Survey*, preface by Hilaire Belloc (New York: Literary Guild of America, 1928).

Ziltener, Werner, *Chrétien und die Aeneis: Eine Untersuchung des Einflusses von Vergil auf Chrétien von Troyes* (Graz-Köln: Böhlau, 1957).

Articles

Adler, Alfred, "The *Pèlerinage de Charlemagne* in New Light on Saint-Denis", *Speculum*, 22 (1947), 550-561.

Aebischer, Paul, "Le Gab d'Olivier", *Revue belge de philologie et d'histoire*, 34 (1956), 659-679.

Ampère, J.-J., "*Le Roman de la Rose*", *Revue des Deux Mondes*, 13, nouvelle série, 3 (1843), 541-581.

Badel, P., "Raison 'fille de Dieu' et le rationalisme de Jean de Meun", *Mélanges... Frappier*, I, 41-52.

Bates, Robert C., "*Le Pèlerinage de Charlemagne: A Baroque Epic*", in *Studies by Members of the French Department of Yale University: Decennial Volume*, ed. Albert Feuillerat (= *Yale Romanic Studies*, 18) (New Haven: Yale Univ. Press, 1941), 1-47.

Becker, Ph. Aug., "Woher stammt Andry de la Vigne?", *Zeitschrift für französische Sprache und Literatur*, 54 (1931), 170.

Beichner, Paul E., "The Allegorical Interpretation of Medieval Literature", *PMLA*, 62 (1967), 33-38.

Bertolucci, Valeria, "Commento retorico all'*Erec* e al *Cligès*", *Studi mediolatini e volgari*, 8 (1960), 9-51.

Beyer, Victor, "Rosaces et roues de Fortune à la fin de l'art roman et au début de l'art gothique", *Zeitschrift für schweizerische Archäologie und Kunstgeschichte*, 22 (1962), 34-43.

Blakey, Brian, "*Aucassin et Nicolette*, XXIV, 4", *French Studies*, 22 (1968), 97-98.

Born, Lester K., "Ovid and Allegory", *Speculum*, 9 (1934), 362-379.

Brault, Gérard J., "Ganelon et Roland: Deux Anecdotes du traître concernant le héros", *Romania*, 92 (1971), 392-405.

Brown, Arthur C. L., "*Iwain:* A Study in the Origins of Arthurian Romance", *Harvard Studies and Notes in Philology and Literature*, 8 (1903), 1-147.

——, "The Knight of the Lion", *PMLA*, 20 (1904), 673-706.

——, "*Chrétiens' 'Yvain'*", *Modern Philology*, 9 (1911-1912), 109-128.

Burger, André, "Le Rire de Roland", *Cahiers de civilisation médiévale*, 3 (1960), 2-11.

Burlingame, Eugene Watson, "The Act of Truth (Saccakiriya): A Hindu Spell and Its Employment as a Psychic Motif in Hindu Fiction", *Journal of the Royal Asiatic Society of Great Britain and Ireland* (1917), 429-467.

Champion, Pierre, "Du succès de l'oeuvre de Charles d'Orléans", in *Mélanges offerts à M. Emile Picot par ses amis et ses élèves*, 2 vols. (Paris: Damascène Morgand, 1913), I, 409-420.

Christmann, Hans Helmut, "Sur un passage du *Tristan* de Béroul", *Romania*, 80 (1959), 85-87.

——, "Nochmals zu Berols *Tristan* v. 4223-4225", *Zeitschrift für französische Sprache und Literatur*, 76 (1966), 243-245.

Cluzel, Irénée, "Jaufré Rudel et l'*amour de lonh*: Essai d'une nouvelle classification des pièces du troubadour", *Romania*, 78 (1957), 86-97.

Cocito, Luciana, "Osservazioni e note sulla lirica di Rutebeuf", *Giornale italiano di filologia*, 11 (1958), 347-357.

Cohen, Anne-Lise, "Exploration of Sounds in Rutebeuf's Poetry", *French Review*, 40 (1967), 658-667.

Cohen, Gustave, "Le Thème de l'aveugle et du paralytique dans la littérature française", in *Mélanges offerts à M. Emile Picot*, II, 393-404.

Cross, Tom Peete, "The Gabs", *Modern Philology*, 25 (1927-1928), 349-354.

Curtis, Renée L., "Le Philtre mal préparé: Le Thème de la réciprocité dans l'amour de Tristan et Iseut", *Mélanges... Frappier*, I, 195-206.

Dahlberg, Charles R., "Macrobius and the Unity of the *Roman de la Rose*", *Studies in Philology*, 58 (1961), 573-582.

——, "Love and the *Roman de la Rose*", *Speculum*, 44 (1969), 568-584.

Defourny, Michel, "Observations sur la première partie du *Roman de la Rose*", *Mélanges... Lejeune*, II, 1163-1169.

——, "*Le Roman de la Rose* à travers l'histoire et la philosophie", *Marche romane*, 17 (1967), 53-60.

Delhaye, Chanoine Philippe, "Le Péché dans la théologie d'Alain de Lille", *Sciences ecclésiastiques*, 17 (1965), 7-27.

Demats, Paule, "D'*Amoenitas* à *Deduit:* André le Chapelain et Guillaume de Lorris", *Mélanges... Frappier*, I, 217-233.

Denomy, Alex J., "An Inquiry into the Origins of Courtly Love", *Mediaeval Studies*, 6 (1944), 175-260.

——, "*Fin'Amors:* The Pure Love of the Troubadours, Its Amorality, and Possible Source", *Mediaeval Studies*, 7 (1945), 139-207.

——, "*Jois* among Early Troubadours: Its Meaning and Possible Source", *Mediaeval Studies*, 13 (1951), 177-217.

——, "The Vocabulary of Jean de Meun's Translation of Boethius' *De Consolatione Philosophiae*", *Mediaeval Studies*, 16 (1954), 19-34.

Dessau, Adalbert, "L'Idée de la trahison au moyen âge et son rôle dans la motivation de quelques chansons de geste", *Cahiers de civilisation médiévale*, 3 (1960), 23-26.

Duggan, Joseph J., "Yvain's Good Name: The Unity of Chrétien de Troyes' 'Chevalier au lion'", *Orbis litterarum*, 24 (1969), 112-129.

Dwyer, R. A., "'Je meurs de soif auprès de la fontaine'", *French Studies*, 23 (1969), 225-228.

Economou, George D., "Januarie's Sin against Nature: The *Merchant's Tale* and the *Roman de la Rose*", *Comparative Literature*, 17 (1965), 251-257.

Egbert, Virginia Wylie, "Pygmalion as Sculptor", *Princeton Univ. Library Chronicle*, 28 (1966-1967), 20-23.

Faral, Edmond, "Le *Roman de la Rose* et la pensée française au XIIIe siècle", *Revue des Deux Mondes*, 35 (1926), 430-457.

Favati, Guido, "Il 'Voyage de Charlemagne en orient'", *Studi mediolatini e volgari*, 11 (1963), 75-159.

Fennley, G. Ward, "Faus-Semblant, Fauvel, and Renart le Contrefait: A Study in Kinship", *Romanic Review*, 23 (1932), 323-331.

Finlayson, John, "*Ywain and Gawain* and the Meaning of Adventure", *Anglia*, 87 (1969), 312-337.

Fisher, John H., "Tristan and Courtly Adultery", *Comparative Literature*, 9 (1957), 150-164.

Fleming, John V., "The Moral Reputation of the *Roman de la Rose* before 1400", *Romance Philology*, 18 (1964-1965), 430-435.

Foulet, Lucien, "Villon et Charles d'Orléans", in *Medieval Studies in Memory of Gertrude Schoepperle Loomis* (Paris: Champion and New York: Columbia Univ. Press, 1927), 355-380.

Fourquet, Jean, "Littérature courtoise et théologie", *Etudes germaniques*, 12 (1957), 34-39.

François, Carlo, "*Tristan et Iseut*, poème d'amour et manuel de la ruse", *Mercure de France*, 338 (1960), 611-625.

Frank, Grace, "Villon at the Court of Charles d'Orléans", *Modern Language Notes*, 47 (1932), 498-505.

——, "The Distant Love of Jaufré Rudel", *Modern Language Notes*, 57 (1942), 528-534.

Frank, Robert Worth, Jr. "The Art of Reading Medieval Personification-Allegory", *ELH*, 20 (1953), 237-250.

Frappier, Jean, "Variations sur le thème du miroir, de Bernard de Ventadour à Maurice Scève", *Cahiers de l'Association internationale des études françaises*, 11 (1959), 134-158.

——, "Vues sur les conceptions courtoises dans les littératures d'oc et d'oïl au XIIe siècle", *Cahiers de civilisation médiévale*, 2 (1959), 135-156.

——, "Structure et sens du *Tristan:* Version commune, version courtoise", *Cahiers de civilisation médiévale*, 6 (1963), 255-280 and 441-454.

——, "Le Motif du 'don contraignant' dans la littérature du Moyen Age", *Travaux de linguistique et de littérature publiés par le Centre de philologie et de littératures romanes de l'Univ. de Strasbourg*, 7.2 (1969), 7-46.

——, "Le Concept de l'amour dans les romans arthuriens", *Bulletin bibliographique de la Société internationale arthurienne*, 22 (1970), 119-136.

Friedmann, Lionel L., "Jean de Meung, 'Antifeminism,' and 'Bourgeois Realism'", *Modern Philology*, 57 (1959-1960), 13-23.

——, "Jean de Meun and Ethelred of Rievaulx", *Esprit créateur*, 2 (1962), 135-141.

——, "Gradus amoris", *Romance Philology*, 19 (1965-1966), 167-177.

Galpin, Stanley Leman, "Fortune's Wheel in the *Roman de la Rose*", *PMLA*, 24 (1909), 332-342.

——, "Dangiers li Vilains", *Romanic Review*, 2 (1911), 320-322.

——, "Influence of the Mediaeval Christian Visions on Jean de Meun's Notions of Hell", *Romanic Review*, 2 (1911), 54-60.

Gérard, Alb, "L'Axe Roland-Ganelon: Valeurs en conflit dans la *Chanson de Roland*", *Moyen Age*, 75 (1969), 445-465.

Gunn, Alan M. F., "Teacher and Student in the *Roman de la Rose*: A Study in Archetypal Figures and Patterns", *Esprit créateur*, 2 (1962), 126-134.

Hall, Robert A., "Ganelon and Roland", *Modern Language Quarterly*, 6 (1945), 263-269.

Ham, Edward Billings, "Régionalismes dans le *Roman de la Rose*", in *Mélanges de linguistique française offerts à M. Charles Bruneau* (= *Société de publications romanes et françaises*, 45) (Geneva: Droz, 1954), 235-239.

Hamilton, George L., "Storm-Making Springs: Rings of Invisibility and Protection. — Studies on the Sources of the *Yvain* of Chrétien de Troyes", *Romanic Review*, 2 (1911), 355-375.

Harden, Robert, "*Aucassin et Nicolette* as Parody", *Studies in Philology*, 63 (1966), 1-9.

Hatzfeld, Helmut, "La Mistica naturalistica di Giovanni di Meung", trans. Ugo Piscopo, *Delta: Rivista di critica e di cultura*, 3rd series, 1 (July, 1962), 25-32.

Heinermann, Theodor, "Zeit und Sinn der Karlsreise", *Zeitschrift für romanische Philologie*, 56 (1936), 497-562.

Heisig, Karl, "Arabische Astrologie und christliche Apologetik im *Rosenroman*", *Romanische Forschungen*, 71 (1959), 414-419.

Hill, Thomas D., "La Vieille's Digression on Free Love: A Note on Rhetorical Structure in the *Romance of the Rose*", *Romance Notes*, 8 (1966), 113-115.

Horrent, Jules, "La Chanson du Pèlerinage de Charlemagne et la réalité historique contemporaine", *Mélanges... Frappier*, I, 411-417.

——, "Pèlerinage de Charlemagne à Jérusalem et à Constantinople", *Moyen Age*, 75 (1967), 489-494.

Jackson, W. T. H., "The *De Amore* of Andreas Capellanus and the Practice of Love at Court", *Romanic Review*, 49 (1958), 243-251.

——, "Allegory and Allegorization", *Research Studies*, 32 (1964), 161-175.

Jauss, Hans Robert, "Ernst und Scherz in Mittelalterlicher Allegorie", in *Mélanges... Frappier*, I, 433-451.

Jenkins, T. Atkinson, "Why did Ganelon hate Roland?", *PMLA*, 36 (1921), 119-133.

Jodogne, Omer, "*Aucassin et Nicolette, Clarisse et Florent*", *Mélanges ... Frappier*, I, 453-481.

——, "La Parodie et le pastiche dans 'Aucassin et Nicolette'", *Cahiers de l'Association internationale des études françaises*, 12 (1960), 53-65.

——, "L'Anticléricalisme de Rutebeuf", *Lettres romanes*, 23 (1969), 219-244.

Johnston, O. M., "The Fountain Episode in Chrétien de Troyes's *Yvain*", *Transactions and Proceedings of the American Philological Association*, 38 (1902), lxxxiii-lxxxiv.

Jones, George Fenwick, "Lov'd I Not Honour More: The Durability of a Literary Motif", *Comparative Literature*, 11 (1959), 131-143.

——, "Friendship in the *Chanson de Roland*", *Modern Language Quarterly*, 24 (1963), 88-98.

Joret, Charles, "La Légende de la rose au moyen âge chez les nations romanes et germaniques", in *Etudes romanes dédiées à Gaston Paris... par ses élèves français et ses élèves étrangers des pays de langue française* (Paris: Emile Bouillon, 1918), 279-302.

Jung, Marc-René, "Der *Rosenroman* in der Kritik seit dem 18. Jahrhunderts", *Romanische Forschungen*, 78 (1966), 203-252.

Keins, Pablo, "Politische Satire und 'poésie personnelle' by Rutebeuf", *Zeitschrift für französische Sprache und Literatur*, 74 (1964), 241-262.

Kelly, Douglas, "Gauvain and *Fin'Amors* in the Poems of Chrétien de Troyes", *Studies in Philology*, 67 (1970), 453-460.

——, "La Forme et le sens de la Quête dans l'*Erec et Enide* de Chrétien de Troyes", *Romania*, 92 (1971), 326-358.

Knowlton, Edgar C., "The Allegorical Figure Genius", *Classical Philology*, 15 (1920), 380-384.

——, "The Goddess Nature in Early Periods", *Journal of English and Germanic Philology*, 19 (1920), 224-253.

——, "Nature in Old French", *Modern Philology*, 20 (1922-1923), 309-329.

——, "Genius as an Allegorical Figure", *Modern Language Notes*, 39 (1924), 89-95.

Knudson, Charles A., "Serments téméraires et gabs: Notes sur un thème littéraire", *Société Rencevals: IVe Congrès international* (1967), *Studia romanica*, 14 (1969), 254-260.

Kressner, A., "Rustebeuf, ein Dichterleben im Mittelalter", *Franco-Gallia*, 10 (1893), 165-170.

——, "Rustebeuf als Satiren-Dichter", *Franco-Gallia*, 11 (1894), 17-23.

Lecoy, Félix, "Sur un passage délicat du *Roman de la Rose* (vers 5532 de l'édition Langlois)", *Romania*, 85 (1964), 372-376.

Leo, Ulrich, "Rutebeuf: Persönlicher Ausdruck und Wirklichkeit", in Ulrich Leo, *Romanistische Aufsätze aus drei Jahrzehnten*, ed. Fritz Schalk (Köln and Graz: Böhlau, 1966).

Lonigan, Paul R., "Ganelon before Marsile ('Chanson de Roland,' laisses XXXII-LII)", *Studi francesi*, 14 (41) (1970), 276-280.

Loomis, Laura Hibbard, "Observations on the *Pèlerinage de Charlemagne*", *Modern Philology*, 25 (1927-1928), 321-322.

Lot-Borodine, Myrrha, "Tristan et Lancelot", In *Medieval Studies in Memory of Gertrude Schoepperle Loomis* (Paris: H. Champion and New York: Columbia Univ. Press, 1927), 21-47.

Louis, René, "Une Coutume d'origine protohistorique: Les Combats sur les gués chez les Celtes et chez les Germains", *Revue archéologique de l'Est et du Centre-Est*, 5 (1954), 186-193.

Luria, Maxwell S., "The Storm-Making Spring and the Meaning of Chrétien's *Yvain*", *Studies in Philology*, 64 (1967), 564-585.

Lyons, Faith, "Sentiment et rhétorique dans l'*Yvain*", *Romania*, 83 (1962), 372-377.

McKean, Sister M. Faith, R. S. M., "The Role of Faux Semblant and Astenance Contrainte in the *Roman de la Rose*". See Holmes, Urban Tigner, ed., *Romance Studies*, 103-107.

——, "Torelore and courtoisie", *Romance Notes*, 3 (1961-1962), 64-68.

Magoun, F[rancis] P[eabody], "Chaucer and the *Roman de la Rose*, vv. 16096-16105", *Romanic Review*, 17 (1926), 69-70.

Méjean, Suzanne, "A propos de l'arbre aux oiseaux dans *Yvain*", *Romania*, 91 (1970), 392-399.

Ménard, Philippe, "*Je meurs de soif auprès de la fontaine:* D'un mythe antique à une image lyrique", *Romania*, 87 (1966), 394-400.

Messiaen, Pierre, "François Villon, le Bon Larron (1431-?)", *Etudes*, 76. 238 (1939), 822-832.

Micha, Alexandre, "Le Discours collectif dans l'épopée et dans le roman", in *Mélanges ...Frappier*, II, 811-821.

——, "*Enéas* et *Cligès*", in *Mélanges de philologie romane et de littérature médiévale offerts à Ernest Hoepffner... par ses élèves et ses amis* (= *Publications de la Faculté des lettres de l'Univ. de Strasbourg*, 113) (Paris: Belles Lettres, 1949), 237-243.

——, "Le Mari jaloux dans la littérature romanesque des XIIe et XIIIe siècles", *Studi medievali*, 17 (1951), 303-320.

——, "*Tristan* et *Cligès*", *Neophilologus*, 36 (1952), 1-10.

——, "En relisant 'Aucassin et Nicolette'", *Moyen Age*, 65 (1959), 279-292.

Micha, Hugues, "Structure et regard romanesques dans l'oeuvre de Chrétien de Troyes" *Cahiers de civilisation médiévale*, 13 (1970), 323-332.

Morgan, Louise B., "The Source of the Fountain-Story in the *Ywain*", *Modern Philology*, 6 (1908-1909), 331-341.

Muscatine, Charles, "The Emergence of Psychological Allegory in Old French Romance", *PMLA*, 68 (1953), 1161-1182.

Neuschäfer, Hans-Jörg, "*Le Voyage de Charlemagne en Orient* als Parodie der Chanson de Geste: Untersuchungen zur Epenparodie im Mittelalter", *Romanistisches Jahrbuch*, 10 (1959), 78-102.

Newstead, Helaine, "The Equivocal Oath in the Tristan Legend", *Mélanges...Lejeune*, II, 1077-1085.

Nichols, Stephen G., Jr., "Ethical Criticism and Medieval Literature: *Le Roman de Tristan*", in *Medieval Secular Literature: Four Essays*, ed. William Matthews (= *Contributions of the UCLA Center for Medieval and Renaissance Studies*, 1) (Berkeley and Los Angeles: Univ. of California Press, 1965), 68-69.

Nitze, William A., "The Fountain Defended", *Modern Philology*, 7 (1909), 145-164.

——, "Yvain and the Myth of the Fountain", *Speculum*, 30 (1955), 170-179.

Noble, Peter, "L'Influence de la courtoisie sur le *Tristan* de Béroul", *Moyen Age*, 75 (1969), 467-477.

Nykrog, Per, "La Composition du *Roland* d'Oxford", *Romania*, 88 (1967), 509-526.

Odegaard, Charles Edwin, "The Concept of Royal Power in Carolingian Oaths of Fidelity", *Speculum*, 20 (1945), 279-289.

Owen, D. D. Roy, "*Voyage de Charlemagne* and *Chanson de Roland*", *Studi francesi*, 33 (1967), 468-472.

Panvini, Bruno, "Ancora sul *Pèlerinage Charlemagne*", *Siculorum gymnasium*, 13 (1960), 17-80.

Parfondry, Max, "A propos d'une ballade de Villon: *Je meurs de seuf auprès de la fontaine*", in *Mélanges... Lejeune*, II, 1453-1467.

Paris, Gaston, "La Chanson du Pèlerinage de Charlemagne", *Romania*, 9 (1880), 1-50.

——, "Le *Carmen de Prodicione Guenonis* et la légende de Roncevaux", *Romania*, 11 (1882), 465-518.

Paris, Paulin, "Notice sur la chanson de geste intitulée *Le Voyage de Charlemagne à Jérusalem et à Constantinople*", *Jahrbuch für romanische und englische Literatur*, 1 (1859), 198-211.

Pellegrini, Silvio, "L'Ira di Gano". See Pellegrini, *Studi rolandiani e trobadorici*, 122-135.

Pézard, André, "Lune et fortune chez Jean de Meung et chez Dante", *Studi in onore di Italo Siciliano*, II, 985-995.

Philipot, E., "Le Roman du *Chevalier au lion* de Chrestien de Troyes", *Annales de Bretagne*, 8 (1892-1893), 33-83, 321-345, and 455-479.

Piaget, Arthur, "Chronologie des epistres sur le *Roman de la Rose*", in *Etudes romanes dédiées à Gaston Paris*, 113-120.

Pike, Robert E., "Note on André de la Vigne", *Philological Quarterly*, 15 (1936), 95-96.

Post, Charles H., "The Paradox of Humor and Satire in the Poems of Rutebeuf", *French Review*, 25 (1951-1952), 364-368.

Ranke, Friedrich, "Isoldes Gottesurteil", in *Medieval Studies in Memory of Gertrude Schoepperle Loomis*, 87-94.

Raynaud de Lage, Guy, "*Natura* et *Genius*, chez Jean de Meung et chez Jean Lemaire de Belges", *Moyen Age*, 58 (1952), 125-143.

——, "Du style de Béroul", *Romania*, 85 (1964), 518-530.

Rigolot, François, "Valeur figurative du vêtement dans le *Tristan* de Béroul", *Cahiers de civilisation médiévale*, 10 (1967), 447-453.

Robertson, D. W., Jr., "The Doctrine of Charity in Mediaeval Literary Gardens", *Speculum*, 26 (1951), 24-49.

Robertson, Howard S., "Blancandrin as Diplomat", *Romance Notes*, 10 (1969), 373-378.

Rösler, Margarete, "Die 'Fontaine perilleuse' in Chrestiens *Yvain*", *Zeitschrift für französische Sprache und Literatur*, 58 (1934), 232-235.

Ruggieri, Ruggero Am., "A proposito dell'ira di Gano", *Cultura neolatina*, 4-5 (1944-1945), 163-165.

Ryding, William W., "Faus Semblant: Hero or Hypocrite?", *Romanic Review*, 60 (1969), 163-167.

Schlauch, Margaret, "The Palace of Hugon de Constantinople", *Speculum*, 7 (1932), 500-514.

Schmidt, Albert-Marie, "Andry de la Vigne et *La Ressource de la chrétienté* (1494)", *Lettres nouvelles*, 4. 41 (1956), 267-278.

Serrigny, Ernest, "La Représentation d'un mystère de Saint-Martin à Seurre, en 1496", *Mémoires de l'Académie des sciences, arts et belles-lettres de Dijon*, 3e série, 10 (1887), 275-477.

Settegast, F., "Die Odyssee oder die Sage vom heimkehrenden Gatten als Quelle mittelalterlicher Dichtung", *Zeitschrift für romanische Philologie*, 39 (1917-1919), 267-329.

Sneyders de Vogel, K., "Marot et le *Roman de la Rose*", *Neophilologus*, 17 (1931-1932), 269-271.

Strohm, Paul, "Guillaume as Narrator and Lover in the *Roman de la Rose*", *Romanic Review*, 59 (1968), 3-9.

Thuasne, Louis, "François Villon et Jean de Meun", *Revue des bibliothèques* (*Paris*), 16 (1906), 93-144 and 204-249.

——, "Les Sources du 'Diomedès' de Villon", in *Villon et Rabelais: Notes et commentaires*, 419-430.

Uitti, Karl D., "Chrétien de Troyes' *Yvain*: Fiction and Sense", *Romance Philology*, 22 (1969), 471-483.

Van Hamel, A. G., "*Cligès* et *Tristan*", *Romania*, 33 (1904), 465-489.

Vàrvaro, Alberto, "L'Utilizzazione letteraria di motivi della narrative popolare nei romanzi di Tristano", *Mélanges... Frappier*, II, 1057-1075.

Wagner, R. L., "Villon et Jean de Bueil (d'un exemple à un mythe)", in *Medieval Miscellany Presented to Eugène Vinaver*, 289-299.

Walpole, Ronald N., "The *Pèlerinage de Charlemagne:* Poem, Legend, and Problem", *Romance Philology*, 8 (1955), 173-186.

Wilcox, John, "Defining Courtly Love", *Papers of the Michigan Academy of Science, Arts and Letters*, 12 (1930), 313-325.

Will, Robert, "Le Climat religieux de l' 'Hortus deliciarum' d'Herrade de Landsberg", in *Recherches théologiques par les professeurs de la Faculté de théologie protestante de l'Univ. de Strasbourg*, II, 122-166 [522-566].

Williams, Arnold, "Medieval Allegory: An Operational Approach", *Poetic Theory/ Poetic Practice: Papers of the Midwest Modern Language Association* (1968; ed. Robert Scholes), 1 (1969), 77-84.

Wind, Bartina, "Ce Jeu subtil, l'Amour courtois", in *Mélanges... Lejeune*, II, 1257-1261.

Woods, William S., "The Symbolic Structure of *La Chanson de Roland*", *PMLA*, 65 (1950), 1247-1262.

——, "The Choice of Ganelon as Messenger to the Pagans", *Studies in Philology*, 48 (1951), 707-716.

York, Ernest C., "Isolt's Ordeal: English Legal Customs in the Medieval Tristan Legend", *Studies in Philology*, 68 (1971), 1-9.

Zaddy, Z. P., "The Structure of Chrétien's *Yvain*", *Modern Language Review*, 65 (1970), 523-540.

Zorzi, Diego, "L' 'Amor de lonh' de Jaufre Rudel", *Aevum*, 29 (1955), 124-144.

Unpublished

Artin, Thomas, "The Allegory of Adventure: Meaning in Chrétien's *Yvain*", Diss., Princeton, 1968.

Bertin, Gerald André, "The Burlesque Elements in Old French Epic", Diss., Columbia, 1953.

Bezanker, Abraham, "An Introduction to the Problem of Allegory in Literary Criticism", Diss., Michigan, 1954.

Brody, Saul Nathaniel, "The Disease of the Soul: A Study in the Moral Associations of Leprosy in Medieval Literature", Diss., Columbia, 1968.

Dahlberg, Charles R., "The Secular Tradition in Chaucer and Jean de Meun", Diss., Princeton, 1953.

Economou, George Demetrios, "The Goddess Natura in Medieval Literature", Diss., Columbia, 1967.

Ferrante, Joan M., "TRISTAN: A Comparative Study of Five Medieval Works", Diss., Columbia, 1963.

Finnie, W. Brice, "A Structural Study of Six Medieval Arthurian Romances", Diss., Ohio State Univ., 1965.

Haller, Robert Spencer, "The Old Whore and Medieval Thought: Variations on a Convention", Diss., Princeton, 1960.

Hicks, Eric C., "Le Visage de l'antiquité dans le *Roman de la Rose:* Jean de Meung, savant et pédagogue", Diss., Yale, 1965.

Jackson, W. T. H., "The Politics of a Poet: The Archipoeta as Revealed by His Imagery", *Festschrift Kristeller*. In Preparation.

Kline, Galen Richard, "Humor in Chrétien de Troyes", Diss., Western Reserve, 1966.

Knowlton, Edgar Colby, "Natura as an Allegorical Figure", Diss., Harvard, 1918.

Kunzer, R. G., *The "Tristan" of Gottfried von Strassburg: An Ironic Perspective*. In Preparation.

Lebovics, Victoria Crane, "The Moral Universe of Charles d'Orléans", Diss., Yale, 1962.

Lonigan, Paul Raymond, "The *Yvain* of Chrétien de Troyes: An Interpretation", Diss., Johns Hopkins, 1967.

Luria, Maxwell Sidney, "The Christian Tempest: A Symbolic Motif in Medieval Literature", Diss., Princeton, 1965.

Ralph, Dorothy Marie, "Jean de Meun, the Voltaire of the Middle Ages", Diss., Illinois, 1940.

Ryding, William W., "Structural Patterns in Medieval Narrative", Diss., Columbia, 1961.

Sklute, Larry Martin, "The Ethical Structure of Courtly Romance: Chrétien de Troyes' *Yvain* and *Sir Gawain and the Green Knight*", Diss., Indiana, 1967.

Smith, Thomas Norris, "The Garden Image in Medieval Literature", Diss., Connecticut, 1967.

Vidal, Elie Robert, "Villon et la critique moderne", Diss., Michigan, 1958.

INDEX

de proprietatibus litterarum

Dfl.

<u>Series Practica</u>

50	Metcalf, A.A.: Poetic Diction in the old English Meters of Boethius		28,-
51	Knowlton, M.A.: The Influence of Richard Rolle and of Julian of Norwich on the Middle English Lyrics		28,-
52	Richmond, H.M.: Renaissance Landscapes		28,-
54	Celler, M.M.: Giraudoux et la métaphore	34 FF/	22,-
55	Fletcher, R.M.: The Stylistic Development of Edgar Allan Poe		34,-
57	Nelson, T.A.: Shakespeare's Comic Theory		18,-
59	Dugan, J.R.: Illusion and Reality		26,-
61	Couchman, G.W.: This our Caesar		32,-
63	Schulz, H.-J.: This Hell of Stories		20,-
69	Godshalk, W.L.: Patterning in Shakespearean Drama		50,-
71	Kostis, N.: The Exorcism of Sex and Death in Julien Green's Novels		22,-
72	Woshinsky, B.R.: La Princesse de Clèves	49 FF/	32,-
75	Hewitt, W.: Through Those Living Pillars	49 FF/	32,-
78	Ferrante, J.M.: The Conflict of Love and Honor	49 FF/	32,-
83	Jones, L.E.: Poetic Fantasy and Fiction		20,-

<u>Series Didactica</u>

1	Swaim, K.M.: A Reading of Gulliver's Travels	38,-